Understanding Credit Derivatives and Related Instruments

Understanding Credit Derivatives and Related Instruments

Antulio N. Bomfim

ELSEVIER
ACADEMIC
PRESS

Amsterdam • Boston • Heidelberg • London • New York • Oxford
Paris • San Diego • San Francisco • Singapore • Sydney • Tokyo

Elsevier Academic Press
525 B Street, Suite 1900, San Diego, California 92101-4495, USA
84 Theobald's Road, London WC1X 8RR, UK

This book is printed on acid-free paper. ∞

For all information on all Academic Press publications
visit our Web site at www.academicpress.com

ISBN-13: 978-0-12-108265-9
ISBN-10: 0-12-108265-2

PRINTED IN THE UNITED STATES OF AMERICA
08   9 8 7 6 5 4

To Kimberly, Sarah, and Emma.

Preface

This book provides a broad introduction to major aspects of the credit derivatives market, including an instrument-by-instrument discussion of the main types of credit derivatives. The book has two main goals. First, the text aims to address the needs of those in industry and academia who want to have a good working knowledge of the growing credit derivatives marketplace, including its history and some of the key regulatory and legal issues facing market participants. Second, the book's intention is to help prepare students and market practitioners who want to delve deeper into the technically demanding modeling and valuation issues surrounding credit instruments in general and credit derivatives in particular.

The book is divided in five parts, each highlighting a particular aspect of "understanding credit derivatives and related instruments." Part I (Chapters 1–3) provides a brief overview of the market for credit derivatives, assuming the reader has little or no familiarity with the topic. Subjects discussed in this part of the book include a brief history of the credit derivatives market, some simple examples that illustrate the main uses of credit derivatives, and an initial discussion of valuation issues.

Part II (Chapters 4–14) goes over each of the main types of credit derivatives in some detail, discussing how each instrument works, how it is used by market participants, and the main factors affecting its pricing in the marketplace. The chapters in this part of the book include diagrams and tables with numerical examples designed to illustrate the basic workings of each instrument. The intention here is to give the reader an intuitive understanding of each instrument while helping set the stage for a more in-depth discussion of valuation issues, which is taken up in subsequent chapters.

Parts III and IV focus on model-based approaches to valuing credit derivatives. Part III (Chapters 15–19), an introduction to modeling single-name defaults, addresses approaches for the modeling of credit risk at the individual debt issuer level, including the "structural" and "reduced-form" approaches to credit modeling. Part IV (Chapters 19–23) is centered on the equally important issue of modeling credit risk at the portfolio level. Part IV builds on some of the techniques introduced in Part III and introduces key concepts, such as default correlation and the loss distribution function, that are crucial for the modeling of multi-name credit derivatives.

The chapters in Parts III and IV provide simple examples designed to illustrate how different credit models can be used to value some of the credit derivatives instruments discussed in Part II, such as credit default swaps and synthetic CDOs. Nonetheless, Parts III and IV are a bit more technically demanding than previous chapters, but not so demanding as to be inaccessible to readers with good introductory courses in statistics, calculus, and fixed-income finance. Furthermore, an appendix at the end of the book should help readers refresh their memories on the technical background needed.

Part V (Chapters 24 and 25) concludes the book with a brief discussion of legal and regulatory issues involving credit derivatives. The aim of this part of the book is to provide a plain-language discussion of some of these issues. A good portion of this part of the book is devoted to a description of the ISDA-sponsored documentation that underlies many credit derivatives transactions, including a simple case study that helps highlight the relevancy of the topic.

A key organizing principle behind the writing of this book has been to help bridge the gap between highly mathematical discussions of modeling and valuation issues and highly superficial descriptions of credit derivatives and credit models. My hope is that readers will see a clear line of thought running throughout the book, where each new chapter builds on results and concepts presented in earlier parts of the book.

The intended audience for this book includes advanced undergraduate students of finance, first-year finance Ph.D. students, MBA students specializing in finance/financial engineering, and finance professionals who are relatively new to credit derivatives.

Acknowledgements

I am grateful to current and former colleagues at OFI Institutional Asset Management and the Board of Governors of the Federal Reserve System, respectively, for providing me with a stimulating intellectual environment that encouraged me to pursue this project. I have benefited from comments and conversations with numerous such colleagues, as well as from thoughtful comments provided by several outside reviewers. Last, but not least, my gratitude goes to the staff at Elsevier/Academic Press for helping me see this project to its conclusion.

Antulio N. Bomfim
OFI Institutional Asset Management
Boston, MA

Contents

V   A Brief Overview of Documentation and Regulatory Issues   283

Part I

Credit Derivatives: Definition, Market, Uses

1

Credit Derivatives: A Brief Overview

In this chapter we discuss some basic concepts regarding credit derivatives. We start with a simple definition of what is a credit derivative and then introduce the main types of credit derivatives. Some key valuation principles are also highlighted.

1.1 What are Credit Derivatives?

Most debt instruments, such as loans extended by banks or corporate bonds held by investors, can be thought of as baskets that could potentially involve several types of risk. For instance, a corporate note that promises to make periodic payments based on a fixed interest rate exposes its holders to interest rate risk. This is the risk that market interest rates will change during the term of the note. For instance, if market interest rates increase, the fixed rate written into the note makes it a less appealing investment in the new interest rate environment. Holders of that note are also exposed to credit risk, or the risk that the note issuer may default on its obligations. There are other types of risk associated with debt instruments, such as liquidity risk, or the risk that one may not be able to sell or buy a given instrument without adversely affecting its price, and prepayment risk, or the risk that investors may be repaid earlier than anticipated and be forced to forego future interest rate payments.

Naturally, market forces generally work so that lenders/investors are compensated for taking on all these risks, but it is also true that investors have varying degrees of tolerance for different types of risk. For example, a given bank may feel comfortable with the liquidity and interest rate risk associated with a fixed-rate loan made to XYZ Corp., a hypothetical corporation, especially if it is planning to hold on to the loan, but it may be nervous about the credit risk embedded in the loan. Alternatively, an investment firm might want some exposure to the credit risk associated with XYZ Corp., but it does not want to have to bother with the interest risk inherent in XYZ's fixed-rate liabilities. Clearly, both the bank and the investor stand to gain from a relatively simple transaction that allows the bank to transfer at least some of the credit risk associated with XYZ Corp. to the investor. In the end, they would each be exposed to the types of risks that they feel comfortable with, without having to take on, in the process, unwanted risk exposures.

As simple as the above example is, it provides a powerful rationale for the existence of a rapidly growing market for credit derivatives. Indeed, credit derivatives are financial contracts that allow the transfer of credit risk from one market participant to another, potentially facilitating greater efficiency in the pricing and distribution of credit risk among financial market participants. Let us carry on with the above example. Suppose the bank enters into a contract with the investment firm whereby it will make periodic payments to the firm in exchange for a lump sum payment in the event of default by XYZ Corp. during the term of the derivatives contract. As a result of entering into such a contract, the bank has effectively transferred at least a portion of the risk associated with default by XYZ Corp. to the investment firm. (The bank will be paid a lump sum if XYZ defaults.) In return, the investment company gets the desired exposure to XYZ credit risk, and the stream of payments that it will receive from the bank represents compensation for bearing such a risk.

It should be noted that the basic features of the financial contract just described are becoming increasingly common in today's financial marketplace. Indeed these are the main characteristics of one of the most prevalent types of credit derivatives, the *credit default swap*. In the parlance of the credit derivatives market, the bank in the above example is typically referred to as *the buyer of protection*, the investment firm is known as *the protection seller*, and XYZ Corp. is called *the reference entity*.[1]

---

[1] The contract may be written either to cover default-related losses associated with a specific debt instrument of the reference entity or it may be intended to cover defaults by a range of debt instruments issued by that entity, provided those instruments meet certain criteria, which may be related to the level of seniority in the capital structure of the reference entity and to the currency in which the instruments are denominated.

1.2 Potential "Gains from Trade"

The previous section illustrated one potential gain from trade associated with credit derivatives. In particular, credit derivatives are an important financial engineering tool that facilitates the unbundling of the various types of risk embedded, say, in a fixed-rate corporate bond. As a result, these derivatives help investors better align their actual and desired risk exposures. Other related potential benefits associated with credit derivatives include:

- Increased credit market liquidity: Credit derivatives potentially give market participants the ability to trade risks that were previously virtually untradeable because of poor liquidity. For instance, a repo market for corporate bonds is, at best, highly illiquid even in the most advanced economies. Nonetheless, buying protection in a credit derivative contract essentially allows one to engineer financially a short position in a bond issued by the entity referenced in the contract. Another example regards the role of credit-linked notes, discussed in Chapter 12, which greatly facilitate the trading of bank loan risk.

- Potentially lower transaction costs: One credit derivative transaction can often stand in for two or more cash market transactions. For instance, rather than buying a fixed-rate corporate note and shorting a government note, one might obtain the desired credit spread exposure by selling protection in the credit derivatives market.[2]

- Addressing inefficiencies related to regulatory barriers: This topic is particularly relevant for banks. As will be discussed later in this book, banks have historically used credit derivatives to help bring their regulatory capital requirements closer in line with their economic capital.[3]

These and other applications of credit derivatives are discussed further in Chapters 2 and 3. They are largely responsible for the impressive growth of the market, more than offsetting the potentially growth-inhibiting influence of the so-called asymmetric-information problems that are often inherent in the trading of credit risk.[4]

---

[2] An important caveat applies. Obviously, whether or not the single transaction actually results in lower costs to the investor than the two combined transactions ultimately depends on the relative liquidity of the cash and derivatives markets.

[3] The notions of regulatory and economic capital are discussed in greater detail in Chapters 3 and 25.

[4] Asymmetric-information problems and the related phenomena of moral hazard and adverse selection are discussed in Chapters 14 and 24.

1.3 Types of Credit Derivatives

Credit derivatives come in many shapes and sizes, and there are many ways of grouping them into different categories. The discussion that follows focuses on three dimensions: single-name vs. multi-name credit derivatives, funded vs. unfunded credit derivatives instruments, and contracts written on corporate reference entities vs. contracts written on sovereign reference entities.

1.3.1 Single-Name Instruments

Single-name credit derivatives are those that involve protection against default by a single reference entity, such as the simple contract outlined in Section 1.1. They are the most common type of credit derivative and account for the majority of the trading activity in the marketplace. We shall analyze them in greater detail later in this book. In this chapter, we only briefly discuss the main characteristics of the most ubiquitous single-name instrument, the credit default swap.

In its most common or "vanilla" form, a credit default swap (CDS) is a derivatives contract where the protection buyer agrees to make periodic payments (the swap "spread" or premium) over a predetermined number of years (the maturity of the CDS) to the protection seller in exchange for a payment in the event of default by the reference entity. CDS premiums tend to be paid quarterly, and the most common maturities are three, five, and ten years, with the five-year maturity being especially active. The premium is set as a percentage of the total amount of protection bought (the notional amount of the contract).

As an illustration, consider the case where the parties might agree that the CDS will have a notional amount of $100 million: If the annualized swap spread is 40 basis points, then the protection buyer will pay $100,000 every quarter to the protection seller. If no default event occurs during the life of the CDS, the protection seller simply pockets the premium payments. Should a default event occur, however, the protection seller becomes liable for the difference between the face value of the debt obligations issued by the reference entity and their recovery value. As a result, for a contract with a notional amount of $100,000, and assuming that the reference entities' obligations are worth 20 cents on the dollar after default, the protection seller's liability to the protection buyer in the event of default would be $80,000.[5]

---

[5] In the event of default, CDS can be settled either physically—the protection buyer delivers eligible defaulted instruments to the protection sellers and receives their par value—or in cash—the protection seller pays the buyer the difference between the face value of the eligible defaulted instruments and their perceived post-default value, where

Other examples of single-name credit derivatives include asset swaps, total return swaps, and spread and bond options, all of which are discussed in Part II of this book.

1.3.2 Multi-Name Instruments

Multi-name credit derivatives are contracts that are contingent on default events in a pool of reference entities, such as those represented in a portfolio of bank loans. As such, multi-name instruments allow investors and issuers to transfer some or all of the credit risk associated with a portfolio of defaultable securities, as opposed to dealing with each security in the portfolio separately.

A relatively simple example of a multi-name credit derivative is the first-to-default basket swap. Consider an investor who holds a portfolio of debt instruments issued by various entities and who wants to buy some protection against default-related losses in her portfolio. The investor can obtain the desired protection by entering into a first-to-default basket with a credit derivatives dealer. In this case, the "basket" is composed of the individual reference entities represented in the investor's portfolio. The investor agrees to make periodic payments to the dealer and, in return, the dealer promises to make a payment to the investor should any of the reference names in the basket default on its obligations. Because this is a first-to-default basket, however, the dealer's obligation under the contract is limited to the first default. The contract expires after the first default, and thus, should a second reference name in the basket default, the dealer is under no obligation to come to the investor's rescue, i.e., the investor suffers the full extent of any losses beyond the first default. Second- and third-to-default products are defined in an analogous way.

Multi-name credit derivatives may be set up as a portfolio default swap, whereby the transfer of risk is specified not in terms of defaults by individual reference entities represented in the portfolio but rather in terms of the size of the default-related loss in the overall portfolio. For instance, in a portfolio default swap with a "first-loss piece" of, say, 10 percent, protection sellers are exposed to however many individual defaults are necessary to lead to a 10 percent loss in the overall portfolio. Second- and third-loss portfolio default swaps are defined similarly.

Portfolio default swaps can be thought of as the building blocks for synthetic collateralized debt obligations (CDOs), which have become an increasingly important segment of the credit derivatives market. Synthetic CDOs and other multi-name credit derivatives are discussed further in Chapters 9, 10, and 14, and in Part IV of this book.

---

the latter is determined by polling other market participants. Chapters 6 and 24 take up these issues in greater detail.

1.3.3 Credit-Linked Notes

Certain investors are prevented from entering into derivatives contracts, either because of regulatory restrictions or owing to internal investment policies. Credit-linked notes (CLN) may allow such investors to derive some of the benefits of credit derivatives, both single- and multi-name.

Credit-linked notes can be broadly thought of as regular debt obligations with an embedded credit derivative. They can be issued either directly by a corporation or bank or by highly rated special purpose entities, often sponsored by dealers. The coupon payments made by a CLN effectively transfer the cash flow of a credit derivatives contract to an investor.

Credit-linked notes are best understood by a simple example: AZZ Investments would like to take on the risk associated with the debt of XYZ Corp., but all of XYZ's debt is composed of bank loans and AZZ Investments cannot simply sell protection in a credit default swap because its investment guidelines prevent it from entering into a derivatives contract. Let us assume that the size of AZZ Investments' desired exposure to XYZ Corp. is $100 million. One way of gaining the desired exposure to XYZ's debt is for AZZ Investments to purchase $100 million in credit-linked notes that reference XYZ Corp. The issuer of the notes may take AZZ Investments' $100 million and buy highly rated debt obligations to serve as collateral for its CLN liability toward AZZ Investments. At the same time, the CLN issuer enters into a credit default swap with a third party, selling protection against a default by XYZ Corp. From that point on, the CLN issuer will simply pass through the cash flows associated with the credit default swap—net of administrative fees— to AZZ investments. In the event of default by XYZ Corp., the CLN issuer will pay its default swap counterparty and the credit-linked note terminates with AZZ Investments receiving only the recovery value of XYZ's defaulted debt. If no default occurs, AZZ Investments will continue to receive the coupon payments associated with the credit-linked note until its maturity date, at which point it will also receive its principal back. It should then be clear that a credit-linked note is simply a funded way of entering into a credit derivatives contract. (Indeed, CLNs can be written based on more complex credit derivatives, such as a portfolio default swap.)

1.3.4 Sovereign vs. Other Reference Entities

Credit derivatives can reference either a corporate entity or a sovereign nation. For instance, in addition to being able to buy and sell protection against default by XYZ Corp., one is also able to buy and sell protection against default by, say, the Brazilian or Chinese governments. Indeed, the core mechanism of a credit default swap market is essentially the same, regardless of whether the reference entity is a corporate or a sovereign debtor, with the differences in the contracts showing up in some of their clauses. For example, contracts written on sovereign debtors may include moratorium and debt repudiation as credit events (events that would trigger the payment by the protection seller), whereas contracts that reference corporate debt generally do not include such events.

Where credit derivatives written on sovereign reference entities differ most from those written on corporates is in the general characteristics of the markets in which they trade. In particular, contracts that reference non-sovereign names, especially those written on investment-grade corporates, are negotiated in a market that is substantially larger than that for contracts that reference sovereign credits. Limiting factors for the market for credit derivatives written on sovereign entities include the fact that the investor base for non-sovereign debt is significantly larger than that for sovereign debt. In addition, modeling and quantifying credit risk associated with sovereign debtors can be more challenging than doing so for corporate borrowers. For instance, sovereign entities, especially in some emerging economies, are more subject to risks associated with political instability than are most corporations based in developed economies. In addition, there are more limited default data for sovereign debtors than for corporations—in part because there are more corporations than countries—which makes it harder to make statistical inferences based on historical experience.

1.4 Valuation Principles

To understand the main factors that enter into the pricing of credit derivatives, we need to consider two basic principles. First, each party in a credit derivative contract faces certain risks. For instance, the protection seller is exposed to the risk that the reference entity will default while the contract is still in force and that it will have to step up to cover the protection buyer's loss. Likewise, the protection buyer is exposed to the risk that the protection seller may be unable to make good on its commitment in the event of default by the reference entity.

The second basic principle in the valuation of credit derivatives is that, as with any other financial market instrument, market forces will be such that the parties in the contract will generally be compensated according to the amount of risk to which they are exposed under the contract. Thus, a first step to understand basic valuation principles for credit derivatives is to examine the nature of the risks inherent in them.

1.4.1 Fundamental Factors

Let us start by considering the four main types of risk regarding most credit derivatives instruments:

- the credit risk of the reference entity;

- the credit risk of the protection seller;

- the default correlation between the reference entity and the protection seller;

- the expected recovery rates associated with the reference entity and the protection seller.

The importance of the first factor is clear: Other things being equal, the greater the likelihood of default by the reference entity, the more expensive the protection, and thus it should come as no surprise that buying protection against default by a company with a low credit rating costs more than buying protection against default by an AAA-rated firm.

The second and third factors highlight a significant issue for purchasers of protection in the credit default swaps market: the credit quality of the protection seller. The protection seller may itself go bankrupt either before or at the same time as the reference entity. In market parlance, this is what is called counterparty credit risk.

As noted later in this chapter, market participants commonly use credit-enhancement mechanisms—such as the posting of collateral—to mitigate the effects of counterparty credit risk in the dynamics of the credit derivatives market. In the absence of these mechanisms, however, other things being equal, the higher the credit quality of a given protection seller relative to other protection sellers, the more it can charge for the protection it provides.

Regarding its credit derivatives counterparty, the protection buyer is subject to two types of risk: Should the protection seller become insolvent before the reference entity, the protection buyer is exposed to "replacement risk" or the risk that the price of default insurance on the reference entity might have risen since the original default swap was negotiated. The protection buyer's greatest loss, however, would occur when both the protection seller and the reference entity default at the same time, and hence the importance of having some sense of the default correlation between the reference entity and the protection seller.[6]

The fourth factor—expected recovery rates—is particularly relevant for credit derivative contracts that specify a payoff in the event of the default

---

[6] The concept of default correlation is discussed in some detail in Chapters 9 and 10 and in Part IV.

that depends on the post-default value of the reference entity's debt. (The typical credit default swap example discussed above is one such contract.) Under such circumstances, the lower the post-default value of the defaulted debt—which the protection provider may have to buy for its par value in the event of default—the more expensive the protection. As a result, the lower the recovery value of the liabilities of the reference entity, the higher the cost of buying protection against a default by that entity.

1.4.2   Other Potential Risk Factors

Are there other risks associated with credit derivatives? If so, how can one protect oneself from such risks? To which extent do these risks affect the valuation of credit derivatives contracts? Here we shall briefly discuss two additional types of risk:

- legal risk

- model risk

Legal Risk.   Consider the case of a credit default swap. The rights and obligations of each party in the swap are specified in a legally binding agreement signed by both parties—the buyer and the seller of protection. For instance, the contract specifies whether the payments made by the protection buyer will be, say, quarterly or monthly, and how, in the event of default, the contract will be settled. Just as important, the contract will determine which kinds of events would "trigger" a payment by the protection seller and under which circumstances. For example, suppose that the reference entity renegotiates the terms of its debt with its creditors. Under which conditions would that constitute a "credit event"? Are these conditions clearly specified in the contract? More generally, uncertainty about how the details of the contract will apply to future unforeseen events constitutes "legal risk."

Since the early days of the credit derivatives market, it was clear to those involved that, if the market were to experience any measure of success, the issue of legal risk was one that had to be addressed head on. As discussed in Chapter 24, market participants have worked together to create and adopt documentation standards for credit derivatives contracts with the aim of minimizing the role of legal risk in the pricing of the contracts. One might even say that the enormous growth of this market in recent years attests that these efforts have been largely fruitful. We say largely because some of the features of early credit derivatives contracts, such as the treatment of debt restructurings, mentioned above, would later prove to be less than satisfactory in the eyes of many market participants. As the market has evolved, however, so have documentation standards and many of the "legal gray areas" of earlier times have been worked out in more recent versions of the contracts, significantly reducing the scope for legal risk to be an important factor in the pricing of credit derivatives.

Model Risk. Suppose a prospective protection buyer has good estimates of the credit quality of both the protection seller and the reference entity. Assume further that the prospective buyer knows with certainty the recovery value of the liabilities of the reference entity and protection seller, and that there is no legal risk. How much should this buyer be willing to pay for obtaining protection against default by the reference entity? Likewise, consider a protection seller who also has good estimates of the credit quality and recovery rate of the same reference entity. How much should this protection seller charge?

What these two potential credit derivatives counterparties need in order to agree on a price for the contract is a way to quantify the risk factors inherent in the contract and then to translate those quantities into a "fair" price. In other words, what they need is an approach or method for arriving at a dollar amount that is consistent with their perception of the risks involved in the contract.

We will briefly discuss different valuation approaches in the next subsection in this chapter and then look at some of them more carefully in subsequent parts of this book. For now, all that we need to know is that the mere fact that there are different ways to arrive at a fair valuation of a credit derivative contract—and that different ways often deliver different answers—suggests that there is always some chance that one's favorite approach or model may be wrong. This is what we shall refer to generically as "model risk," or the risk that one may end up under- or overestimating the fair value of the contract, perhaps finding oneself with a lot more risk than intended.

We should point out that even if one has the right model for translating risk factors into fair valuations, it could well be that the basic ingredients that go into the model, such as, for example, one's estimate of the recovery rate associated with the reference entity, turn out to be wrong. Even the most reliable of models would not be foolproof under such circumstances.

How does one protect oneself from model risk? One might say that the answer is simple. Come up with a pricing methodology that is as foolproof as possible. Easier said than done. As we shall see throughout this book, there is no one "correct" method, and there is never a guarantee that what works well today will continue to do so next year or even tomorrow...

1.4.3 Static Replication vs. Modeling

We have mentioned model risk and the fact that there is no magic formula that tells us how to determine the fair value of a credit derivative. Thus, market participants use various approaches for the valuation of credit derivatives. Broadly speaking, the main approaches can be grouped in two main classes: those based on "static replication" methods and those that rely more heavily on credit risk models. We will discuss the main features of these approaches throughout the book, with the examples of the static replication approach showing up in several chapters in Part II and the credit risk modeling approach taking center stage in Parts III and IV. For now, we shall limit ourselves to introducing some basic terminology and to providing the reader with a flavor of what is to come.

The basic idea of the static replication approach is that the possible payoffs of certain types of credit derivatives can, in principle, be replicated using simple financial market instruments, the prices of which may be readily observable in the marketplace.[7] For instance, as discussed in Part II, in a liquid market without major frictions and counterparty credit risk, a rational investor would be indifferent between buying protection in a credit default swap that references XYZ Corp. or buying a riskless floater while shorting a floater issued by XYZ—where both notes have the same maturity and cash flow dates as the credit default swap. Indeed, such a risky floater/riskless floater combination can be shown to be the replicating portfolio for this CDS contract.

More specifically, as discussed in Chapter 6, in a fully liquid market with no counterparty credit risk, all we need to know to determine the fair value of a CDS premium is the yield spread of a comparable risky floater issued by the reference entity over that of a riskless floater. That is all. Under these idealized market conditions, once we determine the composition of the replicating portfolio, the valuation exercise is done. No credit risk model is required!

Some of the advantages of the static replication approach include the fact that it is completely based on observed market prices, that replication arguments are relatively straightforward to understand, and that replication portfolios are, in principle, easy to implement for many commonly negotiated credit derivatives. The reliance on observed market prices means that one should be able to determine the fair market value of a credit default swap spread without having to know the default probabilities associated with the reference entity. This is indeed a major advantage given that good models of credit risk can be very technically demanding, not to mention the fact that not even the best of models is foolproof.

Nonetheless, there are many situations where the static replication approach is of very limited practical value. For instance, consider the case where there are no readily observed reliable prices of notes issued

---

[7] We use the term "static replication" to refer to situations where, once the replicating portfolio is set up, it requires no rebalancing during the entire life of the derivative. In contrast, the concept of "dynamic replication" requires frequent rebalancing of the portfolio if it is to replicate the cash flows of the derivative.

by the reference entity. What is the credit default swap market participant to do? To take another example of limited applicability of the replication approach, consider a complex multi-name credit derivative such as a synthetic CDO. With many multi-name instruments, creating the replicating portfolio can be difficult in practice, if not impossible. What else can be done? One must venture into the world of credit risk modeling.

Credit risk modeling is the science, some might say "art," of writing down mathematical and statistical models that can be used to characterize the fair market value of different credit instruments such as corporate bonds and loans and credit derivatives. Models have the advantage of being more widely applicable than methods based on the static replication approach. For instance, if static replication is not an option, one can posit a model for the evolution of the creditworthiness of the reference entity and, based on that model, infer the corresponding probabilities of default and protection premiums. We have alluded already to some of the drawbacks of the credit modeling approach. Credit models can be difficult to develop and implement, and their users are clearly subject to model risk, or the risk that the model might fail to capture some key aspect of reality.

1.4.4   A Note on Supply, Demand, and Market Frictions

In principle, the pricing of a credit derivative should essentially reflect the economic fundamentals of the reference entity(ies) and of the counterparty. In practice, however, other factors also affect derivatives prices, driving a wedge between the theoretical prices suggested by fundamentals and observed market prices. For instance, liquidity in the markets for corporate notes and credit derivatives can be significantly different and simple portfolio replication approaches would miss the pricing of the liquidity differential across the two markets. Thus, what may look like an arbitrage opportunity may be simply a function with the relative ease or difficulty of transacting in corporate notes vs. in credit derivatives.

Other factors include the fact that it is often difficult to short a corporate bond—the repo market for corporate bonds is still at a relatively early stage even in the United States—and the fact that there is still quite a bit of market segmentation when credit instruments are concerned. For instance, many institutions participate in the corporate bond market, but not in the credit derivatives market.

The main implication of these and other market frictions is that observed market prices for credit derivatives may at least temporarily deviate from prices implied by either the static replication or credit risk modeling approaches. Thus, while it is true that the price of a credit derivatives contract should reflect the supply and demand for default protection regarding the entities referenced in the contract, because of illiquidity or market segmentation, supply and demand themselves may not always reflect a pure view on the credit risk associated with those entities. It should be noted, however, that large discrepancies between prices of credit derivatives and underlying cash instruments are unlikely to persist: Not only are arbitrageurs expected to take advantage of such discrepancies, but also new participants might be enticed to enter the market, reducing the limiting role of market segmentation.

1.5   Counterparty Credit Risk (Again)

Before we move on, it is worth returning briefly to the subject of counterparty credit risk. How do market participants address this issue? First, just as one would not buy life insurance from an insurance company that is teetering on the verge of bankruptcy, one should not buy default protection from a credit derivatives dealer with a poor credit standing. This obvious point explains why the major sellers of protection in the credit derivatives market tend to be large highly rated financial institutions.

Second, and perhaps not as self-evident as the first point, potential buyers of default protection might want to assess the extent to which eventual defaults by protection seller and the reference entity are correlated. For instance, other things being equal, one may not want to buy protection against default by a large industrial conglomerate from a bank that is known to have a huge exposure to that same conglomerate in its loan portfolio. The bank may not be around when you need it most!

Lastly, a common approach used in the marketplace to mitigate concerns about counterparty credit risk is for market participants to require each other to post collateral against the market values of their credit derivatives contracts. Thus, should the protection seller fail to make good on its commitment under the contract, the protection buyer can seize the collateral. Indeed, while theory would suggest a tight link between the credit quality of protection sellers and the price of default protection, in practice, as is the case with other major types of derivatives, such as interest rate swaps, the effect of counterparty credit risk in the pricing of credit default swaps is mitigated by the use of collateral agreements among counterparties. In Chapter 2 we discuss the nature of these agreements and other factors that help reduce (but not eliminate) the importance of counterparty credit risk in the valuation of credit derivatives. In addition, in Chapter 23 we discuss a simple framework for analyzing the role of counterparty credit risk on the valuation of credit default swaps.

2

The Credit Derivatives Market

The market for credit derivatives has undergone enormous changes in recent years. This chapter provides an overview of the main forces shaping the market, including a discussion of major types of market participants. We also take a quick look at the most common instruments, practices, and conventions that underlie activity in the credit derivatives market.

Credit derivatives are negotiated in a decentralized, over-the-counter market, and thus quantifying and documenting the market's spectacular growth in recent years is no easy task. Unlike exchanged-based markets, there are no readily available volume or notional amount statistics that one can draw upon. Instead, most discussions of the evolution of market, its size, and degree of trading activity tend to center on results of surveys of market participants and on anecdotal accounts by key market players. Regarding the former, we shall focus the discussion in this chapter primarily on two recurrent surveys of market participants, a biannual survey conducted by the British Bankers Association (2002)[4] and an annual survey conducted by *Risk Magazine* (Patel, 2003[66]). In addition, in early 2003, FitchRatings, a major credit-rating agency in the US, conducted a survey of the credit derivatives market.

The FitchRatings (2003)[28] survey was focused on Fitch-rated entities that sell protection in the credit derivatives market. The British Bankers Association (BBA) survey reflects responses from 25 institutions, most of which are significant players in the credit derivatives market. The *Risk Magazine* survey is based on responses from 12 institutions, including the small number of participants that account for a sizable share of the activity in the credit derivatives market. Although results from these surveys differ in some of the details, they all paint a picture of a market that has grown spectacularly in recent years.

2.1 Evolution and Size of the Market

As shown in Figure 2.1, which comes from the *BBA 2001/2002 Credit Derivatives Report*, from virtually nonexistent in the early 1990s, the global credit derivatives market is estimated to have comprised approximately $2 trillion in notional amounts outstanding in 2002 and is projected to grow to $4.8 trillion by 2004. The *Risk Magazine* survey showed similar results regarding the size of the global market in 2002 (about $2.3 trillion). It should be noted, however, that, apart from potential problems related to survey-based results—such as limited participation and incomplete responses—the exact size of the global credit derivatives market is difficult to estimate given the potential for overcounting when contracts involve more than one reporting market participant. In addition, notional amounts outstanding considerably overstate the net exposure associated with those contracts.

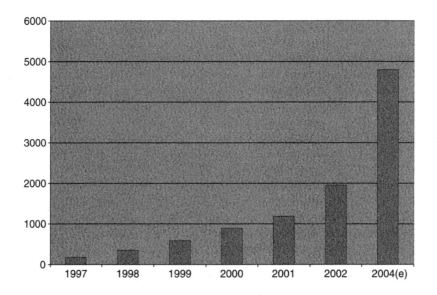

FIGURE 2.1. Global Credit Derivatives Market (US$ billions, excluding asset swaps)
Source: British Bankers Association (2002)

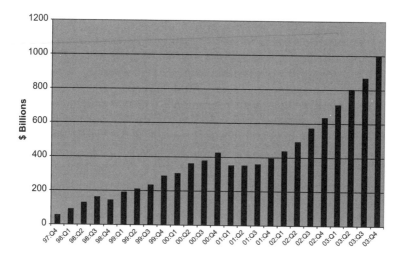

FIGURE 2.2. Notional Amounts of Credit Derivatives at US Commercial Banks
Source: Federal Reserve, Call Reports

Despite its phenomenal growth, the market is small relative to the over-all derivatives market, and by most accounts it has not yet reached the liquidity, transparency, standardization, and widespread market partic-ipation of more mature markets. For instance, according to Bank Call Report data from the US Federal Reserve, credit derivatives represented only a little less than 1.5 percent of the total notional amount of deriva-tives at US commercial banks at the end of 2003, although the credit derivatives' share of the total has risen, on net, in recent years. As shown in Figure 2.2, notional amounts outstanding in credit derivatives at US commercial banks have increased from around $50 billion in late 1997 to $1 trillion in the fourth quarter of 2003.

2.2 Market Activity and Size by Instrument Type

Although still relatively young, the credit derivatives market has already developed to the point where one can characterize its evolution in terms of developments in its various segments, such as the market for single-name credit derivatives or the market for credit derivatives written on sovereign credits.

2.2.1   Single- vs. Multi-name Instruments

Single-name instruments account for the majority of the credit derivatives market, but the use of multi-name products has grown substantially in recent years. As shown in Figure 2.3 BBA estimates that credit default swaps account for about 45 percent of the notional amount outstanding of credit derivatives in the global marketplace. In terms of the sheer volume of negotiated contracts, however, credit default swaps, which typically have much smaller notional amounts than, say, synthetic CDOs, account for a much larger share of the credit derivatives market. Among other single-name instruments, the BBA survey indicates that total return swaps and asset swaps are a distant second in terms of notional amounts outstanding, each accounting for about 7 percent of the market.

The results of the *Risk* 2003 survey regarding the relative market shares of various instruments are qualitatively consistent with those of the BBA survey, but point to an even greater dominance of single-name credit default swaps. According to *Risk*, credit default swaps accounted for about 72 percent of the notional amounts outstanding in the global marketplace. In part, the discrepancy is attributable to the fact that the *Risk* survey did not include asset swaps as a credit derivative instrument.

Both the *Risk* and BBA surveys estimate that portfolio default swaps and synthetic CDOs correspond to the second largest share of the credit derivatives market, accounting for about 20 percent of the notional amounts outstanding in the global market. Respondents to the BBA survey expect portfolio and synthetic CDOs to be the fastest growing credit derivative type over the next few years as they see the use of credit derivatives in active portfolio and asset management becoming increasingly widespread. Among other multi-name instruments, basket products, such as the first-to-default basket discussed in Chapter 1, are said to correspond to a much smaller share of the notional amounts outstanding in the global credit derivatives

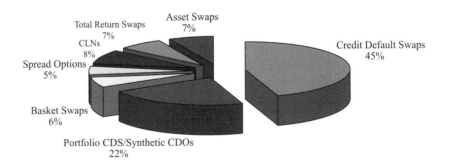

FIGURE 2.3. Market Shares of Main Credit Derivatives Instruments
Source: British Bankers Association (2002)

market: about 6 percent according to the BBA and less than 1 percent according to the *Risk* survey.

2.2.2 *Sovereign vs. Other Reference Entities*

As we mentioned in Chapter 1, credit derivatives are written on both sovereign and non-sovereign reference entities. In practice, however, the vast majority of these instruments reportedly reference non-sovereign entities. The latest BBA survey indicates that only about 15 percent of contracts negotiated in 2001 were written on sovereign entities, with the majority of them referencing sovereign emerging market debt. In addition, according to the BBA survey, the share of contracts written on sovereign entities appears to have been declining steadily since the mid-1990s, from an estimated 54 percent of all credit derivatives contracts in 1996.

In part, the declining share of contracts written on sovereign entities is attributable to explosive growth in contracts that reference other entities. Nonetheless, factors that are germane to the sovereign debt market have also contributed to the slower development of this category of credit derivatives. In particular, market observers have noted that a much smaller number of institutions are willing, or able, to participate in the market for sovereign-debt-based credit derivatives. Moreover, as already noted in Chapter 1, quantifying the nature of the risks involved in sovereign debt, such as pricing the risk that a given emerging market government may decide to repudiate its foreign debt, can be a daunting task even for the most skillful credit risk modeler, especially given the sparseness of the sovereign default data.

Among contracts negotiated on non-sovereign entities (an estimated 85 percent of all contracts negotiated in the global market in 2001), the majority comprised contracts written on nonfinancial corporations, which amounted to 60 percent of all contracts according to the 2002 BBA survey. Respondents to that survey indicated that the growing market share of synthetic CDOs helps explain the predominance of nonfinancial corporations as reference entities as many synthetic CDOs are backed by nonfinancial business debt. Credit derivatives written on financial institutions accounted for 22 percent of contracts negotiated in 2001, also according to the 2002 BBA survey.

2.2.3 *Credit Quality of Reference Entities*

Although credit derivatives are written on both investment- and speculative-grade debt instruments, the market for the former is substantially more developed than that for the latter. Here, too, surveys conducted by the BBA, *Risk*, and FitchRatings help shed some light into key aspects of the credit derivatives market. They indicate that around 90 percent of

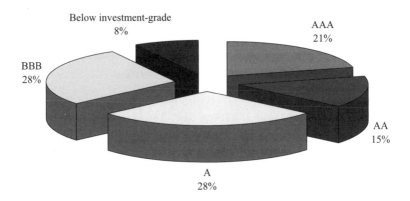

FIGURE 2.4. Reference Entities by Credit Ratings
        Source: FitchRatings (2003)

credit derivatives negotiated in recent years were written on investment-grade entities, with more than half of the contracts negotiated in the global market in recent years referencing entities rated between BBB and A (see Figure 2.4).

One might wonder why the market for credit derivatives written on speculative-grade entities has lagged behind that for investment-grade entities. After all, one might have expected that protection buyers would be more interested in protecting themselves from their riskier debtors rather than from highly rated borrowers.

Anecdotally, some market participants have attributed the predominance of the investment-grade sector in the marketplace to banks' desire to free up regulatory capital related to loans to such corporations so that capital can be put to work in higher-yielding assets. For instance, the terms of the 1988 Basle Accord called on financial regulators to require banks to hold the same amount of capital in reserve for monies lent to, say, an investment-grade, A-rated borrower as they would for a speculative-grade borrower. Nonetheless, lending to the former yields the bank a lower return so some banks prefer to free up the regulatory capital committed to the investment-grade borrower and devote that capital to the speculative-grade client. One way to seek regulatory capital relief, as will shall see later in this book, is to buy adequate default protection in the credit derivatives market from a highly rated credit derivatives dealer.

Looking ahead, respondents to the BBA survey expect that credit derivative uses directly related to regulatory capital management eventually will come to play a less prominent role in the evolution of the market. In part, this will happen as market participants are expected to become more focused on using credit derivatives as tools for overall portfolio management. In addition, protection buyers' attention is expected to continue to shift from regulatory to economic capital in light of the terms of the Basle II Accord, which provide for greater differentiation among differently rated borrowers for the purposes of setting regulatory capital requirements.[1] As a result, some market participants expect that the market share of derivatives written on speculative-grade entities will increase.

2.2.4 Maturities of Most Commonly Negotiated Contracts

As we noted in Chapter 1, credit derivatives have maturities ranging from a few months to many years. In practice, however, about three-quarters of newly negotiated contracts tend to have maturities between one and five years. Contracts with an original maturity of five years are especially common, representing about one-third of the global market, and, indeed, in the credit default swap market, the five-year maturity has come to represent a benchmark for pricing and assessing the credit risk of individual borrowers. Nonetheless, some credit default swap dealers do disseminate indicative quotes for maturities as short as a few months to all the way to ten years.

2.3 Main Market Participants

By far, the main participants in the credit derivatives market are large commercial and investment banks, insurers and re-insurers, and hedge funds. As shown in Figure 2.5, which focuses on end-users of credit derivatives, and

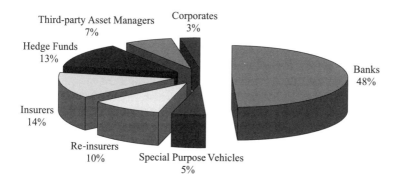

FIGURE 2.5. End-users of Credit Derivatives
Source: Risk Magazine (Patel, 2003)

---

[1] The Basle Accords are discussed briefly in Chapter 3 and in the final part of this book.

thus excludes participation stemming from the market-making activities of dealers, banks account for about half of the credit derivatives market, with insurers and re-insurers representing about one-quarter of the global market, and hedge funds representing about one-eighth.

2.3.1 Buyers and Sellers of Credit Protection

Large banks play a dual role in the credit derivatives market, acting both as major dealers and, as seen in Figure 2.5, end-users. As dealers, they tend to run a "matched book," with their protection selling positions about offset by contracts in which they are buying protection. As end-users, banks in general tend to be net buyers of credit protection. As a result, banks were net beneficiaries of the credit derivatives market during the downturn in credit markets in the early 2000s: Indeed, although corporate default rates rose sharply during that period, most banks were able to maintain or even improve their overall financial condition.

Smaller, but still big, regional banks typically are not dealers, and some, especially in Europe, are said to be net sellers of protection in the credit derivatives market. These institutions view credit derivatives as an alternative way to enhance the return on their capital, essentially viewing the selling of credit protection as an alternative to loan origination. Such banks are relatively small players in the global credit derivatives marketplace however, even if one focuses only on the protection seller's side of the market. Indeed, the main net sellers of protection in recent years are in the insurance industry.

The survey of protection sellers by FitchRatings sheds some light on the role of the insurance industry in the credit derivatives market. The survey suggests three main reasons for the participation of insurers as protection sellers. First, insurers view corporate defaults as being mostly uncorrelated with their underwritten risks, and thus selling credit default protection essentially constitutes a portfolio diversification mechanism. Second, the premiums received from protection buyers are a palpable way to enhance the yield on one's capital, and, lastly, insurers perceive their financial strength as a potentially significant selling point in a market where participants are looking for ways to mitigate their exposure to counterparty credit risk.

Just as credit derivatives were a positive for banks during the wave of corporate defaults in the early 2000s, they proved to be disappointing investment vehicles for some in the insurance industry, especially in Europe. Indeed, anecdotal evidence suggests that insurers may have decided to pull back some from the credit derivatives market in the immediate aftermath of that spike in corporate defaults, but the extent of such pull back is difficult to quantify for the industry as a whole.

TABLE 2.1
Market Shares of Main Buyers and Sellers of Protection
(percent)

	Protection Buyers	Protection Sellers
Banks	52	39
Securities Houses	21	16
Insurers/Re-insurers	6	33
Hedge Funds	12	5
Corporates	4	2
Mutual Funds	2	3
Pension Funds	1	2
Others	2	0

Source: British Bankers Association (2002).

While one may conjecture that reduced credit risk appetite by insurers may turn out to be an impediment to the further development of the credit derivatives market, it appears that other entities, such as pension funds, asset managers, and hedge funds, have been increasing their participation in the sell side of the market. Non-financial corporations have reportedly also increasingly come to the market, but primarily to buy protection to hedge their exposure in vendor financing deals.

Table 2.1 lists the main categories of market players and their estimated relative participation in the buy and sell sides of the market in late 2001, as estimated by the BBA. For instance, 52 percent of the sellers of protection during that period were banks, whereas banks accounted for only 39 percent of the protection sellers. In contrast, as noted, insurers and re-insurers were significant net sellers of protection: They accounted for only 6 percent of the protection buying positions, but corresponded to about one-third of the protection selling positions.

2.4   Common Market Practices

Thus far, this chapter has made a few main points. First, the credit derivatives market has experienced phenomenal growth in recent years. Second, commercial and investment banks, insurers and re-insurers, hedge funds, and a few other mainly financial institutions are the main players in the credit derivatives market, buying and selling credit protection according to their individual needs. Third, the market has continued to grow even in the face of unexpectedly large defaults in the early 2000s. Let us take a few moments now to highlight some of the common practices and procedures that have underlain the evolution of the marketplace.

2.4.1 A First Look at Documentation Issues

As noted in Chapter 1, at its most basic level a credit derivative is a legally binding contract between two counterparties whereby the credit risk of a third party, the reference entity, is transferred from a protection buyer to a protection seller. Consider now a situation where each credit derivatives dealer has its own preferred set of stipulations for, say, a contract detailing a credit default swap. Worse still, consider that each main end-user also has strong preferences for what should and should not be covered in the contract and about how different key terms should be defined.

Now try to imagine how costly it would be to put a contract together that would be mutually agreeable to both counterparties; imagine the difficulties in arriving at fair market values for the premiums associated with each type of contract; imagine all the legal, pricing, and back-office headaches and costs associated with keeping track of a myriad of contracts, each with its own idiosyncrasies. Could a market like that experience the increasing size and liquidity that have characterized the credit derivatives market since the mid-1990s? Unlikely.

The steady convergence of documentation standards for basic credit derivatives contracts has played a key role in facilitating the rapid growth of the marketplace. The adoption of commonly accepted templates for contracts and of marketwide definitions of key terms of the contracts have brought a measure of commoditization to the credit derivatives market, helping the price discovery process and reducing legal risk. The common contract specifications used by over 90 percent of the market are contained in the "Master Agreement," "Credit Derivatives Definitions," and related supplements issued by ISDA, the International Swap and Derivatives Association, a trade group formed by leading swap and derivatives market participants.

Working in consultation with its members, ISDA issued its first set of credit derivatives documents in 1997, and has since continued to improve on them to address evolving market needs. In essence, the standard ISDA confirmation templates are akin to forms that the counterparties fill out and sign. While some core terms and definitions are unchanged across contracts, the parties have the option to choose or "check" different clauses in the standardized contract as they apply to their circumstances. For instance, the standardized contract for a credit default swap gives the parties the choice to either settle the contract "physically" or "in cash."

We will turn to documentation issues in Chapter 24. For now, an important factor to keep in mind about credit derivatives contracts is that the market would probably not be even close to where it is now in terms of participation and growth if it were not for the adoption of standardized contracts and the consequent substantial reduction in transaction costs and legal risk.

2.4.2   Collateralization and Netting

As the credit derivatives market has grown, so have market participants' exposures to one another, and the potential for substantial losses related to a default by a major credit derivatives counterparty has not gone unnoticed. As noted in Chapter 1, an important step that market participants have taken to reduce counterparty credit risk is to require the posting of collateral against the exposures resulting from credit derivatives positions. In reality, however, because posting collateral is expensive, amounts pledged typically cover less than the total net exposure between counterparties. Indeed, a common practice in the interdealer market is for market participants to call for additional collateral after their marked-to-market exposure to a particular counterparty has risen beyond a previously agreed upon threshold level.

Note that the previous paragraph mentioned the "net" exposure between counterparties, and, indeed, this netting of counterparty credit risk exposures is an important feature of market functioning. Consider a simple example. AZZ Bank and XYZ Bank have a large number of credit default swaps between the two of them. AZZ's total exposure to XYZ amounts to $100 billion, whereas XYZ's exposure to AZZ is $90 billion. Netting means that the exposures of the two banks to one another are offset before any collateral is posted so that what matters in the end is the $10 billion net exposure of AZZ to XYZ. This would be the only amount against which any collateral would be calculated, and this would be the claim that AZZ would have on XYZ in the event of a default by XYZ.

Taken together, collateralization and netting, along with standardized documentation, have had the effect of helping overcome some of the "growing pains" of the credit derivatives market. While standardized documentation has helped reduce legal risk and transaction costs, collateralization and netting have eased concerns about counterparty credit risk, especially as potential risk exposures through credit derivatives have grown.

3

Main Uses of Credit Derivatives

As with any other derivative instrument, credit derivatives can be used to either avoid or take on risk, in this case credit risk. Indeed, protection buyers are credit risk avoiders, whereas protection sellers are credit risk takers, and, obviously, the market would not exist without either of them. As we saw in Chapter 2, banks are the main end-users of credit derivatives, generally as net buyers of protection, and we shall start this chapter by discussing bank-specific applications of these instruments. We will then look at the market from the perspective of insurance companies and other typical sellers of credit protection.

3.1 Credit Risk Management by Banks

Taking credit risk is an inherent part of banking. Bankers have traditionally earned a substantial share of their income as compensation for bearing such a risk. In that regard, banks do seek credit risk and view it as a necessary part of doing business. But, as with other aspects of life, it is always possible to "have too much of a good thing"—too much credit risk, that is, not too much income.

Banks monitor the overall credit risk in their portfolios on an ongoing basis and also watch for particular concentrations of credit vis-à-vis a given client or industry. The old adage "don't put all of your eggs in the same basket" applies with force here, especially in this day and age when shareholders, regulators, and the credit-rating agencies have been increasingly focused on stricter controls on risk exposures and capital use by banks.

Consider, as an illustration, the case of a bank that looks at the loan amounts outstanding to various clients and decides that its exposure to a given large corporation (XYZ Corp.) is more than that with which the bank's management and investors can feel comfortable. Short of not renewing existing loans and curtailing its lending to XYZ Corp., what can the bank do? It could, for instance, sell part of its XYZ loans to other lenders directly in the secondary loan market, assuming that market is sufficiently developed. Alternatively, the bank could add some of those loans to a pool of loans to be securitized and effectively sell the loans to investors in the asset-backed securities market.[1] Either way, the bank would end up reducing its credit risk exposure to XYZ Corp., which is what it wanted to do in the first place. The bank would be happy to see its exposure to XYZ reduced. Would XYZ Corp. be happy?

Typically, selling a loan in the secondary market requires the bank to notify and, sometimes, to obtain consent from the borrower. The same principle generally applies to loan securitizations. Borrowers do not always welcome such notifications enthusiastically. Some see them as a vote of no confidence by their bankers. It is as if they are being told by their bank: "Listen, we like having your business and all the income it brings to us, but we think you are a bit too risky for our taste so we will pass some of the loans we made you along to other banks and investors..." A lot of banking is about maintaining and nurturing client relationships so the banker will be the first to receive a call when the client decides to embark in a new venture or expand the range of financial services it purchases from the banking sector. This is especially relevant nowadays, when banks and their affiliates are much more like financial supermarkets that offer a whole gamut of services ranging from bond underwriting to equity placements. Loan sales and transfers are not always consistent with this goal.

Let us go back to the XYZ Corp. example. What if the bank decided that it did not want to jeopardize its relationship with XYZ Corp.? It could turn to the credit derivatives market. Suppose the bank goes out and buys default protection in a credit default swap that references XYZ Corp. The bank has effectively reduced its exposure to XYZ Corp., just as it would if it had sold or transferred loans made to XYZ to someone else. (Should XYZ Corp. go under, the bank would go to its credit derivatives counterparty and receive the par value of XYZ's defaulted assets.) Unlike a loan sale or securitization, however, XYZ Corp.'s debt remains on the bank's books. More important for bank relationship purposes, XYZ Corp. need not be notified about the credit default swap transaction. In a

---

[1] We shall discuss securitizations further in Part II of this book.

nutshell, the bank was able to reduce its exposure to XYZ Corp. anonymously because the reference entity is typically not a party in a credit derivatives contract. In market parlance, by purchasing default protection through a credit default swap, the bank was able to "synthesize" the effects of a loan transfer or securitization—it shed the credit risk associated with those loans—but the loans themselves never left the bank's books. In effect, credit default swaps, and credit derivatives more generally, help banks manage their credit risk exposure while maintaining client relationships.

Synthetic loan transfers through credit derivatives have other advantages over traditional sales and securitizations. They often involve lower legal and other setup costs than do sales and securitizations. Moreover, buying protection in the credit derivatives market can be a more tax efficient way of reducing one's risk exposure. In particular, banks can shed the credit risk of a given pool of assets without having to face the tax and accounting implications of an outright sale of the asset pool.

Lastly, we should point out that even though the above example centered on buying protection through a single-name credit default swap, banks can, and very often do, use other credit derivatives instruments, such as synthetic CDOs, to transfer large pools of credit risk and manage their credit risk exposure. We shall discuss these instruments in greater detail in Part II of this book.

3.2 Managing Bank Regulatory Capital

Banks are required by law to hold capital in reserve in order to cover eventual default-related losses in their loan portfolios. The general framework detailing guidelines on how much capital to hold vis-à-vis loans extended to different types of borrowers were first spelled out at the international level in the 1988 Basle Bank Capital Accord. The 1988 Accord was later followed up by the so-called Basle II Accord, which is discussed in Chapter 25, but the underpinnings of the original Accord have historically provided banks with an additional motivation to use credit derivatives: the management of their regulatory capital requirements. As a result, understanding banks' participation in the credit derivatives market requires some discussion of the 1988 Basle Accord.

3.2.1 A Brief Digression: The 1988 Basle Accord

The 1988 Accord assigned specific "risk weights" to different types of borrowers and prescribed how much of the banks' exposure to such borrowers should be held in reserve as a sort of "rainy-day fund." Most borrowers received a 100 percent risk weight under the Accord, which means that banks were required to set aside 8 percent of their total exposure to such

TABLE 3.1

Risk Weights Specified in the 1988 Basle Accord for Selected Obligors

Type of Exposure	Risk Weight (percent)	Capital Charge (percent)
OECD Governments	0	0.0
OECD Banks	20	1.6
Corporates and Non-OECD Banks & Gov'ts	100	8.0

borrowers in reserve. For instance, if a bank extended $10 million to a borrower that fell under the 100 percent risk weight rule, it should incur a $800,000 "capital charge," i.e., it should set aside that much as a capital reserve related to that loan.[2] What if the borrower had a different risk weight under the Accord? Then the capital charge would change accordingly. For instance, for a borrower with a 1988 Basle Accord risk weight of, say, 20 percent, banks are allowed to hold only 20 percent of the capital they would hold for a borrower with a 100 percent risk weight, resulting in a capital charge of 1.6 percent of the bank's exposure to that borrower.

More generally, the regulatory capital charge specified in the 1988 Accord obeyed the following formula

$$\text{regulatory capital charge} = r \times .08 \times \text{notional exposure} \qquad (3.1)$$

where r is the risk weight assigned to the borrower—e.g., $r = .20$ for a borrower with a 20 percent risk weight—and the notional exposure denotes the extent to which the bank is exposed to that particular borrower.

In practice, the 1988 Accord specified only a small number of possible values for the risk weight r. For instance, Table 3.1 shows the 1988 Basle risk weights assigned to the most common types of entities referenced in the credit derivatives market: (i) governments of member countries of the Organization for Economic Cooperation and Development (OECD) were assigned a 0 percent risk weight, meaning that banks needed to hold no regulatory capital for loans extended to OECD countries; (ii) OECD banks were given a 20 percent risk weight, resulting in the 1.6 capital charge

---

[2] The 1988 Basle Accord differentiated assets held in the banking book, typically assets held by the banks as part of their normal lending activities, from those held in the trading book, mainly assets held for short periods as part of the bank's trading activities. Our focus in this brief review is on the former.

cited in the above example, and (iii) corporates and non-OECD banks and governments were subject to a 100 percent risk weight.[3]

One obvious limitation of the 1988 Accord was that it lumped all (non-OECD bank) corporate debt under one single borrower category, assigning a 100 percent risk weight to all corporate borrowers regardless of their creditworthiness. In particular, a loan extended to an AAA-rated corporation would result in the same 8 percent regulatory capital charge as one made to a corporation with a below-investment-grade credit rating. In addition, the 0 and 20 percent risk weights assigned to all OECD governments and OECD banks are also viewed as somewhat arbitrary by many banks as not all OECD member countries and their banks are alike. For instance, both Mexico and the United Kingdom, two countries with very different credit histories, are OECD member countries and thus were subject to the same risk weight of 0 percent for their sovereign debt and 20 percent for their banks. In market parlance, the 1988 Basle Accord did not allow for sufficient "granularity" in its assignment of risk weights to different categories of borrowers.

The end result of this lack of granularity in the 1988 Accord was that the notion of regulatory capital was often misaligned with that of "economic capital," or the capital that a prudent bank would want to hold in reserve given its overall credit risk exposure. For instance, a bank may well want to hold more than the prescribed 8 percent charge against a loan made to a firm that is now financially distressed—nothing in the 1988 Accord would have prevented it from doing so—but that same bank might feel that the risks associated with a loan to a top-rated firm are significantly less than what would be suggested by the mandated 8 percent charge—but here the bank would be legally prevented from reducing its capital charge. Holding too much capital in reserve is expensive—the bank would have to forego the income that the held capital could generate, for instance, if it were lent to prospective borrowers—and banks have taken measures to reduce their regulatory capital requirements while staying within the limits prescribed by bank regulators.

3.2.2   Credit Derivatives and Regulatory Capital Management

One general approach banks followed to better align regulatory and economic capital has been to move loans to highly rated borrowers—for whom the regulatory capital charge might be deemed excessive—off their balance sheets, while retaining loans to lower-rated borrowers on the balance sheet. One way to achieve such a goal is for the bank to sell or securitize

---

[3] OECD membership is composed of primarily industrialized economies, although some emerging market economies are now member countries.

loans made to highly rated borrowers, the net effect of which would be the freeing up of capital that was previously tied to such loans. While banks do engage in such sales, they are mindful, as we noted in the previous section, of possible adverse effects on their customer relationships. Here again, banks have found that the anonymity and confidentiality provided by the credit derivatives market make it a desirable venue for managing their regulatory capital.

The credit derivatives market is so young that it was not even covered by the 1988 Basle Accord. Nonetheless, national bank regulators attempted to treat issues related to credit derivatives in a way that is consistent with the spirit of that Accord. For instance, when banks sell default protection through a credit default swap, most regulators treat that as being analogous to extending a loan to the reference entity specified in the swap. For instance, if the reference entity is a nonfinancial corporation, banks have to incur a capital charge equal to 8 percent of the notional amount of the contract.

Consider now a bank that has extended a loan to a highly rated corporation. As we argued above, under the terms of the original Basle Accord, that loan would be subject to the same capital charge assigned to a less creditworthy borrower, even though it would typically embed much less credit risk and, consequently, a lower yield to the bank. One way for the bank to reduce the regulatory capital charge associated with this loan, short of selling or transferring the loan off its balance sheet, would be to buy protection against default by that corporation from an OECD bank.

If the bank regulators were satisfied that the credit risk associated with the loan had been effectively transferred to the OECD bank, then the regulatory capital charge of the protection-buying bank would fall from 8 percent to 1.6 percent, reflecting the fact that, from the perspective of the protection-buying bank, the only remaining risk exposure associated with the loan is the counterparty credit risk associated with the OECD bank. (The OECD bank, of course, would have to hold the full 8 percent capital reserve in conjunction with the protection sold under the contract.)

The use of credit derivatives by banks in this type of regulatory capital management under the 1988 Basle Accord played a significant role in the evolution of the credit derivatives market. Banks used not just credit default swaps, but also, and by some accounts mainly, portfolio products such as synthetic CDOs to bring their regulatory capital requirements more in line with what they perceive to be their economic capital needs. In this context, the credit derivatives market has helped make banks' use of capital more efficient, freeing up capital set aside in excess of true fundamental risk and putting that capital to work elsewhere in the banking system.

There is still much debate about the implications of the Basle II Accord for the future of the credit derivatives market. While some market observers have noted that regulatory capital management will likely be less of a drive for banks' participation in the credit derivatives market, others have noted that, with capital charges that more closely correspond to debtors' creditworthiness, banks will have a greater incentive to move lower-quality credits off their balance sheets, and that some of that activity will take place in the credit derivatives market. In addition, credit derivatives are treated explicitly in the context of the Basle II Accord, and there is some disagreement among market observers on the question of how the credit derivatives provisions of the new Accord will affect banks' incentives to participate in the credit derivatives market.[4]

3.3   Yield Enhancement, Portfolio Diversification

There are two sides to every story, and if banks see benefits in using the credit derivatives market to lay off some of the credit risk in their portfolios, there must be others for whom that market has some appeal as a place to take on credit risk. We have mentioned already, in Chapter 2, that insurers and re-insurers tend to be sellers of protection in the credit derivatives market. In particular, we argued that some insurance companies see credit risk as being essentially uncorrelated with their underwritten risks and that protection sellers in general see credit risk exposure as a way to enhance the return on their portfolios and diversify their risks.

Having said all that, however, there are other ways for protection sellers to obtain the desired exposure to credit risk. They could, for instance, and they do, turn to the corporate bond and secondary bank loan markets to essentially buy credit risk. Is there anything about the credit derivatives market, other than banks' desire to buy protection, that entices protection sellers not to limit themselves to the cash (bonds and loans) markets?

3.3.1   Leveraging Credit Exposure, Unfunded Instruments

Certain credit derivatives, including credit default swaps, are "unfunded" credit market instruments. Unlike buying a corporate bond or extending a loan, which requires the investor to come up with the funds to pay for the deal upfront, no money actually changes hands at the inception of many credit derivatives contracts.[5]

---

[4] Regulatory issues are treated in greater detail in Chapter 25.

[5] As noted in Chapter 2, it is not uncommon for credit derivatives contracts to require some degree of collateralization, but posting collateral is expensive. Still, it was also argued in that chapter that the collateral pledged often covers less than the total net exposure between the counterparties. Moreover, even when full collateralization of net exposures is in place, net exposures are computed with respect to marked-to-market values of the contracts involved, and, as discussed in Chapter 16, marked-to-market values are typically substantially less than the underlying notional amounts.

Take the example of a credit default swap. In its most common form, the two parties in the contract agree on a value for the annualized premium that the protection buyer will pay to the protection seller such that the contract has zero market value at its inception. As a result, provided both the protection buyer and the reference entity remain solvent while the contract is in place, the protection seller is guaranteed a stream of payments during the life of the contract without initially putting up any cash. In contrast, were this same protection seller to buy a bond issued by the reference entity, it would have to pay for the bond, either by using its scarce capital or by raising the funds in the marketplace, before it could enjoy the periodic payments made by the bond issuer. In other words, typical cash instruments such as bonds and loans have to be funded on the investors' balance sheet; typical credit default swaps, as well as many other forms of credit derivatives, largely do not. This crucial difference between cash and derivatives instruments allows investors (protection sellers) effectively to leverage up their credit risk exposure.

Let us look at another example to see how the unfunded nature of some credit derivatives makes them particularly appealing relative to traditional cash instruments. Consider a leveraged investor with a relatively high cost of funds. That investor would likely find it unattractive to invest in a bond issued by a highly rated reference entity, the reason being that the yield it would earn on the bond would tend to be lower than the investor's own cost of funds. The story would be different in the credit derivatives market, however. The investor could enter into a credit default swap with a highly rated dealer where it sells protection against default by the corporation. The investor would earn the credit default swap premium paid by the dealer, all while avoiding at least part of its funding disadvantage in the credit markets and being subject to a relatively low level of credit risk.

3.3.2 Synthesizing Long Positions in Corporate Debt

Another potentially appealing application of credit derivatives to investors is the ability to obtain credit risk exposures that would otherwise not be available through traditional cash instruments. Suppose a given institutional investor would like to take on some of the credit risk associated with XYZ Corp., but all of XYZ's debt is locked up in loans held on banks' books. The investor can essentially synthesize a long position in XYZ's debt by selling default protection in the credit derivatives market. In principle, the income earned via the credit derivatives contract would be closely related to what it would be earning had it lent to XYZ Corp. directly.

3.4   Shorting Corporate Bonds

In highly liquid financial markets, such as the market for US Treasury securities and some equity markets, investors who have a negative view regarding future market prices can hope to profit from their opinions by establishing short positions in those markets. For example, if one thinks that US Treasury yields are headed higher, and that this sentiment is not fully reflected in market prices, one could sell Treasuries short in the very active repo market for Treasury securities in hopes of buying them back later at a profit when their prices will presumably be lower.[6]

While a short selling strategy can generally be implemented without significant difficulties in sufficiently liquid markets, its applicability to corporate debt markets can be problematic. Indeed, even in the United States, which has the most advanced corporate debt market in the world, the ability to short sell individual corporate bonds is, at best, very limited. In particular, the market for these securities has not yet reached the level of liquidity and transparency that facilitate the emergence of a viable repo market. What is the aspiring short seller to do? One option is to go, you guessed, to the credit derivatives market.

Consider an investor who has a negative view on XYZ Corp. and thus expects that its credit quality will deteriorate in the near term. Moreover, the investor thinks that market prices have not yet fully accounted for such a scenario regarding XYZ's fortunes. While that investor may be unable to establish a short position on XYZ's debt, it may be able to mimic at least part of the economic effects of such a position by buying protection against XYZ Corp. in the credit default swap market. Here is how it would work. The investor buys protection against XYZ today. Should the investor's views on that reference entity prove to be right, the market value of the original credit default swap will now be positive, i.e., a newly entered credit default swap that references XYZ would require a higher premium from protection buyers than the one written into the investor's contract. The investor can thus unwind its credit default swap position at a profit, essentially cashing in on its earlier view, now confirmed, that XYZ's credit quality was headed lower.[7]

The example just described offers two important insights into the many uses of credit derivatives. First, one need not have any risk exposure to a

---

[6] In the repo market, short sellers sell borrowed securities now, hoping that by the time that they have to repurchase the securities to return them to their original owners—repo is the market term for repurchase—their prices will have fallen enough to produce a profit.

[7] In Chapter 6 we discuss how a credit default swap can be unwound. For now it suffices to note that by unwinding we mean the effective termination of the contract where the part for whom the contract has positive market value is compensated accordingly.

given reference entity in order to have a reason to buy protection against it. Second, in addition to providing protection against the possibility of default by particular reference entities, credit default swaps can also be used to express views about the prospective credit quality of such entities, and thus one can financially benefit from them even when no default by the reference entity takes place.

3.5   Other Uses of Credit Derivatives

Banks and would-be short sellers are not the only ones who stand to benefit from buying protection in the credit derivatives market, just as leveraged investors are not the only ones with something to gain from selling protection. Nonfinancial corporations, certain classes of investors, and even some banks have found other uses for credit derivatives and increased their market participation accordingly.

3.5.1   Hedging Vendor-financed Deals

Once again, let us look at a hypothetical example to better understand this alternative use of credit derivatives. Consider an equipment manufacturer with a few large corporate clients. To facilitate its business, the manufacturer also provides its customers with at least some of the financing they need to fund their orders. While that may be good for sales, such vendor-financed deals have one obvious drawback to the manufacturer. They leave the manufacturer exposed to the risk that its customers may default on their obligations. One way to hedge against such risk would be to buy protection in credit derivatives contracts that reference the individual customers. As a result, the manufacturer can concentrate on its core business, producing and selling equipment, while hedging out its credit risk in the credit derivatives market.

While this use of credit derivatives is not yet widespread, market participants see the potential for it to become more so in the future. For instance, respondents to the 2002 British Bankers Association Credit Derivatives Report expect corporations to increase their participation in the credit derivatives market, although they have revised down their forecasts relative to the 2000 report.

3.5.2   Hedging by Convertible Bond Investors

Convertible bonds are corporate bonds with an embedded call option on the bond issuer's stock. Equity-minded investors would be natural buyers of such securities, except that some may not want to have to bother with the associated credit risk. One strategy apparently followed by many convertible bond investors, including certain hedge funds, is to buy the bonds and simultaneously buy protection against the bond issuer in the credit default swap market. The end result of these transactions is to synthesize a pure call option on the issuer's stock. While the bond purchase involves buying both credit risk and the call option, the former is offset by the credit default swap position.

Of course, the attractiveness of the approach just described depends on how it compares to the cost of buying a call option on the bond issuer's stock directly from an options dealer. Apparently, many investors occasionally do find that the call option embedded in the bonds is cheap relative to the direct purchase approach. Indeed, when liquidity in the credit derivatives market is thin, the cost of buying protection against a convertible issuer can temporarily go higher even when the market's assessment of the issuer's creditworthiness is unchanged.[8]

3.5.3 Selling Protection as an Alternative to Loan Origination

In discussing the ways banks use credit derivatives we have thus far portrayed banks as protection buyers. While available information on banks' participation in the credit derivatives market tends to confirm their role as net buyers of protection, banks do sell protection over and beyond that amount required by their market making activities.

From a bank's perspective, selling protection in the credit derivatives market can be thought of as an alternative to originating loans.[9] More generally, a bank may view protection selling as portfolio diversification and yield enhancement mechanisms, i.e., as a way to obtain exposure to particular credits that would otherwise not be easily obtainable in the loan and bond markets.

3.6 Credit Derivatives as Market Indicators

We have thus far focused on the main uses of credit derivatives strictly from the standpoint of the entities that participate in the credit derivatives market. Not so obvious, but potentially very important, is the growing use by participants and non-participants alike of prices of credit derivatives,

---

[8] This is one example where temporary demand factors, discussed in Chapter 1, can affect the pricing of credit derivatives. We will encounter more examples later in the book.

[9] We mentioned an example of this phenomenon when we discussed regional European banks in Chapter 2.

especially credit default swaps, as indicators of market sentiment regarding specific reference entities (and credit risk in general).

Investors, credit analysts, and financial regulators already have at their disposal several indicators regarding the creditworthiness of particular firms. For instance, in the United States, such indicators include yield spreads of corporate bonds over US Treasury debt, as well as a few equity-market-based measures of credit risk developed by well-known analytical firms. Increasingly, credit default swap premia have been added to the ranks of major indicators of perceived credit risk. Indeed, some market observers have even suggested that prices in the credit default swap market have a tendency to incorporate information more quickly than prices in the corporate bond market given that, at times, it may be easier to enter into swap positions than to buy or sell certain corporate bonds and loans. Whether information truly is reflected first in the credit derivatives or cash markets remains a point of empirical debate, but the fact that both investors and regulators have started to pay closer attention to signals sent out by the credit default swap market is difficult to deny.

An additional potential indirect benefit of the credit default swap market is the possibility that it may encourage greater integration between the corporate bond and bank loan markets, two segments of the credit markets that have remained largely segregated despite their natural common ground. In particular, in part because most credit default swaps generally are physically settled and allow the delivery of either bonds or loans in the event of default, and in part because banks have been stepping up their use of credit derivatives to manage their economic capital, one might expect that banks will increasingly turn to prices observed in the credit derivatives market as important inputs into their own lending decisions. Should this phenomenon come to pass, it will have the potential to encourage greater efficiency and discipline in the credit markets in general, with credit risk being more transparently and consistently priced across the marketplace.

Part II

Main Types of Credit Derivatives

4

Floating-Rate Notes

Floating-rate notes, FRNs or floaters for short, are among the simplest debt instruments. They are essentially bonds with a time-varying coupon. In this chapter we go over the basics of FRNs and introduce some notation and concepts that will be used throughout the remainder of the book.

4.1 Not a Credit Derivative...

Floating-rate notes are not credit derivatives, but they are featured prominently in the discussion of so many of them—such as credit default swaps, asset swaps, and spread options—that we decided to give them their own chapter in this book.

The main reason for the close link between FRNs and credit derivatives is that, as we shall see below, the pricing of a floater is almost entirely determined by market participants' perceptions of the credit risk associated with its issuer. As such, floaters are potentially closer to credit default swaps than to fixed-rate corporate notes, which, as the name suggests, are bonds with a fixed coupon.

4.2 How Does It Work?

The variable coupon on a floating-rate note is typically expressed as a fixed spread over a benchmark short-term interest rate, most commonly three- or six-month LIBOR (London Interbank Offered Rate). LIBOR is the rate at which highly rated commercial banks can borrow in the interbank market. Therefore, one can think of LIBOR as reflecting roughly the credit quality of borrowers with credit ratings varying between A and AA, and thus such borrowers are able to issue FRNs with a spread that is either zero or close to it. Intuitively, someone with a lower/higher credit quality than these borrowers would presumably issue floaters with a positive/negative spread over LIBOR.

The mechanics of an FRN is quite simple and can be best understood with an example. Consider a corporation that needs to raise $100 million in the capital markets and that has decided to do so by issuing four-year floaters that will pay coupons semiannually. Floaters are typically issued at "par" or very close to par, meaning that their initial market price will be equal or very close to their face value, $100 million in this case. Suppose that in order for the corporation's floaters to be issued at par, they have to be issued with a fixed spread of 80 basis points over six-month LIBOR. This is called the par floater spread or the spread that makes the floater be priced at its face value. (We will address pricing issues in further detail later. For now, we can deduce that this issuer has a credit rating that is likely inferior to A given that it had to offer a positive spread over LIBOR in order to be able to sell its floaters at par.)

When the floater is issued, investors know what their first coupon payment will be, although the actual coupon payment will be received only six months forward. In particular, that coupon will be the sum of the current value of six-month LIBOR plus the 80 basis point spread required to sell the floater at par. Thus, assuming that six-month LIBOR is 6 percent, the first coupon will be equal to 6.8 percent, or 3.4 percent on a semiannual basis. Future coupons are not known in advance as they will be reset on each payment date according to the then prevailing six-month LIBOR. For instance, suppose that when the first coupon becomes due, six-month LIBOR happens to be 6.2 percent. That would result in the floater's second coupon being reset to 7 percent on an annual basis. The process continues like this until the end of the four-year period covered by the floater. As with standard fixed-income bonds, the last payment will also include the repayment of the full $100 million face value of the floater.

Table 4.1 details the cash flows of the four-year floater under consideration using hypothetical values for six-month LIBOR over the life of the instrument. Again, at any point in time, investors only know the value of the next coupon payment. The size of subsequent payments will be determined one at a time at each reset date of the floater. All that investors know about these future payments is that they will be based on an annualized coupon 80 basis points higher than the six-month LIBOR prevailing at the immediately preceding reset date.

TABLE 4.1

Cash Flows of a Hypothetical Floater[a]

(Face value = $100 million; Spread = 80 basis points)

Reset Date (years from now)	6-month LIBOR (percent)	Coupon (percent, annual)	Cash Flow ($ millions)
(1)	(2)	(3)	(4)
0	6.0	6.8	−100.00
.5	6.2	7.0	3.40
1	6.2	7.0	3.50
1.5	6.1	6.9	3.50
2	6.0	6.8	3.45
2.5	5.8	6.6	3.40
3	5.8	6.6	3.30
3.5	5.7	6.5	3.30
4	5.4	—	103.25

[a] A negative cash flow denotes a payment from the investor to the note issuer.

4.3 Common Uses

Banks are relatively frequent issuers of FRNs, especially in Europe. US corporations occasionally do issue floaters as well, but it is fair to say that the market for FRNs is significantly smaller than that for fixed-rate corporate bonds. Some sovereign debt is also issued in the form of FRNs.

From the credit investor's standpoint, FRNs have one key advantage over their fixed-rate cousins. As noted, the value of a portfolio of floaters depends almost exclusively on the perceived credit quality of their issuers represented in the portfolio. Thus, similar to someone who has sold protection in a credit default swap, the FRN investor has primarily bought some exposure to credit risk. In contrast, an investor who is long a corporate bond with a fixed coupon is exposed primarily to both credit and interest rate risk, the latter arising from the fact that prices of fixed-coupon bonds move in the opposite direction of market interest rates. (As we shall see below, floaters have very little interest rate risk.)

4.4 Valuation Considerations

Let us take a closer look at the factors that influence the pricing of a floating-rate note. As the above example suggested, the most important factor is, by far, the credit quality of the issuer. Our intuition should tell us that the riskier the issuer, the higher the spread over LIBOR will it have to offer in the marketplace in order to attract willing investors. At the same time, an AAA-rated issuer would generally be able to sell its notes at a negative spread relative to LIBOR as its creditworthiness would be superior to that of even the highly rated banks that borrow and lend in the interbank market.

While understanding the relationship between FRN spreads and credit risk is straightforward, the fact that floaters are relatively insensitive to other types of risk, particularly interest risk, may not be so obvious. To see this, let us consider first a fixed-rate note, perhaps the corporate debt security with which people are the most familiar. For simplicity, assume that the note was bought for its par value. Suppose a couple of months go by and market interest rates rise unexpectedly. What happens to the market value of the note? The purchaser of the note finds itself in the unenviable position of holding a security that now pays a coupon based on a below-market interest rate. The market value of the bond naturally falls. Of course the opposite would have been true if market interest rates had fallen. The main point here is that the fixed-rate note investor does not know whether market interest rates will rise or fall. That is the nature of interest rate risk![1]

Would the holder of a floating-rate note, also bought for par and at the same time as the fixed-rate note, fare any better than the fixed-rate note investor under the same circumstances? Suppose that the sudden rise in market interest rates happened just before a reset date for the floater. That means that the floater's coupon will soon be increased to reflect the recent rise in market rates. More important, the rise in the coupon will be such that, provided the credit quality of the issuer has remained the same, the floater will continue to be valued at par. Not much interest rate risk here! When market rates increase, the coupon increases; when rates decline, the coupon declines... and the floater continues to be valued at par. (We will show this in a numerical example below, after we introduce some simple valuation principles more formally.)

The careful reader probably noticed that we assumed that the sudden rise in market interest rates happened just before one of the floater's reset dates. What if the increase in market rates had happened right after a reset date? Given that the floater's coupon changes only at reset dates, the holder of the floater would temporarily be receiving a coupon based on

---

[1] There is one sense in which a fixed-rate note investor may not care about interest rate risk. Suppose the investor paid par for the note, plans to hold on to it until its maturity, and is not particularly concerned about what will happen to its value during the intervening time. Assuming no default by the note issuer, the investor will receive par back when the note matures regardless of where market interest rates are at that point.

a below-market rate. The key word here is "temporarily" as the floater's coupon would eventually adjust to prevailing market rates and thus the resulting effect on the market price of the floater is generally very small. The risk of movements in market rates in between reset dates is what market participants call "reset risk." We will examine reset risk more closely below. For now it suffices to say that reset risk is not a major factor in the pricing of floaters as the time between reset dates is typically short, generally six months at the most.

Table 4.2 uses a numerical example to highlight key aspects regarding the pricing of floating-rate notes and to draw some comparisons with fixed-rate notes. Let us continue to use the hypothetical four-year floater detailed in Table 4.1; indeed columns (1) through (3) and (5) are taken directly from Table 4.1. What is new in Table 4.2 is the fact that we now also consider a hypothetical fixed-rate note issued by the same corporation. By assumption, the fixed-rate note pays a fixed-coupon of 6.8 percent per annum—the same initial coupon of the floater—and has the same maturity, face value, and payment dates as the floater. We now also make the explicit simplifying assumption that the corporation faces a flat term structure of interest rates, i.e., it can borrow at a fixed rate of 6.8 percent regardless of the maturity of its debt. The table shows, in the first row of columns (5) and (6) that the investor paid the par value of both securities at time 0. How can we show that these are "fair" market prices? Let us start with the fixed-rate note, which in some respects is easier to price than the floater.

A basic valuation principle for any financial security is that its market value today should reflect the (appropriately defined) expected present (discounted) value of its future cash flows. In the absence of default, we know exactly what the cash flows of the fixed-rate security will be. The only thing we need to do to derive the market value of the fixed-rate note is discount these future cash flows to express them in terms of current dollars and add them up. Let $D(0,t)$ denote the discount factor that corresponds to today's (time-0) value of a dollar to be received at time t. Those familiar with simple bond math will recognize $D(0,t)$ as today's price of a zero-coupon bond that will mature at time t—see Appendix A for a brief refresher on basic concepts from bond math. Assuming that the debt instruments of the issuer have no recovery value in the event of default, we can write today's value of the four-year fixed-rate note, denoted below as $V^{FX}(0,8)$, as

$$V^{FX}(0,8) = \left[\sum_{t=1}^{8} \left(D(0,t)\frac{\bar{C}}{2} \right) + D(0,8) \right] P \qquad (4.1)$$

where $\bar{C}$ is the fixed annual coupon rate paid by the note at time t—as shown in Table 4.2, $\bar{C} = 6.8$ percent or 0.068—P is the face value of the note—$100 million—and $D(0,t)$ is the discount factor, as seen from time 0,

TABLE 4.2

Valuation of Fixed- and Floating-rate Notes[a]

(Face value = $100 million; Spread = 80 basis points)

Reset Date (yrs hence)	6-month LIBOR (percent)	Coupons (percent, annual)		Cash Flows ($ millions)	
		Floater	Fixed	Floater	Fixed
(1)	(2)	(3)	(4)	(5)	(6)
0	6.0	6.8	6.8	−100.00	−100.00
.5	6.2	7.0	6.8	3.40	3.40
1	6.2	7.0	6.8	3.50	3.40
1.5	6.1	6.9	6.8	3.50	3.40
2	6.0	6.8	6.8	3.45	3.40
2.5	5.8	6.6	6.8	3.40	3.40
3	5.8	6.6	6.8	3.30	3.40
3.5	5.7	6.5	6.8	3.30	3.40
4	5.4	—	6.8	103.25	103.40

[a] A negative cash flow denotes a payment from the investor to the note issuer.

relevant for a cash flow received at time t.[2] Thus, for instance, given the assumption of semiannual payments, $D(0,2)\frac{\bar{C}}{2}P$ is today's value of the coupon payment that will be received one year from the present date.

Which zero-coupon bond prices should we use to discount the future payments promised by the note issuer? If there were not default risk associated with the issuer, one might just use zero-coupon bond prices derived, say, from the US Treasury yield curve, which is typically assumed to be a good representation of the term structure of default-free interest rates. In the presence of credit risk, however, the prudent investor might want to discount these future payments at a higher rate. How much higher? The answer is in the issuer's own yield curve, which we assumed to be flat at 6.8 percent in this example. Given this yield curve, one can derive the prices of zero-coupon bonds associated with the issuer. For now we will focus on discretely compounded rates. As shown in Appendix A, for $j = 1, 2, \ldots, 8$, one can write $D(0,j)$ as

$$D(0,j) = \frac{1}{(1 + R(0,j)/2)^j} \tag{4.2}$$

---

[2] The zero-recovery assumption means that the note becomes worthless upon default. We make this assumption here for the sake of simplicity only. Different recovery assumptions are discussed in Part III.

where $R(0, j)$ is the semiannually compounded zero-coupon bond yield, derived from the issuer's yield curve, that corresponds to the maturity date j. Given the flat yield curve assumption, $R(0, j) = .068$ for all maturities j. Thus, we obtain $D(0, 1) = 0.9671$, $D(0, 2) = 0.9353$, etc. By carrying on with these calculations and substituting the results into equation (4.1) we find that $V^{FX}(0, 8) = \$100$ million, which is what is shown in Table 4.2.

We can use similar principles to value the floater, except that in this case the associated future cash flows are unknown even in the absence of default. For instance, we do not know today what six-month LIBOR will be in one year's time. How can we verify that the floater is indeed worth par given the assumptions underlying Table 4.2?

It can be shown that the following relationship holds for a par floater:

$$P = \left[\sum_{t=1}^{N} \left(D(0, t) \frac{F^*(0, t-1, t) + \hat{S}}{2} \right) + D(0, N) \right] P \qquad (4.3)$$

where $F^*(0, t-1, t)$ is the discretely compounded forward LIBOR rate, as seen at time 0, that corresponds to a future loan that will start at a future date $t - 1$ and end at t, and $\hat{S}$ is the issuer's par floater spread. Thus, the forward rate that applies to this particular issuer would be $F^*(0, t-1, t)+\hat{S}$. By definition of the forward rate, see Appendix A, we have

$$F^*(0, t-1, t) + \hat{S} \equiv \frac{1}{\delta} \left(\frac{D(0, t-1)}{D(0, t)} - 1 \right) \qquad (4.4)$$

where δ is the accrual factor that corresponds to the period between $t - 1$ and t. For instance, if $F^* + \hat{S}$ is expressed on an annual basis, $\delta = .5$ corresponds to the case where the period $[t - 1, t]$ is equal to one-half of a year.

If we substitute the above expression for the forward rate into equation (4.3) we find that the term in square brackets simplifies to 1 so that (4.3) holds, verifying what we wanted to show.

Going back to the example in Table 4.2, we can use equation (4.4) to compute the forward rates associated with the note issuer and check whether the assumed spread of 80 basis points over LIBOR is indeed consistent with the floater being sold par at time 0. It is!

Note that we can use an expression analogous to (4.3) to price any floater, not just a par floater. In particular, we can write:

$$V^{FL}(0, N) = \left[\sum_{t=1}^{N} \left(D(0, t) \frac{F^*(0, t-1, t) + S}{2} \right) + D(0, N) \right] P \qquad (4.5)$$

where S is the floater's spread, which is not necessarily the same as the par spread $\hat{S}$. Thus, if we know the discount curve for a particular issuer, we can find the fair market value of a floater paying a generic spread S over LIBOR.

We are now in a position to take another look at the floater's sensitivity to changes in market interest rates (reset risk) and to changes in the credit quality of the issuer. Let us consider first a surprise across-the-board 50 basis point increase in market rates—a parallel shift in the yield curve. We consider two scenarios. In the first scenario, six-month LIBOR increases 50 basis points six months after it was issued, just before the floater's first reset date, but immediately after the first coupon payment is received. In the second, the rise in rates happens immediately after the floater was issued.

As noted, the first case illustrates a situation of minimum, virtually zero, reset risk. Rates rise just before the reset date so the higher level is immediately reflected in the floater's coupon. The end result, which can be verified with help from equation (4.5) is that the market value of the floater is not affected by the rise in market interest rates.

The second scenario illustrates a case of maximum reset risk. Market interest rise unexpectedly but investors have to wait for a full accrual period (six months) before the floater's coupon will be adjusted. What happens to the market value of the floater? It falls 0.24 percent, from its par value of $100 million to $99.76 million. Once the reset date does arrive, however, the floater's coupon is adjusted to the prevailing LIBOR, and the floater's price reverts to par.

How does the interest rate sensitivity of the hypothetical floater in the example in Table 4.2 compare to that of the fixed-rate note? Using equation (4.1), we find that the price of the fixed-rate security falls about 1.5 percent and 1.7 percent in the first and second scenarios, respectively. Another way to compare the interest rate sensitivities of the floating- and fixed-rate notes is to look at their durations, which one can approximate with the following calculation:

$$\text{Duration} = -\left(\frac{\text{change in price}}{\text{change in interest rate}}\right)\left(\frac{1}{\text{initial price}}\right) \qquad (4.6)$$

This calculation puts the duration of the floater between 0 and just under 6 months and that of the fixed-rate note at between 3 and $3\frac{1}{2}$ years.

An interest rate sensitivity measure that is closely related to duration is PV01 sensitivity, defined as the change in the price of an instrument in response to a parallel one basis point shift in both the issuer's and benchmark yield curves. The PV01 sensitivities of the hypothetical floating-rate note in Table 4.2 were $0 and $-$4,835 in the two scenarios examined, given the $100 million initial price of the floater. For the fixed-rate note, the PV01 sensitivities were substantially more pronounced, at $-$30,681 and $-$34,506 for the two cases analyzed and same initial price.

While the floater has very little sensitivity to changes in market interest rates, a sudden deterioration in the credit quality of the issuer would have a noticeable effect on the prices of both the floating- and fixed-rate notes. In particular, continuing to use Table 4.2 as an illustration, suppose the issuer's yield curve shifts up 50 basis points in a parallel fashion while other market interest rates remain unchanged. Looking at the floater first, both the forward LIBOR curve and the 80 basis spread written into the floater are unchanged in equation (4.5). Nonetheless, all future payments to be received from the issuer will now be discounted at a higher rate to reflect the issuer's lower credit quality. As a result, assuming the widening in spreads happens immediately after the notes were issued, the price of the floater declines 1.7 percent. In this particular example the price of the fixed-rate note also declines 1.7 percent as a result of the deterioration in the issuer's credit quality.[3]

To sum up, the above examples highlight two key points about floating-rate notes. First, they have very little sensitivity to changes in market interest rates. Second, changes in their prices reflect mainly changes in the creditworthiness of issuers. As such, floating-rate notes are closely related to many types of credit derivatives, an issue we shall discuss in greater detail in the next two chapters.

---

[3] A related concept is that of spread duration, which measures the sensitivity of a bond's price to a change in its yield spread over a given benchmark rate—typically the yield on a comparable government bond. In the above example, both the floater and the fixed-rate bond have a spread duration of about $3\frac{1}{2}$ years.

5

Asset Swaps

Asset swaps are a common form of derivative contract written on fixed-rate debt instruments. The end result of an asset swap is to separate the credit and interest rate risks embedded in the fixed-rate instrument. Effectively, one of the parties in an asset swap transfers the interest rate risk in a fixed-rate note or loan to the other party, retaining only the credit risk component. As such, asset swaps are mainly used to create positions that closely mimic the cash flows and risk exposure of floating-rate notes.

5.1 A Borderline Credit Derivative...

There is some disagreement among credit derivatives market participants on whether an asset default swap is a credit derivative. Some apparently focus on the fact that the asset swap can be thought of as not much more than a synthetic floater, and a floater is definitely not a credit derivative. Others seem to emphasize the fact that asset swaps can be thought of as a way to unbundle the risks embedded in a fixed-rate security, isolating its credit risk component, much like what other credit derivatives do. For these and other reasons, the difference in opinions regarding asset swaps persists. Indeed, while *Risk Magazine*'s 2003 Credit Derivatives Survey (Patel, 2003) decided to exclude asset swaps from its range of surveyed products, the 2002 British Bankers Association Credit Derivatives Report included assets swaps in its credit derivatives statistics. The BBA acknowledged the ongoing debate among market participants, but reported that a majority of key participants considers asset swaps as part of their credit derivatives activities.

Regardless of where the asset swap debate settles, however, asset swaps are important in their own right if one's goal is to develop a better understanding of credit derivatives. For instance, similar to floating-rate notes, asset swaps are closely related to credit default swaps, which are probably the best-known type of credit derivative.

5.2 How Does It Work?

Those familiar with interest rate swaps will find several similarities between the mechanics of an asset swap and that of an interest rate swap. As with an interest rate swap, an asset swap is an agreement between two parties to exchange fixed and variable interest rate payments over a predetermined period of time, where the interest rate payments are based on a notional amount specified in the contract. Unlike the vanilla interest rate swap, however, where the variable rate is LIBOR flat and the fixed rate is determined by market forces when the contract is agreed upon, the fixed rate in an asset swap is typically set equal to the coupon rate of an underlying fixed-rate corporate bond or loan, with the spread over LIBOR adjusting to market conditions at the time of inception of the asset swap.

But this is not a book about interest rate swaps, nor is detailed knowledge about such instruments a prerequisite for reading this chapter.[1] Figure 5.1 lays out the basic features of an asset swap. Consider an investor who wants to be exposed to the credit risk of XYZ Corp. (the reference entity), but who wants to minimize its exposure to interest rate risk. Assume further that XYZ Corp.'s debt is issued primarily in the form of fixed-rate bonds, which, as we saw in Chapter 4, embed both credit and interest rate risk. The investor can enter into an asset swap with a dealer where the investor will be a floating-rate receiver. (In market parlance, the investor is called the asset swap buyer and the dealer is the asset swap seller.)

The typical terms of the agreement are as follows.

- The investor (the asset swap buyer) agrees to buy from the dealer (the asset swap seller) a fixed-rated bond issued by the reference entity, paying par for the bond regardless of its market price. This is shown in the upper panel of Figure 5.1.

- The investor agrees to make periodic fixed payments to the dealer that are equal to the coupon payments made by the reference bond. The investor essentially passes through the coupon payments made by

---

[1] See Hull (2003)[41] for an overview of interest rate swaps.

Purchase of fixed-rate bond for par

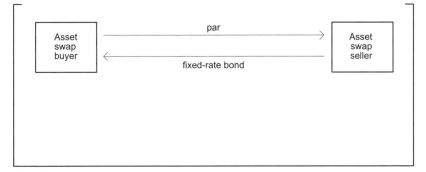

Embedded Interest Rate Swap

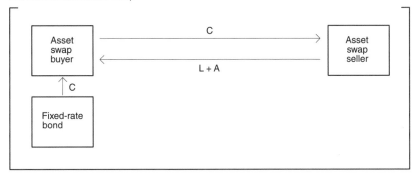

FIGURE 5.1. Diagram of an Asset Swap

the bond to the dealer. In return the dealer agrees to make variable interest rate payments to the investor, where the variable payments are based on a fixed spread over LIBOR, and the notional principal is the same as the par value of the reference bond. This is shown in the lower panel of Figure 5.1. The coupon payments made by bond and passed along by the investor are denoted as C, and the variable rate payments made by the dealer are denoted as $L + A$, where L stands for the relevant LIBOR—typically corresponding to the three- or six-month maturity—and A is the so-called asset swap spread.

- A is typically set so that the initial market value of the asset swap is zero. This implies, for instance, that if the reference bond is trading at a premium over its face value, dealers must be compensated for the fact that they sell the bond to the asset swap buyer for less than its market value. That compensation comes in the details of the interest rate swap embedded in the asset swap. In the case of a bond that is trading at more than its par value, A must be such that the dealer's position in the swap has a sufficiently positive market value at the time of inception of the swap so it will compensate the dealer for selling the bond to the investor "at a loss."[2]

Assuming there is no default by the reference entity during the life of the asset swap, what happens at its maturity date?

- The investor receives the par value of the reference bond.

- The dealer and the investor are freed from their obligations under the swap after they make their last exchange of payments. As with an interest rate swap, there is no exchange of notional principals at the end of the swap.

What if the reference entity defaults while the asset swap is still in force?

- The asset swap lives on, that is, all rights and obligations of the dealer and the investor are unaffected by the reference entity's default.

- The investor, however, loses the original source of funding for the fixed rate payments that it is obliged to make to the dealer. The investor also loses its claim on the full par value of the bond, receiving only the bond's recovery value upon the reference entity's default.

If the reference entity defaults, the investor and the dealer may decide to terminate the interest rate swap by cash settling it. They will look at the market value of the interest rate swap at that point in time, and the party for whom the interest rate swap has positive market value will be paid accordingly by the other in order to terminate the swap. For instance, suppose both parties agree that the interest rate swap has positive market value of Y to the dealer. In order to the terminate the swap, the investor will pay Y to the dealer.

5.3 Common Uses

Investors who want exposure to credit risk, without having to bother much about interest rate risk, but who cannot find all the floaters they want, can go to the asset swap market to "buy synthetic floaters." Likewise, investors

---

[2]We will look at this more explicitly in Section 5.4.

who fund themselves through floating-rate instruments but who hold fixed-rate assets might want to transfer the interest rate risk of their assets to someone else by becoming buyers of asset swaps.

Banks are significant users of asset swaps as they tend to fall in the category of investors mentioned at the end of the last paragraph. Banks traditionally fund themselves by issuing floating-rate liabilities, e.g. deposits, but may hold some fixed-rate assets on their balance sheets, such as fixed-rate bonds and some fixed-rate loans. As we saw in Chapter 4, the interest sensitivity of floating-rate instruments is vastly smaller than that of fixed-rate instruments. As a result, banks and other investors with potentially sizable mismatches between the durations of their liabilities and assets may benefit from buying asset swaps. For instance, a floater-funded investor who invests in fixed-rate bonds could be substantially adversely affected by a sudden rise in market interest rates: Although the value of its liabilities would be relatively unaffected by the rise in rates, that of its assets could potentially plunge.

Some market participants, such as hedge funds, use the asset swap market to exploit perceived arbitrage opportunities between the cash and derivatives market. As discussed above, buying an asset swap is akin to buying a synthetic floater issued by the entity referenced in the swap. It should then be the case that, in the absence of market frictions such as segmentation, poor liquidity, and other transactions costs, par asset swap spreads will tend to remain close to par floater spreads.[3] When the two spreads are deemed to be sufficiently out of line that associated transactions costs of taking positions in both markets are not binding, arbitrageurs will spring into action. For instance, suppose the asset swap spread associated with contracts referencing XYZ Corp. are perceived to be too narrow relative to the spreads paid by floaters issued by XYZ. An arbitrageur could exploit this apparent misalignment in prices in the asset swap and floater markets by selling asset swaps written on XYZ fixed-rate debt and buying XYZ floaters.[4]

Asset swaps can be used to leverage one's exposure to credit risk. For instance, consider an investor who wants to buy a corporate bond that is trading at a substantial premium over its face value. The investor can either buy the bond in the open market for its full market value or buy it through a par asset swap where the initial cash outlay would be only the bond's face value. Of course, as with other leveraging strategies, buying the asset swap in this case has the implication that the investor could lose more than the initial cash outlay in the event of default by the bond issuer: If you bought the bond through a par asset swap, and thus paid less than

---

[3] We will take a closer look at the relationship between asset swap spreads and floater spreads towards the end of this chapter.

[4] This arbitrage strategy is discussed further in Section 5.4.2.

the market price of the bond because you also entered into an asset swap that had negative market value to you. Thus, if and when the bond defaults, you may find yourself in a situation where not only you incur a default-related loss in the bond, as would an investor who bought the bond directly in the open market, but you could also find yourself with an interest rate swap that is still against you. In contrast, if you bought the bond directly in the open market, your maximum loss will be your initial cash outlay.

5.4   Valuation Considerations

To understand what goes into the pricing of an asset swap (AP), it is best to think of it as a "package" involving two products: (i) a fixed-rate bond (B), which is bought by the investor from the dealer for par, and (ii) an interest rate swap (IRS) entered between the investor and the dealer. Thus, from the perspective of the asset swap buyer (the investor), the market value of the asset swap can be written as

$$V^{AP}(0, N) = [V^{B}(0, N) - P] + V^{IRS}(0, N) \tag{5.1}$$

where P denotes the face value of the bond, and the notation $V^{Y}(.)$ is used to represent the market value of Y, whatever Y may be. For the interest rate swap, we express its market value to the asset swap buyer; the market value to the asset swap seller would be the negative of this quantity.

In words, equation (5.1) says that the value of the asset swap to its buyer at its inception is essentially given by the sum of its two components. The buyer paid par for the bond, but its actual market value, $V^{B}(0, N)$, could well be different from par, and thus the buyer could incur either a profit or a loss if the bond were to be immediately resold in the open market. This potential profit or loss is shown by the term in brackets on the right side of the equation. The second component in the valuation of the asset swap is the market value of the embedded interest rate swap between the buyer and the dealer, denoted above as $V^{IRS}(0, N)$. That swap too may have either positive or negative market value to the buyer.

We see then that the market prices of the reference bond and the embedded interest rate swap determine the market value of the asset swap. Now, the market value of the bond is given to both the dealer and the investor so the main issue of negotiation between the two of them would be the interest rate swap component, more precisely, the spread A over LIBOR that will be part of the variable-rate payment made to the investor—both LIBOR and the bond's coupon, which determines the fixed leg of the swap, are also outside of the control of either the dealer or the investor.

Market convention is to set the asset swap spread so that the market value of the entire package, the asset swap, is zero at the inception of the contract. This means that, if the market price of the bond is above its face value—effectively meaning that the investor bought the bond from the dealer for less than its market price—the dealer must be getting something in return. Indeed, for the privilege of buying the bond at below its market price in this example, the investor agrees to enter into an interest rate swap that has positive market value to the dealer. Thus, for a par asset swap, the asset swap spread will be set such that the market value of the interest rate swap will exactly offset the difference between the par and market values of the bond.

5.4.1 Valuing the Two Pieces of an Asset Swap

Valuing the bond piece of the asset swap is relatively straightforward. We have seen how to do it in Chapter 4—equation (4.1). For convenience, let us repeat the relevant equation here:

$$V^B(0, N) = \left[\sum_{i=1}^{N} \left(D(0,i)\delta_i\bar{C} \right) + D(0,N) \right] P \qquad (5.2)$$

where $V^B(0, N)$ is the time-0 price of a fixed-rate bond that matures at time N; $\bar{C}$ is the fixed annual coupon paid by the bond at time i; P is its face value; and $D(0,i)$ is the time-0 discount factor, derived from the issuer's yield curve, that represents the present value of $1 payable by the issuer at a future time i.[5] δ_i is the accrual factor that corresponds to the period between $i-1$ and i—for instance, if the bond pays coupons semiannually, $\delta_i = .5$. In practice, of course, the price of the fixed-rate bond may be directly observable in the market, but we write down the above expression here as it will come in handy in the valuation of the embedded interest rate swap.

To find the market value of the embedded interest rate swap, we should remember the fundamental principle that the market price of any security essentially is equal to the appropriately discounted value of the future cash flows associated with the security (see Chapter 4). Now consider the fact that an interest rate swap can be thought of as an exchange of a fixed- for a floating-rate liability and we are essentially home! Recall that the asset swap buyer agrees to pay fixed in the interest rate swap, which is akin to selling a fixed-rate bond to the dealer. In particular the market value of the so-called fixed leg of the swap, denoted below as $V^{XL}(0, N)$ can be

---

[5] To keep things simple at this point, it is assumed that the bond has no recovery value.

written as

$$V^{XL}(0, N) = \left[\sum_{i=1}^{N} \left(D^*(0, i) \delta_i \bar{C} \right) \right] P \qquad (5.3)$$

where, as is customary for an asset swap, we assumed that the fixed leg has the same coupon, notional principal, and payment dates as the underlying bond. Before moving ahead, let us take notice of two points. First, we omitted the principal payment at the end of the swap, given that there is no exchange of notional amounts in these contracts. Second, and more important, we used a different set of factors, $D^*(0, i)$, to discount the future payments of the swap.[6] These should reflect the credit quality of the swap counterparties, either on a stand-alone basis or enhanced via collateral agreements and other mechanisms. For simplicity, let us assume that $D^*(0, i)$ is derived from the LIBOR curve, which tends to correspond to the average credit quality of the main participants in the asset and interest rate swap markets.

Turning to the other leg of the interest rate swap, the dealer has agreed to make variable-rate payments to the asset swap buyer. This is analogous to selling a floating-rate note to the asset swap buyer. From Chapter 4, equation (4.5), we know how to value a floater. Let $V^{LL}(0, N)$ represent the market value of the floating-leg of the interest rate swap. Then, we can write

$$V^{LL}(0, N) = \left[\sum_{i=1}^{N} \left(D^*(0, i) \delta_i (F^*(0, i-1, i) + A) \right) \right] P \qquad (5.4)$$

where A is the spread to be paid over LIBOR, which in the current context shall be called the asset swap spread, and $F^*(0, i-1, i)$ is forward LIBOR, as seen from time 0, for a deposit to be made at time $i-1$ with maturity at time i. Notice again that we are discounting the future payments of the swap using the LIBOR curve and that we are omitting the repayment of principal at the end of the contract.

We are now in a position to derive the market value of the IRS embedded in the asset swap. From the point of view of the asset swap buyer, who receives the floating and pays fixed, we have:

$$V^{IRS}(0, N) = V^{LL}(0, N) - V^{XL}(0, N) \qquad (5.5)$$

and thus we now have all necessary ingredients for valuing the entire asset swap.

---

[6] $D(0, i)$ corresponds to discount factors that reflect the credit quality of the reference entity.

Remember again that the market practice is to choose a value for A, the asset swap spread, such that the asset swap has zero market value at its inception. To see how we can find this value of A, called the par asset spread, let us rewrite (5.1) using the results derived thus far:

$$V^{AP}(0, N) = [V^B(0, N) - P] + [V^{LL}(0, N) - V^{XL}(0, N)] \qquad (5.6)$$

Finding the par asset swap spread, $\hat{A}$, amounts to solving the above equation for A while setting $V^{AP}(0, N)$ to zero. To do this note that we can rewrite (5.4) as

$$V^{LL}(0, N) = \left[\sum_{i=1}^{N} (D^*(0, i)\delta_i F^*(0, i - 1, i)) + A \sum_{i=1}^{N} (\delta_i D^*(0, i)) \right] P \quad (5.7)$$

Adding and subtracting $D^*(0, N)P$ to equation (5.7), and remembering that

$$\left[\sum_{i=1}^{N} (D^*(0, i)\delta_i F^*(0, i - 1, i)) + D^*(0, N) \right] P$$

is nothing more than the market value of a par floater with a zero spread over LIBOR—see equation (4.3) and recall the definitions of $D^*(0, i)$ and $F^*(0, i - 1, i)$—we can write:

$$V^{LL}(0, N) = \left[1 + A \sum_{i=1}^{N} (\delta_i D^*(0, i)) - D^*(0, N) \right] P \qquad (5.8)$$

After substituting the above expression into (5.6) and rearranging some terms, one obtains

$$0 = V^B(0, N) + A \sum_{i=1}^{N} \delta_i D^*(0, i)P - V^{XL}(0, N) - D^*(0, N)P \qquad (5.9)$$

Note now that the last two terms of the above expression have a natural financial interpretation. They represent the present discounted value of the cash flows of the bond underlying the asset swap, where the discount factors were derived from the LIBOR curve, instead of from the bond issuer's yield curve. Let us denote this quantity $V^{B*}(0, N)$, which is consistent with the notation of using the superscript * to denote variables derived from the LIBOR curve. Then we can write

$$0 = V^B(0, N) - V^{B*}(0, N) + A \sum_{i=1}^{N} \delta_i D^*(0, i) P \qquad (5.10)$$

and it is easy to see that the par asset swap spread $\hat{A}$ is

$$\hat{A} = \frac{V^{B*}(0, N) - V^B(0, N)}{\sum_{i=1}^{N} D^*(0, i) \delta_i P} \qquad (5.11)$$

which has the intuitive interpretation that the par asset swap spread will be positive if $V^{B*} > V^B$, which in turn means that the discount factors associated with the reference entity, $D(0, i)$, are lower than those derived from the LIBOR curve, $D^*(0, i)$. Recall that lower discount factors mean heavier discounting of future cash flows. The fact that the cash flows of the bond issued by the reference entity are discounted more heavily than the cash flows of the fixed leg of the swap leads to $V^{B*}(0, N) > V^B(0, N)$, which would imply that the issuer has a lower credit quality than that embedded in LIBOR and thus its asset swap spread should be positive.

5.4.2 Comparison to Par Floaters

Let us look at the cash flows associated with the par asset swap just described, focusing on the investor's (asset swap buyer's) position. As Figure 5.1 showed, the investor paid par at the time of inception of the asset swap, and in return was promised a net cash flow of $L + A$ for as long as the reference entity does not default. Recall that, by the nature of the contract, the cash flow received from the bond is exactly offset by the fixed-rate payments made by the investor to the dealer. Should the reference entity default while the asset swap is still in place, the investor loses the bond—assume for simplicity that the bond has no recovery value—and is left with a position in an interest rate swap that may have either positive or negative value.

Notice that the net cash flow of the asset swap looks very much similar to the cash flows of a par floater. As discussed in Chapter 4, the par floater buyer pays par for the note and, assuming the note issuer does not default on its obligations, receives variable interest rate payments based on $L + S$ each period until the the floater's maturity date. Should the par floater issuer default during the life of the floater, and continuing to assume zero recovery, the investor is left with nothing.

Thus, setting aside the topic of counterparty credit risk in the interest rate swap for the moment, were it not for the possibly non-zero value of

TABLE 5.1

Cash Flows of a Par Floater and a Par Asset Swap[a]

(Assuming that the swap is terminated upon default by the reference entity,
without regard to its market value.)

Year	Floater	Asset Swap	Difference
(1)	(2)	(3)	(2) minus (3)
A. Assuming no default by the reference entity			
0	-1	-1	0
1	$L + S$	$L + A$	$S - A$
2	$L + S$	$L + A$	$S - A$
3	$L + S$	$L + A$	$S - A$
4	$1 + L + S$	$1 + L + A$	$S - A$
B. Assuming default by the reference entity at $t = 2$.[b]			
0	-1	-1	0
1	$L + S$	$L + A$	$S - A$
2	0	0	0

[a]From the perspective of the buyer. Notional amount = $1.
[b]Assuming default occurs at the very beginning of year 2.

the interest rate swap at the time of the reference entity's default, the cash flow of the asset swap would be identical to that of this par floater. To see this, let us take a look at Table 5.1 where we consider an asset swap where, unlike the asset swap described in Figure 5.1, the embedded interest rate swap is terminated without regard to its market value upon default by the reference entity.

Table 5.1 shows the cash flows of two hypothetical par products, a floater paying a spread of S over LIBOR and an asset swap with a spread of A, also over LIBOR. We assume that the asset swap is written on a bond issued by the same reference entity that issued the floater and that they have the same maturity, payment dates, and principal amounts. For simplicity, we assume that payments are annual. If there is no default by the reference entity, the floater and the asset swap will pay $L + S$ and $L + A$, respectively each period. In addition, the last period includes the par values of the floater and asset swap. This is shown in the upper panel of the table.

Suppose now the reference entity defaults on its obligations at year 2 before making its annual interest rate payments and assume that these obligations have no recovery value. The cash flows of the two products are shown in the lower panel of Table 5.1.

What is the relationship between the par floater and par swap spreads shown in Table 5.1? Notice that the two investment alternatives have the same initial cost, same payment dates, and same risk exposure. In either case, the investor is exposed to the credit risk of the reference entity. Thus, it must be the case that $S - A = 0$, i.e., they must generate the same cash flow. To see this, consider what would happen if, say, $S > A$. In this case one could buy the floater and sell an asset swap. Notice that this investment strategy costs nothing at year 0; one can finance the purchase of the floater with the sale of the asset swap. One would then enjoy a positive net income of $S - A$ per period during the life of the swap for as long as the reference entity remains solvent. If the reference entity does default during the life of the swap, both the floater and the asset swap become worthless. The point here is that this is an arbitrage opportunity that cannot persist in an efficient market. Other investors would see this opportunity and attempt to exploit it, putting downward pressure on the floater spread—faced with strong demand for its floaters, the floater issuer would be able to place them in the market with a lower spread—and upward pressure in the asset swap spread—asset swap buyers would be able to ask for a higher spread if people are rushing to sell them. Thus, the asset swap and par floater spreads illustrated in Table 5.1 should be the same.[7]

Unlike the hypothetical example in Table 5.1, however, the typical asset swap does not specify the automatic termination of its embedded IRS without regard to its market value upon default by the reference entity. As a result, the par asset swap spread will generally not be equal to the par floater spread of the reference entity. In particular, the asset swap spread will take into account the fact that the value of the embedded IRS will commonly be nonzero and thus the asset swap buyer has some exposure to the value of the IRS should the reference entity default. In practice, however, such exposure tends to be small, especially when the reference bond is trading at close to par at the time of inception of the asset swap and so par asset swap and par floater spreads tend not to diverge significantly from one another.[8]

Thus far, we have abstracted from counterparty credit risk in the embedded IRS, or the risk that one of the IRS counterparties will default on its IRS obligations. If that risk were significant, it could drive a substantial

---

[7]Note that we have just encountered the first example of pricing a credit derivative via the static replication approach discussed in Chapter 1. We will do a lot more of this in the remainder of the book.

[8]With the bond trading at close to par at the time of inception of the asset swap, the market value of the embedded IRS will be close to zero. That would suggest about even odds that future values of the IRS will be positive to the asset swap buyer—if the IRS were more/less likely to have positive than negative value to the asset swap buyer in the future, the market value of the IRS to the asset swap buyer would have been positive/negative.

wedge between par asset swap and par floater spreads as investing on a par floater involves only the credit risk of the floater issuer, whereas entering into the asset swap would encompass both this risk and the risk associated with default in the embedded IRS. In reality, however, counterparty credit risk tends to be mitigated in the asset swap market via the use of credit enhancement mechanisms such as netting and collateralization.

To sum up, similar to the pricing of a par floater, the main determinant in the pricing of a par asset swap is the credit quality of the reference entity. Nonetheless, other factors potentially enter into the pricing of asset swaps, such as counterparty credit risk and the default-contingent exposure of the asset swap buyer to the market value of the embedded interest rate swap. Still, the contribution of these factors to the determination of the asset swap spread tends to be small relative to that of the credit risk of the reference bond. That is why asset swaps are viewed essentially as synthetic floating-rate notes. Having said that, however, as mentioned in Chapter 1, other "technical" factors do affect asset swap spreads in practice, such as differences in liquidity between the corporate bond and asset swap markets, market segmentation, and other supply and demand influences.

6

Credit Default Swaps

Credit default swaps (CDS) are the most common type of credit derivative. According to different surveys of market participants, which were summarized in Chapter 2, CDS are by far the main credit derivatives product in terms of notional amount outstanding. Their dominance of the marketplace is even more striking in terms of their share of the total activity in the credit derivatives market.[1] As actively quoted and negotiated single-name instruments, CDS are important in their own right, but their significance also stems from the fact that they serve as building blocks for many complex multi-name products.[2]

The rising liquidity of the credit default swap market is evidenced by the fact that major dealers now regularly disseminate quotes for such contracts. Furthermore, along with risk spreads in the corporate bond market, CDS quotes are now commonly relied upon as indicators of investors' perceptions of credit risk regarding individual firms and their willingness to bear this risk. In addition, quotes from the CDS market are reportedly increasingly used as inputs in the pricing of other traditional credit products such as bank loans and corporate bonds, helping promote greater integration of the various segments of the credit market.

---

[1] CDS transactions are much more common than multi-name credit derivatives such as synthetic collateralized debt obligations, but the latter have substantially larger notional amounts.

[2] We shall examine some multi-name instruments in Chapters 9 through 11 and in Part IV.

6.1   How Does It Work?

A credit default swap is a bilateral agreement between two parties, a buyer and a seller of credit protection. In its simplest "vanilla" form, the protection buyer agrees to make periodic payments over a predetermined number of years (the maturity of the CDS) to the protection seller. In exchange, the protection seller commits to making a payment to the buyer in the event of default by a third party (the reference entity). As such, a credit default swap shares many similarities with traditional insurance products. For instance, car owners generally go to an insurance company to buy protection from certain car-related financial losses. The car insurance company collects a stream of insurance premiums from its customers over the life of the contract and, in return, promises to stand ready to make payments to customers if covered events (accidents, theft, etc.) occur.

Figure 6.1 illustrates the basic characteristics of a credit default swap. In a typical credit default swap, a protection buyer purchases "default insurance" from a protection seller on a notional amount of debt issued by a third party (the reference entity). The notional quantity, in effect, represents the amount of insurance coverage. In the credit default swap market, the annualized insurance premium is called the "credit default swap spread," or "credit default swap premium," which is quoted as a fraction of the notional amount specified in the contract and generally set so that the contract has zero market value at its inception. As an illustration, the credit default swap represented in the diagram has a notional amount of $100 and an associated premium of 40 basis points. Thus, the protection buyer pays 40 cents per year for each $100 of notional amount in exchange for protection against a default by the reference entity. Typically, CDS premiums are paid quarterly so that, in this example, the protection seller agrees to pay 10 cents per quarter for each $100 of desired credit protection.

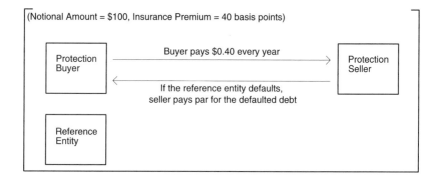

FIGURE 6.1. Example of a Credit Default Swap

In the event of default by the reference entity, a CDS can be settled physically or in cash, with the settlement choice determined upfront when entering the contract. In a physically settled swap, the protection buyer has the right to sell (deliver) a range of defaulted assets to the protection seller, receiving as payment the full face value of the assets. The types of deliverable assets are also prespecified in the contract. For instance, the typical CDS determines essentially that any form of senior unsecured debt issued by the reference entity is a deliverable asset, and thus any bank loan or bond that meets this criterion is a deliverable asset.

In a cash settled swap, the counterparties may agree to poll market participants to determine the recovery value of the defaulted assets, and the protection seller is liable for the difference between face and recovery values. The asset or types of assets that will be used in the poll are prespecified in the contract. Cash settlement is more common in Europe than in the United States, where, by far, the majority of CDS are physically settled.

As mentioned in Chapters 1 and 3, the adoption of standardized documentation for credit default swap agreements has played an important role in the development and greater liquidity of the CDS market. The use of master agreements sponsored by the International Swaps and Derivatives Association (ISDA) is now a common market practice, significantly reducing setup and negotiation costs. The standard contract specifies all the obligations and rights of the parties as well as key definitions, such as which situations constitute a "credit event"—a default by the reference entity—and how a default can be verified. Regarding the former, for instance, CDS contracts generally allow for the following types of default events:

- bankruptcy

- failure to pay

- debt moratorium

- debt repudiation

- restructuring of debt

- acceleration or default

Some of these events are more common in contracts involving certain types of reference names. For instance, moratorium and repudiation are typically covered in contracts referencing sovereign borrowers. In addition, especially in the United States, CDS contracts are negotiated both with and without restructuring included in the list of credit events. In Chapter 24 we discuss the standardized ISDA contract for credit default swaps in some detail, including the specific definitions of each of these credit events.

The maturity of a credit default swap does not have to match that of any particular debt instrument issued by the reference entity. The most common maturities of credit default maturities are 3, 5, and 10 years, with the five-year maturity being especially active.

It is possible, and increasingly easier, to terminate or unwind a credit default swap before its maturity (and this is commonly done) in order to extract or monetize the market value of the position. Typically, unwinding a CDS position involves agreement by both parties in the contract regarding the market value of the position.[3] The party for whom the position has negative market value then compensates the other accordingly. Alternatively, a party may be able to close out its position by assigning it to a third party, but this generally requires mutual approval of both new counterparties.

6.2   Common Uses

From the analogy with traditional insurance products, it becomes obvious what the most direct uses of credit default swaps are. At the most basic level, protection buyers use credit default swaps to buy default insurance, and protection sellers use them as an additional source of income. In practice, however, market participants' uses of credit default swaps go well beyond this simple insurance analogy. Indeed, because credit default swaps are the main type of credit derivative, we have indirectly discussed many of their most common applications in the general discussion of uses of credit derivatives in Chapter 3. We shall only briefly review them here, devoting more space in this chapter to those applications that are more germane to the credit swaps or that were not specifically covered in Chapter 3.

6.2.1   Protection Buyers

As we saw in Chapter 3, credit derivatives in general, and credit default swaps in particular, allow banks and other holders of credit instruments to hedge anonymously their exposure to the credit risk associated with particular debtors. Thus, while the credit instruments may remain in the holder's balance sheet—which may be important particularly to banks for relationship reasons—the associated credit risk is transferred to the protection seller under the CDS contract. From the perspective of the protection buying end of the market, here is where the car insurance analogy works best: you can keep your car while shifting some of the associated financial risk to an automobile insurance company.

---

[3]The valuation of CDS positions (marking to market) is discussed in Part III.

As discussed in Section 3.4, however, some market participants may want to buy protection through credit default swaps even if they have no exposure to the reference entity in question. In particular, buying protection is akin to shorting the reference entity's debt as the market value of the protection buyer's position in the swap would increase in the event of a subsequent deterioration in the credit quality of the reference entity.

6.2.2   Protection Sellers

On the other side of the market, as we also discussed in Chapter 3, sellers of default protection see the credit default swap market as an opportunity to enhance the yields on their portfolios and diversify their credit risk exposure. Here again there is a straightforward analogy to selling traditional insurance policies. For as long as the events covered in the contract do not occur, protection sellers receive a steady stream of payments that essentially amount to insurance premiums.

Of course, prospective protection sellers could, in principle, simply buy debt instruments issued by the desired reference entities directly in the marketplace in order to obtain potentially yield enhancement and portfolio diversification benefits similar to those provided by credit default swaps. Furthermore, buying credit risk through outright long positions in, say, corporate bonds and loans, has the advantage of not exposing one to counterparty credit risk in the CDS contract.

One may thus ask the following question: In addition to the fact that there are so-called natural buyers of default protection, what motivates someone to sell protection in the CDS market? As noted in Section 3.3, the unfunded nature of many credit derivatives, including typical credit default swaps, distinguishes them importantly from cash market instruments such as bonds and bank loans.

For instance, credit default swaps allows an investor to obtain, say, exposure to $10 million worth of debt issued by XYZ Corp. with essentially no upfront cost other than a possible initial posting of collateral. In contrast, that same exposure would have required a sizable initial cash outlay by the investor if the exposure were obtained in the form of a direct purchase of bonds or loans issued by XYZ Corp. In other words, the investor would have to use its scarce capital to fund its purchase of credit risk if that risk were obtained via an outright purchase of bonds or loans, whereas credit risk obtained through credit default swaps involves essentially little or no funding requirement.[4]

---

[4] If the investor could finance the cost of the outright purchase in the repo market for bonds or loans issued by XYZ Corp., the transaction could also be characterized as one requiring little or no funding. The investor would buy the bond or loan for its market price of, say, Y and immediately repo it out, essentially using the bond or loan

In Section 3.3 we also mentioned the use of credit derivatives to create synthetic long positions in corporate debt—instead of holding the credit risk assets outright, one sells protection in the credit derivatives market. This use of credit derivatives highlights the fact that, in addition to their unfunded nature, credit default swaps might be particularly attractive to investors in situations where outright positions in the cash market regarding an individual reference entity are difficult to establish. Consider, for instance, a firm whose debt is closely held by a small number of investors. For an investor who wants to obtain some credit risk exposure to that firm, but who cannot buy its debt instruments directly in the cash market, selling protection via a CDS contract becomes a potentially appealing alternative. Our financial intuition should tell us—and this will be confirmed below— that the income that the investor will receive under the CDS contract will be closely linked to the cash flow that it would have received if buying the reference entity's debt directly.

6.2.3 Some Additional Examples

We shall consider two simple, specific applications of credit default swaps from the perspective of both sellers and buyers of protection. First, we examine the case of a highly rated investor who wants to generate some additional income while minimizing the exposure to credit risk. Second, we discuss the situation of a below-investment grade investor who wants exposure to high-quality credits, but who faces high funding costs in the financial markets. These examples highlight the importance of investors' funding costs, an issue we will turn back to in the discussion of valuation issues regarding credit default swaps.

Synthesizing a (relatively) riskless asset. Consider an investor who establishes a hedged position in a certain credit: The investor buys bonds issued by a given reference entity and simultaneously buys protection in a credit default swap that references that same entity. The investor funds the purchase of the bonds by borrowing in the financial market. The investor's net income on the bond is then given by the spread between the yield paid by the bond and its funding costs. If that spread is wide enough, i.e., if the investor's creditworthiness is strong enough that it can fund itself at a relatively low cost, the net income derived from the purchase of the bond

---

as collateral for a loan in the amount of Y. The net result of these two simultaneous transactions would be that an initial cash outlay of zero for the investor—the purchase of the bond was financed by the proceeds of the repo transaction involving the bond—and a net income of $C_y - C_r$, where C_y is the coupon payment made by the bond and C_r is the payment made by the investor to its repo counterparty. While this works well in theory, in practice the repo market for corporate debt is still at a very early stage of development even in the United States, where the market for corporate debt instruments is generally more developed than in other parts of the world.

may well exceed the payments made by the investor under the terms of the credit default swap. The net result of this hedged credit position is thus a synthetic asset that is relatively free from credit risk. We say relatively free because the investor is still exposed to the credit risk of its default swap counterparty, although the extent of that exposure can be mitigated via netting and collateralization.

Adding highly rated assets to one's portfolio. The previous example works well for investors with relatively low funding costs. For a less creditworthy investor, the net income derived from holding the bond on the balance sheet may well be lower than the cost of buying protection in a credit default swap, resulting in a net negative income stream from the hedged portfolio position. Worse still, if the yield on the corporate bond is lower than the investor's cost of funds, it might make little sense for the investor to buy the bond in the first place. What if the investor wanted to add the credit risk of this particular issuer to its portfolio? A potentially more cost effective way to do it would be to sell protection in a CDS that references that issuer. Because CDS are unfunded instruments, the investor can effectively bypass the funding market, where its costs are high, and more profitably "add" higher-quality credits to its portfolio.

6.3 Valuation Considerations

Suppose you are asked to estimate the cost of buying protection against default by a given reference entity. Consistent with the car insurance analogy discussed at the beginning of this chapter, you know that the higher the credit risk associated with the entity, the higher the price of protection. (A car that is more prone to accidents will command a higher insurance premium.) But you need to come up with a specific number. How high should the credit default swap premium be for this particular reference entity?

As we did in Chapter 5, when we priced a simple variant of the asset swap, we will make use of the static replication approach to valuing financial assets. That approach tells us that if we can devise a portfolio made up of simple securities that replicates the cash flows and risk characteristics of the contract we want to price, the price of that contract is, in the absence of arbitrage opportunities, simply the price of setting up the replicating portfolio.[5]

---

[5] There are other technical conditions that the replicating portfolio must satisfy, such as the requirement that it must constitute a self-financing investment strategy, but we will just assume that all these conditions are satisfied here. Baxter and Rennie (2001)[6] provide an intuitive discussion of this topic. For a more rigorous, but still accessible exposition of replicating strategies, see, e.g., Bjork (1998)[7].

We shall consider two highly stylized, though increasingly realistic, examples. Together, they provide us with some basic insights regarding the valuation of credit default swaps, in particular, and the static replication approach in general.[6]

Example 6.1 Consider an investor who is offered the choice of either of two portfolios

- a long position in a risky floater yielding $R^f + S$ combined with a short position in a riskless floater yielding R^f;

- a short position (protection seller) in a CDS written on the risky floater.

We assume that both floaters have the same maturity, coupon dates, and face values ($1), and that they sell at par immediately after their coupon payment dates. To keep things even simpler, let us postulate further that the recovery rate on the risky floater is zero and that default can only occur immediately after the coupon payment dates.[7]

What are the cash flows associated with each portfolio? For as long as the issuer of the risky floater does not default, the first portfolio yields S every period. As for the second portfolio, the CDS has a cash flow of S_{cds} every period, where S_{cds} is the CDS premium.

In the event of default, the holder of the portfolio of floaters ends up with a short position in the riskfree floater, which translates into a liability of $1, given that the floater is valued at par on its coupon payment dates. The protection seller in the CDS is liable for the CDS payoff, which is also worth $1. Thus, when there is a default, both portfolios have the same payoff.

At this point, we should pause to make two key points:

- With time-varying interest rates, the static replication argument outlined above would generally fail if, instead of using floating-rate notes to replicate the CDS cash flows, we had used fixed-rate notes. This occurs because a fixed-rate note is not generally valued at par after it is issued and thus the liability of the short seller in the event of default could well be different from $1.

- Neither portfolio required a cash outlay when they were set up: The proceeds of the short sale of the riskless floater were used to finance the purchase of the risky floater, and it costs nothing to enter into a vanilla CDS.

---

[6] These examples are extracted from Bomfim (2002)[11].

[7] These assumptions can be relaxed and the basic results would still hold.

Given the same initial cost, the same payoffs in the event of default, and the same risk exposure of the CDS transaction and the portfolio of floaters, it must be the case that the CDS and the floater portfolio must have the same cash flow in the absence of a default by the reference entity. This requires that $S_{cds} = S$. Thus, under the conditions set out above, the premium that should be specified in a CDS written on a given corporation is the same as the risk spread associated with a par floater issued by that corporation.

The above example made an important point, highlighting the tight correspondence between the CDS spread for a given reference entity and the borrowing costs facing that entity. However, we are still missing a few important aspects of reality. For instance, we have thus far ignored the fact that the first portfolio ultimately has to be funded on the balance sheet, whereas the CDS does not. We turn now to a slightly more realistic example that addresses this issue.

Example 6.2 Using the same notation and assumptions of example 1, consider the following two scenarios:

- The investor finances the purchase of the risky floater, by repoing it out, paying the repo rate $R^f + F$. (Alternatively, we can think of $R^f + F$ as the rate at which the investor can obtain financing for the portfolio.) Assuming no default by the issuer of the risky floater, the investor receives $R^f + S$ every period and pays out $R^f + F$ to its repo counterparty. In the event of default, the risky floater becomes worthless, and the investor ends up owing \$1 to its repo counterparty. To sum up, the investor's cash flows are: $S - F$ (no default) and $-\$1$ (default).

- The investor sells \$1 worth of protection in a CDS written on the issuer of the same risky floater considered in the previous scenario. The cash flows associated with such a CDS position are: S_{cds} (no default) and $-\$1$ (default).

Again, notice that neither strategy required an initial cash outlay and both have the same payoff in the event of default. Thus, in the absence of arbitrage opportunities and market frictions, it must be the case that they have the same payoff in the absence of default, i.e., the CDS premium S_{cds} must be the equal to the difference between the risky floater spread S and the investor's funding cost F:

$$S_{cds} = S - F \tag{6.1}$$

where the above differs from the result obtained from example 1 because we are now explicitly taking into account the fact that the first portfolio has to be funded on the balance sheet of a leveraged investor whereas the CDS is an unfunded instrument.

To bring the discussion of the above examples even closer to the real world, we should note the following: Although the above approach for pricing a CDS relied on rates on par floaters issued by the reference entity, most corporate debts issued in the United States are fixed-rate liabilities. In practice, however, one can circumvent this problem by resorting to the asset swap market—see Chapter 5.[8] In particular, the above examples can be made more realistic as illustrations of how to obtain an (approximate) value for the CDS premium if we (i) substitute the par floater spread, S, with the par asset swap spread associated with the reference entity in question and (ii) redefine R^f as a short-term LIBOR rate in order to conform with the quoting convention for asset swaps.

6.3.1   CDS vs. Cash Spreads in Practice

We can use observed market quotes to verify how well the data support the simple valuation relationships uncovered by the above examples. As an illustration, the four panels in Figure 6.2 show quotes on credit default swaps and asset swaps for four investment-grade reference entities that underlie some of the most frequently negotiated credit default swaps of the late 1990s: Bank of America, General Motors Acceptance Corp. (GMAC), Tyco International, and Walmart, which, at the end of the period shown in the figure, were rated A+, A, A−, and AA by Standard and Poor's, respectively.

The CDS and par asset swap spreads shown for Bank of America and GMAC do line up closely and are thus broadly consistent with the results of the static replication approach outlined in the previous section. In contrast, charts for Tyco and Walmart show CDS spreads that are substantially above what would be suggested by the asset swap market, displaying what market participants call "positive bias" or a positive "CDS-cash basis."

The divergence between CDS and asset swap spreads for the reference entities shown in Figure 6.2 highlights the role that market segmentation and idiosyncratic supply and demand factors still play in the CDS market. For instance, the substantial positive bias associated with Tyco during the period shown in the figure was attributable in part to strong demand by convertible bond investors for buying protection against Tyco: Tyco had issued substantial amounts of convertible debt during the period featured in the chart, but the investors who bought such bonds were focusing primarily on the cheapness of embedded call options on Tyco's stock. In particular,

---

[8]When neither floaters nor fixed-rate instruments are actively traded, valuation approaches based on credit risk models become particularly relevant, as discussed in Section 6.3.3.

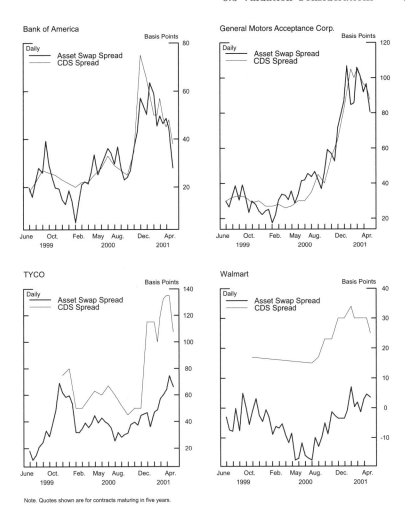

FIGURE 6.2. An Informal Test of the Static Replication Approach
Source: Bomfim (2002)[11]

they used the CDS market to shed the credit risk associated with Tyco and liquidity and market segmentation factors led to a widening of the CDS-cash basis.

In addition, administrative and legal costs are also factored into CDS premiums in practice, and even CDS for reference entities that borrow at LIBOR flat or below, such as Walmart in the late 1990s, tend to be slightly positive. Another factor that contributes to positive bias is the fact that participation in the CDS market is limited either by some investors' lack of familiarity with credit derivatives or by regulatory restrictions and internal investment policies of certain institutional investors. In addition, for some reference entities, a liquidity premium on CDS, reflecting the poorer liquidity of the CDS market relative to the cash (corporate bond) market for those entities, may also be a factor leading to positive bias.

6.3.2 A Closer Look at the CDS-Cash Basis

We used Figure 6.2 to highlight the fact that the theoretical result that suggests the equality of CDS premiums and par asset swap spreads for the same reference entity does not always hold in practice. In other words, the so-called CDS-cash basis, defined as

$$\text{CDS-cash basis} = \text{CDS premium} - \text{par asset swap spread} \qquad (6.2)$$

is often nonzero.

Should an arbitrageur who sees, for instance, a negative CDS-cash basis for a given reference entity (par asset swap spread above CDS premium) jump to buy protection in a CDS contract and buy the asset swap in the hopes that the gap between the two will close? Not necessarily. In many realistic situations, a nonzero CDS-cash basis can be perfectly justified by fundamental factors that were not included in the stylized examples discussed in the beginning of this section. The arbitrageur's challenge is then to identify those movements in the basis that are driven by fundamentals from those that are the result of temporary supply and demand dislocations that can be profitably exploited.

Fundamental factors behind a nonzero CDS-cash basis include

- cheapest-to-deliver feature of CDS contracts,

- default-contingent exposure in asset swaps,

- accrued premiums in CDS contracts,

- funding risk in asset swaps,

- counterparty credit risk,

- liquidity risk differentials.

As noted, most CDS contracts are physically settled and allow for a wide range of deliverables (typically all senior unsecured debt). In principle, in the event of default, all obligations of the reference entity that meet the deliverability criterion should have the same recovery value. This would imply that buyers and sellers of protection should be indifferent about which assets are actually delivered to settle the CDS contract. As is often the case, things are not so simple in the real world.

In many realistic circumstances, the values of deliverable obligations can differ at the time of settlement of the CDS contract. The most obvious case is that of a CDS triggered by a restructuring of the reference entity's debt because restructuring tends to affect the market values of bonds and loans differently as they are most often applied to loans. In effect, this means that the protection buyer is long a cheapest-to-deliver (CTD) option, i.e., the buyer can look at the full range of deliverables and hand over the cheapest ones to the protection seller. Now consider the buyer of an asset swap. If the reference entity defaults for whatever reason, the asset swap buyer will receive the post-default value of the specific fixed-rate bond or loan underlying the asset swap. There is no cheapest-to-deliver option! (The same argument would apply to someone who bought a par floater directly instead of synthesizing one in the asset swap market.)

As the old saying goes, "there is no free lunch," and thus protection sellers in the CDS market will "charge" for the embedded CTD option in their product by demanding a higher CDS premium than the spread paid in either the par asset swap or par floater markets. Thus, other things being equal, the embedded CTD option in a credit default swap results in a positive CDS-cash basis that is perfectly in line with economic and financial fundamentals. In such cases, the positive CDS-cash basis is not indicative of an arbitrage opportunity. We should point out, however, that the value of the embedded CTD option has likely diminished in recent years in light of changes in the way restructurings are treated in CDS contracts (see Chapter 24).

But other things are not equal. In particular, as we saw in Chapter 5, the asset swap buyer has a default-contingent risk exposure to the marked-to-market value of the interest rate swap embedded in the asset swap. To recap briefly, unlike the credit default swap, the asset swap does not completely terminate with a default by the reference entity. In particular, the interest rate swap embedded in the former continues even after the reference entity defaults. Thus, it could well be the case that, in addition to losing the difference between the par and recovery values of the bond underlying the asset swap, the asset swap buyer may find itself with a position in an interest rate swap that has negative market value. When this is likely, the CDS-cash basis has a tendency to be negative, going in the opposite direction of the CTD effect.

Another factor that tends to pressure cash spreads above CDS premium is the fact that, in the event of default by the reference entity, the protection seller in a CDS still receives that portion of the CDS premium that accrued between the last payment date of the CDS and the time of default. The asset swap buyer does not enjoy that benefit and thus must be compensated in the form of a higher asset swap spread than would otherwise be the case.

Also contributing to a negative CDS-cash basis is the fact that the asset swap buyer is generally subject to funding risk. This stems from the fact that the asset swap buyer may have to fund the purchase of the underlying bond through a short-term loan—for instance, terms in the repo market rarely go beyond a few months—and roll over the loan for the duration of the asset swap at uncertain future costs. In contrast, participants in a CDS contract face no such uncertainties.

Lastly, we mentioned liquidity and counterparty credit risk as factors that may potentially affect the CDS-cash basis. For certain reference entities, such as some US corporations with large amounts of bonds out-standing, the CDS market may be less liquid than the cash market. That would tend to push CDS premiums above corresponding cash market spreads as protection sellers would have to be compensated for the greater illiquidity they face.[9] Regarding counterparty credit risk, one should be aware that, while it is a potential factor in the pricing of both credit default and asset swaps, that is certainly not the case for conventional floaters, and comparisons between CDS spreads and par floater spreads need to be considered accordingly.

To sum up, a number of factors drive a wedge between CDS premiums and spreads in the par floater and asset swap markets, some contributing to a positive CDS-cash basis, some to a negative one. As a result, if you are asked to assess the fair value of a particular CDS premium, cash spreads are definitely a good place to start, but they are almost certainly not going to give you the whole answer.

6.3.3 *When Cash Spreads are Unavailable...*

Thus far, our main inputs for determining the fair value of a CDS premium have been spreads in the cash market, such as par asset swap spreads and par floater spreads. Certain reference entities, however, may not have marketable debt outstanding, or the market for their debt may be very illiquid and available quotes may be uninformative.

An alternative approach to valuing credit default swaps that is especially useful when reliable spreads in the cash market are not available is the one based on credit risk models.[10] For standard credit default swaps, an impor-tant starting point is the basic insight that, because the contract has zero market value at its inception, the CDS premium is set such that the value of the "protection leg"—defined as the present value of the expected pay-ment made by the protection seller in the event of default by the reference entity—is equal to the value of the "premium leg"—defined as the present value of the premium payments made by the protection buyer.

---

[9] The reverse has reportedly been true for some sovereign reference names, where liquidity in the cash markets at times has fallen short of liquidity in the CDS market.

[10] In Part III of this book, we discuss some modeling approaches.

As a preview of what is to come, suppose we have a model that gives us the default probabilities associated with a given reference entity. Consider now the (extremely) simple case of a one-year CDS with a $1 notional amount and a single premium payment, S_{cds}, due at the end of the contract. Let us make the artificial assumption that a default by the reference entity, if any, will only occur at the maturity date of the contract. (To keep things even simpler, assume no counterparty credit risk and no market frictions such as illiquidity or market segmentation.)

The current value of the protection leg is simply the present value of the premium:

$$PV[\text{premiums}] = PV[S_{cds}] \tag{6.3}$$

where $PV[.]$ denotes the present value of the variable in brackets.

How about the present value of the protection leg? Let ω denote the probability that the reference entity will default in one year's time. The protection seller will have to pay $1 - X$ with probability ω and 0 otherwise, where X is the recovery rate associated with the defaulted instrument.[11] Thus we can write the present value of the protection leg as

$$PV[\text{protection}] = PV[\omega \times (1 - X) + (1 - \omega) \times 0] \tag{6.4}$$

If the CDS is to have zero market value at its inception, the present values in equations (6.3) and (6.4) must be equal, and that will happen when

$$S_{cds} = \omega \times (1 - X) \tag{6.5}$$

and we get the result that the cost of protection S_{cds} is increasing in the probability of default and decreasing in the recovery rate associated with the reference entity. In particular, in the limiting case of no recovery, the CDS premium is equal to the probability of default. Thus, if we have a theoretical model that gives us the default probabilities associated with the reference entity, we can price a CDS written on that entity accordingly. As we shall see later in this book, these results can be generalized, with a few modifications, for more realistic cases, such as multi-period credit default swaps.

---

[11] We are being intentionally vague here regarding the nature of ω and the discount factors implicit in $PV[.]$. We will address the issues of discounting and risk-neutral vs. objective probabilities in Part III. For now, let us simply assume that market participants are risk-neutral, i.e., they are indifferent between, say, receiving $\bar{Y}$ for sure and receiving an uncertain amount Y, where the expected value of Y is $\bar{Y}$.

6.4 Variations on the Basic Structure

There are several variations on the "vanilla" CDS discussed thus far in this chapter, but none of these variants are nearly as liquid and widely negotiated as the standard form of the contract. We shall very briefly discuss three structures that are closely related to the basic CDS contract.

Binary or fixed-recovery credit default swaps, also called digital credit default swaps, are similar to vanilla CDS contracts except that the payoff in the event of default by the reference entity is known ahead of time and written into the contract. (Recall that in the vanilla CDS, the payoff is equal to the notional amount of the contract minus the post-default value of the underlying assets, but this value is only known following the default.) While the binary CDS eliminates the uncertainty about recovery rates, it is generally a less effective hedging vehicle than its vanilla cousins. One use of binary credit default swaps is to enhance the yield on one's portfolio: Selling protection in a binary CDS with an implied fixed recovery rate that is lower than the market consensus should result in a higher premium than in a vanilla CDS.

Certain credit default swaps, especially those written on reference entities that are viewed as potentially headed for trouble, require upfront payment of at least some of the protection premiums. (Recall that no money changes hands in the inception of a vanilla CDS.) In the case of highly distressed reference entities, the upfront payments help attract protection sellers to a market that could otherwise be severely one-sided.

An alternative to buying protection through a vanilla CDS is to buy an option on credit default swap, commonly referred to as a credit default swaption. As the name suggests, CDS options are contracts that give their buyers the option, but not the obligation, to enter into a CDS at a future date if the CDS premium on the reference entity goes higher than some "strike level."[12]

---

[12] We discuss the closely related topic of spread options in Chapter 8. The valuation of credit default swaptions is addressed in Chapter 18.

7

Total Return Swaps

In a total return swap (TRS), an investor (the total return receiver) enters into a derivatives contract whereby it will receive all the cash flows associated with a given reference asset or financial index without actually ever buying or owning the asset or the index. The payments are made by the other party in the TRS contract, the total return payer. Unlike an asset swap, which essentially strips out the credit risk of fixed-rate asset, a total return swap exposes investors to all risks associated with the reference asset—credit, interest rate risk, etc.[1] As such, total return swaps are more than just a credit derivative. Nonetheless, derivatives dealers have customarily considered their TRS activity as part of their overall credit derivatives business.

7.1   How Does It Work?

Total return swaps come in different variations. We shall describe the most basic form first. Like other over-the-counter derivatives, a TRS is a bilateral agreement that specifies certain rights and obligations for the parties involved. In the particular case of the TRS agreement, those rights and obligations are centered around the performance of a reference asset.

---

[1] The fact that an asset swap involves the actual purchase of the asset is another difference between the asset swap and the total return swap.

For instance, suppose an investor wants to receive the cash flows associated with a fixed-rate bond issued by XYZ Corp., but is either unwilling or unable to purchase the bond outright. The investor approaches a derivatives dealer and enters into a total return swap that references the desired XYZ bond. The dealer promises to replicate the cash flows of the bond and pay them out to the investor throughout the maturity of the swap, provided, of course, the issuer of the reference bond does not default. What does the dealer get in return? The investor promises to make periodic payments to the dealer, where the payments are tied to short-term LIBOR plus a fixed spread applied to the same notional amount underlying the coupon payments made by the dealer. This basic arrangement is shown in Figure 7.1. The investor (the total return receiver) receives payments that exactly match the timing and size of the reference bond's coupons (C) and, in return, pays LIBOR (L) plus the TRS spread T to the dealer (the total return payer).

Figure 7.1 looks very much like the lower panel of Figure 5.1, where we illustrated the interest rate swap embedded in a par asset swap. But there are some important differences. First, the investor is now making a floating-rate payment to the dealer, as opposed to making fixed-rate payments in the asset swap. Second, the reference asset in a total return swap need not be a fixed rate asset; it could actually be a floating-rate asset. Thus, in principle, the exchange of payments between dealer and investor in Figure 7.1 could well be an exchange of two floating-rate payments. Lastly, unlike the asset swap buyer, the total return receiver has not bought the reference asset. After all, not having to purchase the asset outright is typically a major reason for the TRS contract.

While the contract is in place...

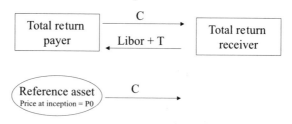

At termination/maturity date of the swap...

If P1>P0, TR payer pays TR receiver P1-P0.

If P1<P0, TR receiver pays TR payer P0-P1.

Note: P1 is the price of the reference asset at the swap termination date.

FIGURE 7.1. Total Return Swap

What happens at maturity of the TRS? Assuming no default by the reference entity, the total return receiver is paid the last coupon of the bond, along with the difference between the market value of the bond at the maturity of the TRS and the market value of the bond at the inception of the TRS. If that difference is negative, the total return receiver pays that amount to the total return payer. As a result, the TRS replicates not just the coupon stream of the bond but also the capital gain or loss that would be experienced by an investor who had actually bought the bond at the inception of the TRS and sold it at the maturity date of the TRS.

What if the issuer of the reference bond defaults? The fact that the TRS is designed to replicate the cash flows of the bond means that the total return receiver will bear the default-related loss. Once again, the total return receiver pays the difference between the price of the bond at the inception of the TRS and the recovery value of the bond at the time of default. Typically, the TRS is terminated upon the reference entity's default.

We should also make one additional remark about the workings of a TRS. The maturity of the contract need not coincide with that of the reference bond. Indeed, as we shall see, a TRS can be used to synthesize assets that suit the maturity preferences of individual investors.

7.2 Common Uses

Investors with relatively high funding costs can use TRS contracts to synthetically own the asset while potentially reducing their funding disadvantage. For instance, consider an investor who can fund itself at LIBOR + 120 basis points and who wants to add a given bond to its portfolio. The investor can either buy the bond outright and fund it on its balance sheet or it can buy the bond synthetically by becoming a total return receiver in a TRS, where, say, it would have to pay LIBOR+50 basis points to the total return payer in exchange for receiving the cash flows associated with the same bond. In this example, it is clear that the investor would be better off by tapping the TRS market. The example also illustrates that the total return payer is essentially providing financing to the total return receiver so it can synthetically "buy" the bond, and that the TRS market makes it easier for investors to leverage their credit risk exposure.

From the perspective of highly rated counterparties, the TRS market also offers some potentially attractive opportunities. Suppose that the total return payer in the above example is an AA-rated entity that funds itself at LIBOR flat. To carry on with the funding analogy, the total return payer is extending a synthetic loan to the total return receiver where it is earning a 50 basis point spread over its cost of funding. Thus, the TRS market allows highly rated entities to benefit from their funding advantage.

One might question the plausibility of the numerical example just discussed. Why would the total return payer provide financing to the TRS counterparty essentially at a below-market spread over LIBOR? After all, the cash market requires a 120 basis point spread over LIBOR as compensation for the credit risk associated with the total return receiver, but the total return payer in the example seems perfectly willing to extend a synthetic loan at the much lower spread of 50 basis points. In part, this apparent inconsistency owes to at least two factors. First, counterparty credit risk in the TRS contract can be mitigated via collateral and netting arrangements that are common in other over-the-counter derivatives contracts. Second, the TRS market offers opportunities to total return payers that, in practice, may not be easily available in the cash market. The existence of such opportunities in one market but not the other may create a wedge between otherwise comparable spreads. Indeed, as we shall see below, market participants' uses of total return swaps go well beyond issues relating to their relative funding costs.

One opportunity afforded by a total return swap that may not be available in the cash market is the ability to short certain debt instruments. Suppose, for instance, that a market participant has a negative view regarding the future prospects of a given corporation. That participant may want to express and (hopefully) profit from its view by taking a short position in bonds issued by that corporation. For most corporate bonds, however, that may not be a practical alternative given the inexistence of a fully functional corporate repo market. A more feasible approach would be to become a total return payer in a TRS contract that references a bond issued by that corporation. For instance, assuming the participant is not actually holding the reference bond, should the corporation default during the life of the TRS, the total return payer would realize a profit equal to the difference between the market value of the bond at the time of inception of the TRS and its recovery value.

Paying positions in total return swaps can be viewed as hedging vehicles for investors who are actually long the reference asset. The investor holds the reference entity, but essentially transfers all risks associated with the asset to the total return receiver. Similar to a credit default swap, this risk transfer can be done anonymously without requiring notification of the reference entity, a feature that may be particularly attractive to a bank that would like to diminish its exposure to particular customers without risking bank relationships. Likewise, total return swaps can be used to obtain exposure to debt instruments that may not be easily bought in the cash market. For instance, one might want to be long the bonds issued by a given corporation, but those bonds are in the hands of "buy-and-hold" investors who are not interested in selling. Through a receiver's position in a total return swap, one may synthetically "buy" those bonds in the desired amounts. Lastly, as we mentioned above, because the maturity of the TRS contract need not coincide with that of the underlying bonds, TRS contracts can be used to create assets that match the needs of individual investors.

7.3   Valuation Considerations

Going back to Figure 7.1, most determinants of the cash flows of a total return swap come from outside the TRS market: The coupon (C) and the initial and final prices of the reference bond come from the corporate bond market, and the values of short-term LIBOR (L) throughout the life of the contract are determined in the interbank loan market. The one exception is the TRS spread T. Indeed, pricing a TRS is essentially synonymous to finding the value of T that would prevail in a competitive market.

As we have done in previous chapters, we shall rely on the static replication approach to price the TRS contract, but here we will take this opportunity to look at the replicating portfolio from a slightly different angle. In particular, if we can come up with a replicating portfolio for the TRS contract, one can essentially combine long and short (or short and long) positions in the TRS and the replicating portfolio, respectively, to create a hedged portfolio, i.e., a portfolio that is completely riskfree. To see this, simply recall that, by definition, the replicating portfolio exactly mimics the cash flows of the TRS contract. Thus, any gains and losses associated with, say, a long position in the contract, will be perfectly offset by losses and gains in a short position in the replicating portfolio. In other words, the replicating portfolio can be recast as that portfolio that provides "the perfect hedge" for the derivatives position. Thus, just as we noted before that one can value a derivatives contract by looking at the costs associated with establishing its replicating portfolio, we can now say that determining the price of a derivatives contract essentially involves determining the costs of setting up "the perfect hedge," i.e., the costs of hedging the derivatives position.

For the case of the total return swap, it is very straightforward to find the replicating portfolio. Consider the position of the total return payer in a market that is free of frictions and where counterparty credit risk is not an issue. The TR payer pays a cash flow to the total return receiver that is supposed to mimic exactly the cash flow of a given reference bond. Thus, a short position in the reference bond is the replicating portfolio! Consequently, if the TR payer is long the reference bond, he has a fully hedged position in the TRS contract. To see this, consider a TRS contract between two parties who can fund themselves at LIBOR $+ X$. For additional simplicity, assume that the reference bond is selling for its par value at time 0 and has the same maturity of the contract. Column (2) in Table 7.1

TABLE 7.1
Determining the Total Return Swap Spread[a]

	Cash Flows		
Year	TRS (TRS payer)	Ref. Bond (long position)	TRS+Bond
(1)	(2)	(3)	(2) plus (3)
A. Assuming no default by the reference entity			
0	0	0	0
1	$-C + L + T$	$C - L - X$	$T - X$
2	$-C + L + T$	$C - L - X$	$T - X$
3	$-C + L + T$	$C - L - X$	$T - X$
4	$-C + L + T$	$C - L - X$	$T - X$
B. Assuming default by the reference entity at $t = 2$[b]			
0	0	0	0
1	$-C + L + T$	$C - L - X$	$T - X$
2	$-C + L + T + 1 - R$	$C - L - X + 1 - R$	$T - X$

[a]Negative cash flows represent cash outlays. Notional amount = $1.
[b]Assuming default occurs immediately after the coupon payments are made.

shows the cash flows of the total return payer. Let us look at the upper panel first, which shows cash flows corresponding to a scenario involving no default by the reference entity. At the inception of the contract—time 0—the TR payer receives no cash flow, but thereafter on each payment date the TR payer will pay the reference bond's coupon C and receive $L + T$ from its counterparty in the TRS contract. Column (3) shows the cash flows associated with the outright purchase of the bond, funded on the balance sheet of the TR payer. Again, at time 0 there is no cash outlay as the bond purchase is financed through a loan with an interest rate of $L + X$. Thereafter, the long position in the bond entails receiving the bond coupon C and paying the cost of funding that position $L + X$. The last column in the table shows the cash flow of a portfolio composed by the payer's position in the TRS and a long position in the reference bond. This portfolio involves no initial outlay at time 0 and a net cash flow of $T - X$ in all subsequent periods in the absence of a default by the reference entity.

What happens in the event of default? The lower panel shows a scenario where the bond issuer makes its coupon payment in period 2 and immediately proceeds to declare bankruptcy. In addition to the regular exchange of payments in the TRS, the TR payer receives the difference between the value of the bond at time 0 ($1) and its post-default value (R) and the contract is terminated. Likewise, the long position entails the usual coupon and funding cost flows plus repayment of the $1 loan obtained at time 0 and receipt of the recovery value of the bond. Again we find that the cash flow of the portfolio in the last column is zero at the inception of the contract and $T - X$ for as long as the contract remains in force.

What is the value of $T - X$ that is consistent with a market that is free from arbitrage opportunities? Note that one spends nothing a time 0 and is assured to receive $T - X$ during the life of the contract no matter what.[2] Suppose $T - X$ is a positive quantity. One would be getting something for sure out of nothing. That would clearly be an arbitrage opportunity. Indeed, the opportunity to get something for nothing would make paying positions in this TRS so attractive that prospective payers would be willing to accept a lower TRS spread (T) for as long as $T - X$ were positive. Consequently, in equilibrium T would be such that $T - X = 0$. The case where $T - X$ is negative is entirely analogous: for as long as $T - X < 0$, prospective TRS payers would demand a higher T in order to enter into the TRS contract.

The simple example in Table 7.1 yielded the basic insight that an important factor in the pricing of a TRS contract is the funding cost of the total return payer. While this is a key determinant of the TRS spread, other factors also come into play under more realistic situations. In particular, the total return payer may be concerned about the credit risk associated with its TRS counterparty. As with other over-the-counter derivatives, this risk can be mitigated via collateralization and netting arrangements.[3]

7.4 Variations on the Basic Structure

This chapter described the basic structure of a total return swap. We conclude by noting that there are several variations around this basic structure. For instance, instead of terminating automatically upon default by the reference entity, the contract may continue until its maturity date. In addition, instead of having a single bond or loan as the reference asset, the contract might specify a given portfolio or a bond index as the reference "asset."

---

[2] The reader can verify that, under the assumptions made in Table 7.1, the portfolio consisting of the TR paying position and the bond would pay $T - X$ for as long as the reference entity remains solvent regardless of when default occurs.

[3] The total return receiver may also be concerned about counterparty credit risk, but that too can be mitigated. For instance, the total return payer may post the underlying bond as collateral.

So-called index swaps can be a more efficient way of getting exposure to a market aggregate, compared to buying all the individual securities in the index. Other variants of the basic structure include the forward-starting TRS, which allows investors to enter into a TRS today that will start only at some future date at a predetermined spread, and contracts with an embedded cap or floor on the reference asset.

8

Spread and Bond Options

The credit derivatives instruments we have examined thus far have in common the fact that their final payoffs are essentially tied to "default events" involving the reference entity. Spread and bond options deviate from this norm. Spread option payoffs are generally specified in terms of the performance of a reference asset relative to that of another asset. Bond options are options to buy or sell bonds at a future date at a predetermined price. Both types of options can be exercised regardless of whether or not the issuers of the underlying assets have defaulted. They are credit derivatives because they involve the yield spread of a credit risky asset over that of some benchmark asset—the spread option—or the market price of a risky bond—the bond option. As we shall see below, the basic structure of spread and bond options is similar to that of standard call and put options.

8.1 How Does It Work?

To understand the workings of a credit option it is best to start with a simple example. Suppose you want to have the option, but not the obligation, to buy a particular five-year asset swap one year from today.[1] You want the asset swap to reference a fixed-rate bond issued by XYZ Corp. and to have a prespecified par spread of $\bar{A}$. You approach an options dealer and

---

[1] Recall, from Chapter 5, that buying an asset swap means buying the underlying bond and receiving floating-rate payments in an interest rate swap.

agree to pay her an amount X today so that she will be ready to sell you that asset swap in one year, should you decide to buy it then. We have just described the basic structure of a simple spread option.

In the above example, the five-year XYZ asset swap is the "underlying instrument" in the spread option, the predetermined spread $\bar{A}$ is called the "strike spread" of the option, and the upfront payment made to the dealer is the "option premium" or the price of the option. The "expiration date" of this option is one year from today. The "exercise date" is also one year from now, given that the contract only allows you to exercise the option in one year's time.[2]

Under which conditions would you decide to exercise your option to buy the asset swap? At the exercise date, you will compare the strike spread $\bar{A}$ to the then prevailing asset swap spread on the underlying bond. You will buy the underlying asset swap if the strike spread is above the prevailing asset swap spread for the relevant bond, otherwise you let the option expire unexercised. (If the prevailing spread is above the strike spread and you still want to enter into a five-year XYZ asset swap, you would be better off buying the asset swap in the open market and receiving the higher spread.) Referring back to standard call and put options, one can think of the above example as a put option on the spread. The holder of the option will benefit if the spread prevailing in the marketplace at the expiry date of the option is lower than the strike spread.

In some dimensions, a put option on the spread is analogous to a call option on the underlying bond, where the latter option is a bilateral contract in which one party pays for the option to buy a given bond at a future date at a predetermined price. Consider a call option written on the same bond that was referenced in the asset swap underlying the spread option just discussed. For a given position of the LIBOR curve, a narrowing in the asset swap spread, which we know would benefit the holder of the put option on the spread, would be associated with an increase in the market price of the bond, which would benefit the holder of a call option on the bond. By the same token, a call option on the spread—for instance, an option to sell an asset swap at a future date with a predetermined asset swap spread—is akin to a put option on the reference bond—or an option to sell the bond at a future date at a predetermined price.

We have compared spread and bond options while holding the LIBOR curve constant. But the analogy between spread and bond options breaks down somewhat when we consider the effects of shifts in the LIBOR curve. For instance, suppose the LIBOR curve shifts up but the asset swap spread for the underlying bond remains the same. In this case the values of the

---

[2] The single fixed exercise date makes this a "European" option. We briefly discuss other exercise date structures—"American" and "Bermudan" options—towards the end of this chapter.

bond and spread options are affected differently. Intuitively, one can think of the effect on the value of the spread option as being limited to the discounting of its expected future payoff, but the effect on the value of the bond option also stems from the fact that higher rates will drive the bond price lower, affecting the payoff directly. This highlights the fact that bond options involve a joint bet on both the general level of interest rates and the credit risk of the bond issuer, whereas spread options pertain mainly to the latter.[3]

We mentioned above that the payoffs of spread and bond options are specified in terms of the performance of the reference asset relative to that of a benchmark security. If this was not clear at the beginning of this chapter, it should be so by now. Take, for instance, the spread option examined above. Given that asset swap spreads are generally defined in terms of a spread over short-term LIBOR, the payoff of the spread option can be thought of as being a function of how the synthetic floating-rate note embedded in the asset swap will perform during the life of the option vis-à-vis a floater that pays LIBOR flat. Likewise, the payoff of a bond option may well depend on how its price moves relative to the prices of other bonds; for instance, a decrease in the credit quality of the bond issuer will lower the underlying bond's price and make it underperform relative to other bonds. Nonetheless, as we noted above, the payoff of a bond option also depends on the general level of interest rates.

8.2   Common Uses

Similar to other credit derivatives, spread and bond options can be used to express a view on the future credit quality of a given issuer. Take the put spread option discussed above and assume that the strike spread is set at the current asset swap spread associated with the underlying bond. When the option buyer is not holding the underlying bond, she is essentially placing a bet that the credit quality of the issuer will improve during the coming year. If she turns out to be right, she will profit from her view by being able to buy an asset swap in one year's time that pays a higher spread than the one then prevailing in the market place. (Likewise, an investor with a bearish view on the issuer might want to buy a call spread option struck at or close to the current asset swap spread of the bond.)

As we noted above, pure credit views are more effectively expressed with spread options than with bond options because the payoff of the latter also depends importantly on the general level of interest

---

[3] This is analogous to the distinction between fixed- and floating-rate notes, which we discussed in Chapter 4.

rates—the "LIBOR curve." Nonetheless, if one wants to express a combined credit and interest rate view, one might want to consider a bond option. For instance, if one expects market interest rates to go higher and the credit quality of a given reference entity to deteriorate, one might consider buying a put option on a bond issued by that entity. Indeed, bond options are commonly used by some hedge funds to place such joint bets, which implicitly involve a view on the correlation between interest rate levels and credit quality.

Spread and bond options can be used to express a view on volatility that is independent of the direction taken by either the underlying spread or bond price. Consider, for instance, someone who expects greater volatility regarding both market interest rates and the prospects of a given firm, but who has no particular view on the direction of the resulting movements in either market rates or the bond spreads associated with the firm. That investor can buy an option written on a bond issued by the firm and hedge it by taking short positions in the underlying bond. If the investor is appropriately hedged, should the bond price move, the investor's portfolio will be little affected as the change in the market value of the long position in the option will be offset by the change in the value of the short position in the underlying. Should uncertainty (volatility) surrounding the price of the underlying bond increase, however, the value of the long option position will increase, benefiting the investor.[4] An analogous argument applies to spread options.

Investors who hold a particular bond, or who may be buyers in an asset swap, can use spread and bond options to potentially increase the yield on their portfolios. For instance, a bond investor may want to sell call options on that bond with a strike price that is well above the current price of the bond. After collecting the option premium, the investor waits for the option buyer's decision on whether or not to buy the bond at the option's exercise date. Should the option buyer decide not to exercise its right to buy the bond, the investor keeps both the bond and the premium. If the buyer does exercise the option, the investor sells the bond to the option buyer for the strike price, which could still be higher than the price the investor originally paid for the bond.

Other than allowing investors to take financial positions that reflect their views on prospective credit and interest rate developments, spread and bond options are used as hedging vehicles by banks and other institutions that have exposures to spread risk. As an example, consider an institution that is holding a debt instrument of a given corporation. If the institution wants to reduce its exposure to the credit risk associated with that corporation, it could buy a put option on the debt instrument it holds. Should the

---

[4]The relationship between option prices and volatility is discussed briefly in the following section and in Part III of this book.

credit quality of the corporation deteriorate, which would result in a decline in the market value of the debt instruments issued by the corporation, the institution could exercise its put option to offset the associated losses in its credit portfolio. In this regard, the put option is akin to buying protection in a credit default swap (see Chapter 6). The credit default swap gives the protection seller the right to put (sell) an underlying asset to the protection buyer for its par value upon default by the reference entity. There are some differences, however. For instance, the put option allows the contract to be exercised even if no default event takes place, and its premium is typically paid upfront.

Lastly, prospective borrowers may want to buy spread options with the purpose of capping their future borrowing costs. For instance, a corporation may buy an option to obtain a two-year loan from a bank at a spread of LIBOR plus, say, 150 basis points in one-year's time. This is essentially an option to sell a two-year floater to the bank in one year, where the strike spread is set at 150 basis points. If the corporation's funding costs for a two-year loan have risen above 150 basis points by the exercise date of the option, the corporation exercises its right under the option, otherwise it lets the option expire unexercised.

8.3   Valuation Considerations

We have been able to rely on the static replication approach to price the various credit derivatives examined thus far in this part of the book. For instance, under the assumption of liquid and frictionless markets, all we needed to do to, say, determine the arbitrage-free value of a credit default swap premium was to examine the costs of setting up a portfolio consisting of a long position in a risky floater and a short position in a riskless floater. Moreover, once that portfolio was set up, we could essentially rest assured that a short position in the portfolio would exactly offset any gains and losses associated with the credit default swap. (Again, as we saw in Chapter 1, that is what makes this a static replication.) With bond and spread options, we encounter our first example in this part of the book where static replication on the basis of simple cash instruments does not work. It can be shown that a replicating portfolio does exist, but that portfolio needs to be rebalanced dynamically, on a continuous basis, so it can truly replicate the option.[5] For now, however, we will limit ourselves to discussing briefly the main determinants of the market price of spread and bond options. We will revisit the valuation of these derivatives in greater depth later, in Chapter 18.

---

[5] See, e.g., Baxter and Rennie (2001)[6] and Bjork (1998)[7] for a discussion of replicating portfolios for standard call and put options.

Those familiar with call and put options written on stocks should have no difficulty understanding the main factors that determine the prices of spread and bond options. As an illustration, we will examine the case of a call option on a bond, but the basic points made here are also applicable to put options on bonds and to puts and calls on spreads, as we shall see in Chapter 18. The payoff $V(T)$ of a call option on a bond can be written as

$$V(T) = \text{Max}[B(T) - K, 0] \tag{8.1}$$

where T is the exercise date of the option, $B(T)$ is the market price of the underlying bond at that date, and K is the strike price. In words, if the price of the bond happens to be above the strike price at time T, the option holder will exercise the option, buying the bond for the strike price K and selling it in the open market for its market price $B(T)$ for an immediate profit of $B(T) - K$. In contrast, if the market value of the bond happens to be below the strike price, the option has no value to its holder, i.e., $V(T) = 0$ when $B(T) < K$.

Equation (8.1) shows that, from the perspective of the buyer of a call option, the further the bond price rises above the strike price written into the option the better. Thus, other things being equal, a call option with a lower strike price should be more expensive than an otherwise identical option of a higher strike price. The former presents an easier "hurdle" for the bond price and thus a potentially higher payoff to the option holder. For a put option on a bond, the reverse is true. Puts with lower strike prices are more valuable than comparable puts with higher strike prices.

The volatility of the bond price is a key determinant of the option price. Higher volatility increases the chances that $B(T)$ in equation (8.1) will end up above K so that the option will expire "in the money." Thus options written on bonds whose prices are subject to greater volatility are more expensive than otherwise comparable (same maturity and strike and initial bond prices) options written on bonds with relatively stable prices.

8.4   Variations on Basic Structures

There are several variants of the basic spread and bond options described so far in this chapter. For instance, an even simpler spread option than the ones described above is one written directly on a floating-rate note, instead of on an asset swap. Alternatively the underlying in a spread option may well be a credit default swap. Indeed, we mentioned credit default swaptions at the end of Chapter 6 when we discussed variations on the vanilla credit default swap agreement.

For the sake of simplicity, this chapter has focused on European options, or those with a single, fixed exercise date. Spread and bond options are also negotiated with "American" and "Bermudan" exercise structures. American-style spread and bond options allow the option holder to exercise the option at any time during the life of the option (some contracts may stipulate an initial "no-exercise" period, e.g., a five-year option that becomes exercisable any time starting in one year). Bermudan-style options give the option buyer the right to choose one of several fixed exercise dates. For instance, the option may be exercised on any one of the coupon dates of the underlying bond.

There are many other variations in spread and bond option contracts as these tend to be less standardized than, say, credit default swap agreements. For instance, while many options are physically settled, others are settled in cash, and some spread options may be written in terms of spreads over a given US Treasury yield, rather than short-term LIBOR.

9

Basket Default Swaps

Unlike the basic forms of the contracts discussed in Chapters 4 through 8, basket default swaps are credit derivatives written on a "basket" or portfolio of assets issued by more than one reference entity. In particular, a payment by the protection seller in a basket swap can be triggered by a default of any one of the entities represented in the basket, provided that default meets the requirements specified in the contract.

We briefly encountered a common variety of a basket default swap—the first-to-default basket—in Chapter 1 when we introduced different types of credit derivatives. We will now take a closer look at this instrument, this time to illustrate the basic structure of basket default swaps. We also use this chapter to highlight the importance of default correlation in the pricing of multi-name credit derivatives, an issue we will examine in greater detail in Part IV of this book.

9.1 How Does It Work?

Let us look at a particular example. Consider an institution that wants to hedge its exposure to five different reference entities. The institution enters into a first-to-default (FTD) basket contract with a derivatives dealer where the reference basket is composed of those five entities. The institution, which is the protection buyer in the contract, agrees to make periodic premium payments to the dealer (the protection seller), much like in a single-name credit default swap. In return, the dealer commits to making

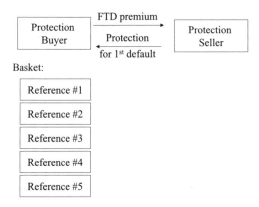

Basket:

FIGURE 9.1. Diagram of a First-to-default Basket

a payment to the institution (the protection buyer) if and when any one of the entities included in the reference basket defaults during the life of the contract. The catch is that the payment will be made for only the first default. The FTD basket contract is terminated after the protection coverage regarding the first default in the basket is settled.

Figure 9.1 illustrates the basics of an FTD basket. In this example, we assume that the notional amount of debt covered by the contract is $10 million for each of the five entities in the basket reference. Let us say that the FTD basket premium is quoted as 200 basis points per year and that recovery rates are zero. That means that the annual payment made by the protection buyer would be

$$\frac{200}{100^2} \times \$10 \text{ million} = \$200{,}000$$

or, typically, $50,000 per quarter. Why was the premium payment based on only $10 million, rather than on $50 million, which is the sum of the notional amounts covered for each reference entity? Because the protection seller will cover only the first default, and the notional amount associated with each individual default is only $10 million.

If none of the reference entities defaults during the life of the FTD basket, the protection seller simply keeps on collecting the premium payments made by the protection buyer. What happens when the first default takes place? Similar to a single-name credit default swap, which we discussed in Chapter 6, the protection seller pays the buyer the difference between the face value of the defaulted debt and its recovery value. The contract can be either cash or physically settled.

Carrying on with the example in Figure 9.1, suppose reference entity #3 defaults and the contract calls for physical settlement. The protection buyer will deliver to the protection seller $10 million worth of par value of eligible debt instruments issued by reference entity #3. These instruments are now worth only their recovery value, but the protection seller will pay par for them. The FTD basket swap terminates once the protection payment related to the first default is made. The protection seller has no further exposure to the remaining names in the reference basket.

9.2   Common Uses

Protection buyers find basket swaps attractive because they tend to be less expensive than buying protection on each name in the basket separately through single-name credit default swaps. Of course, the lower cost of protection in, say, the FTD basket swap stems from the fact that the protection seller is only really protected from the first default. Still, in the case of the FTD basket, protection buyers find some comfort in the fact that it will take more than one default in their portfolio before they actually experience a loss. In market parlance, the credit risk associated with the "first loss" in the reference basket has been transferred to the protection seller.

From the perspective of investors (protection sellers), basket swaps provide an opportunity for yield enhancement with a limited downside risk. For instance, we will see below that the FTD basket premium is typically above the credit default swap premiums of any one individual entity referenced in the basket. This is because the protection seller is exposed to the credit risk of all names in the reference basket. As a result, a protection seller in an FTD basket composed of, say, A-rated names, could conceivably earn a premium that would be typical of, say, a credit default swap written on a single BBB-rated name, without actually having to expose itself to a BBB-rated entity.

We mentioned above that the protection seller has a limited downside risk. Why? Because the seller will ultimately be liable to cover at most one default among the names included in the basket. The protection seller can thus substantially leverage its credit exposure: Going back to the example in Figure 9.1, the protection seller was exposed to assets totaling $50 million in notional amount, but the most it could lose was $10 million.

9.3   Valuation Considerations

What determines the premium paid by the protection buyer in a credit basket swap? The main determinants are (i) the number of entities in the reference basket, (ii) the credit quality and expected recovery rate of each basket component, and (iii) the default correlation among the reference entities.[1]

Understanding the role of the first two determinants—number and credit quality of the reference entities—is relatively straightforward. In general, other things being equal, the larger the number of entities included in the basket the greater the likelihood that a default event will take place and thus the higher the premium that protection buyers will pay. Likewise, for a given number of names in the basket, the lower the credit quality and recovery rates of those names, the more expensive the cost of protection will be.

Though important, the number and credit quality of the entities in the reference basket only tell part of the story when it comes to pricing a credit basket swap. Indeed, the role of default correlation is so important in the pricing of basket swaps that market participants tend to characterize these instruments mostly as default correlation products. To see why this is so we will examine the simplest FTD basket one can imagine, one that is composed of only two reference names, which we shall refer to as XYZ Corp. and AZZ Bank.

Consider an investor who is exposed to both XYZ Corp. and AZZ Bank, but who wants to use credit derivatives to at least reduce this exposure. One option for such an investor is simply to buy protection in two separate credit default swaps—one referencing XYZ, the other written on AZZ. Assume that the notional amount of protection sought for each reference entity is $1, the relevant recovery rates are 0, and the maturity of the desired credit default swaps is one year. If we make the same simplifying assumptions adopted in Section 6.3.3, the premium for the CDS written on XYZ is simply given by the probability ω_X that XYZ will default in one year's time, and the cost of buying protection against a default by AZZ is analogously determined. Thus the cost of buying protection through two separate single-name CDS in this case would be:

$$S_{CDSs} = \omega_X + \omega_A \tag{9.1}$$

What if, instead of buying protection against defaults by both XYZ and AZZ through two separate credit default swaps, the investor were to buy protection through an FTD basket with the same maturity as the CDS and with a notional amount of $1 for each of the names in the basket? Note that in this case, the protection bought and sold applies to a default by either XYZ or AZZ, whichever comes first. Let $\omega_{X\,or\,A}$ denote the probability that at least one of the entities will default in one year's time. Thus, the protection seller will be required to make a payment of $1 to the protection

---

[1] Default correlation is discussed further in Part IV—see also Appendix B.

buyer with probability $\omega_{X \text{ or } A}$—no payment from the protection seller will be due otherwise. Carrying on with the simple methodology outlined in Chapter 6, we can write the present value of the "protection leg" of this basket swap as

$$\text{PV[protection]} = \text{PV}[\omega_{X \text{ or } A} \times \$1 + (1 - \omega_{X \text{ or } A}) \times \$0] \qquad (9.2)$$

where PV[.] denotes the present value of the variable in brackets.

Recall now from elementary statistics that one can write $\omega_{X \text{ or } A}$ as

$$\omega_{X \text{ or } A} = \omega_X + \omega_A - \omega_{X \& A} \qquad (9.3)$$

where $\omega_{X \& A}$ denotes the probability that both XYZ and AZZ will default in one year's time.[2] Thus, we can rewrite (9.2) as

$$\text{PV[protection]} = \text{PV}[\omega_X + \omega_A - \omega_{X \& A}] \qquad (9.4)$$

Let us now value the premium leg of the basket. Let S_{basket} denote the premium paid by the protection buyer under this basket agreement. The present value of the premium leg is simply given by

$$\text{PV[premiums]} = \text{PV}[S_{basket}] \qquad (9.5)$$

and thus, if the basket has zero market value at its inception, the present values of the premium and protection legs must be the same, which implies that

$$S_{basket} = \omega_X + \omega_A - \omega_{X \& A} \qquad (9.6)$$

Equation (9.6) allows us to make several important points regarding the valuation of basket swaps. As discussed in Part IV, the probability that both XYZ and AZZ will default in one year's time is closely related to the default correlation between the two reference entities. In particular, if the one-year default correlation between the two entities is positive and high, $\omega_{X \& A}$ will be a larger number.[3]

---

[2] This basic result is illustrated graphically in Chapter 19.

[3] The generalization to the case of nonzero recovery is straightforward. The reader can verify that the expression for the FTD premium becomes:

$$S_{basket} = (\omega_X + \omega_A - \omega_{X \& A})(1 - X)$$

where X is the recovery rate associated with the reference entities.

9.3.1 A First Look at Default Correlation

We can use equation (9.6) to take a preliminary look at how default correlation affects the pricing of the FTD basket. Let us examine first the case of very high default correlation between XYZ and AZZ, a default correlation close to 1. Suppose

$$\omega_X > \omega_A$$

i.e., XYZ is more likely to default than AZZ. It can be shown—we will see this in Part IV—that as the default correlation approaches its maximum at 1, the probability of both XYZ and AZZ defaulting in one year's time approaches the default probability of the higher-quality entity (AZZ in this example). Intuitively, if the financially stronger entity has defaulted, chances are that the lower-quality firm has almost surely defaulted if the default correlation involving the two companies is very high. Thus, if $\omega_X > \omega_A$,

$$\omega_{X\&A} \approx \omega_A \quad \text{when the default correlation } \approx 1$$

and, given (9.6),

$$S_{basket} \approx \omega_X$$

i.e., the FTD basket premium approaches the default probability of the entity with the lowest credit quality (XYZ) as the default correlation between the names in the basket approaches 1.

We will also see in Part IV that, when (i) default correlation is close to zero and (ii) the product of individual default probabilities is sufficiently small, $\omega_{X\&A}$ will be low. Indeed, equation (9.6) implies that the FTD basket premium will approach the sum of the individual credit default swap premiums of the reference entities as $\omega_{X\&A}$ approaches zero. Using the above notation:

$$\omega_{X\&A} \approx 0 \quad \text{when conditions (i) and (ii) above are met}$$

and, given equation (9.6),

$$S_{basket} \approx \omega_X + \omega_A$$

To sum up, and generalizing to baskets with more than two reference entities, protection bought through a first-to-default basket will be more expensive when the degree of default correlation among the entities in the basket is low and cheaper when that correlation is high. In plain words, with low default correlation, the protection seller in the above example is exposed to two largely uncorrelated sources of risk and must be compensated accordingly with a higher FTD basket spread. In contrast, when default correlation is close to one, the protection seller is exposed mainly to one type of risk, the common factor driving the fortunes of the reference entities. Intuitively, the FTD basket premium will approach the CDS spread of the entity that is most vulnerable to that common factor, i.e., the one with the highest default probability. For intermediate values of default correlation, the FTD basket premium will fall in between the highest (single-name) CDS premium in the portfolio and the sum of all the CDS premiums.

One final point: Note that when the probability that both XYZ and AZZ will default is zero or very nearly so—$\omega_{X\&A} \approx 0$—the cost of buying protection through the basket approaches that of buying protection separately through two credit default swaps, one written on XYZ and the other on AZZ, where each contract has a notional amount of \$1, the same notional amount associated with each reference entity included in the basket. Under such circumstances, the protection buyer may be better off with the two separate CDS contracts. Why? Together, the two CDS contracts cost about the same as the basket, but they effectively provide protection against defaults by both XYZ and AZZ, whereas the basket only provides protection against the first default. Thus, it makes more sense to buy protection through an FTD basket when there is some default correlation among the reference entities.

9.4 Variations on the Basic Structure

There are several variations around the basic structure discussed thus far in this chapter. The most straightforward one is the second-to-default swap, which, as the name suggests, is a contract where a payment by the protection seller is triggered only by the second default in the basket. For instance, for a basket where each reference entity is associated with a notional amount of \$1, that payment will be equal to \$1 minus the recovery value of the debt instruments of the second entity to default. Third-, fourth-, and, more generally, nth-to-default swaps are defined accordingly. From the perspective of investors, these products still offer the opportunity to take a leveraged exposure to credit, albeit at a lower risk (and thus with a lower yield).[4]

Unlike the simple example discussed in the previous section, which involved only two reference entities, basket swaps tend to reference five to

---

[4] Nth-to-default baskets have similarities to tranched structures, which we discuss in Chapter 14.

ten entities. Nonetheless, the main pricing results derived above regarding default correlations can be generalized for baskets written on a larger number of entities, although the required computations become substantially more complicated. We will address these more realistic cases in Part IV of this book.

10
Portfolio Default Swaps

Portfolio default swaps are similar to basket swaps (Chapter 9) in that they transfer portions of the credit risk associated with a portfolio from a protection buyer to a protection seller. A key difference is that the risk transfer is specified in relation to the size of the default-related loss in the reference portfolio instead of in terms of the number of individual defaults among the reference entities. For instance, whereas protection sellers in a first-to-default basket are exposed to the first default in the reference basket, protection sellers in a "first-loss" portfolio default swap are exposed to default-related losses that amount up to a prespecified share of the reference portfolio.

In Chapter 9 we introduced some key ideas about the role of default correlation in the pricing of multi-name credit derivatives. We continue to highlight this role here and introduce another key concept for valuing derivatives that reference more than one entity: the loss distribution function. Lastly, by discussing the basics of portfolio default swaps, this chapter lays some of the groundwork for discussing synthetic collateralized debt obligations (CDOs), which are the subject of Chapter 14.

10.1 How Does It Work?

Consider a hypothetical bank with a large portfolio of loans. The bank wants to reduce its exposure to the credit risk embedded in the portfolio, but does not want to sell or transfer the underlying loans. In addition, the

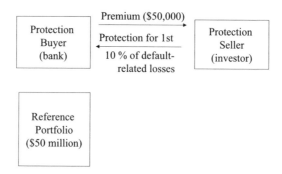

FIGURE 10.1. Diagram of a Simple Portfolio Default Swap with a First-loss Piece of 10 Percent (Size of Portfolio = $50 million; Premium = 100 basis points, paid annually)

number of reference entities represented in the portfolio is large enough that simple basket products, such as a first-to-default basket, would offer only very limited protection. The bank could, of course, buy protection in several baskets—e.g., first-, second-, third-to-default baskets...—or even enter into several single-name credit default swaps to achieve its goals. Alternatively, the bank could buy protection through a single portfolio default swap.

The basic features of a simple portfolio default swap are illustrated in Figure 10.1. Suppose the bank feels that the chances that it will experience default-related losses in excess of, say, 10 percent over the next year are sufficiently small that it is willing to bear that risk. The bank can enter into a one-year portfolio default swap with an investor who is willing to sell protection against the first 10 percent in default-related losses in the portfolio. The investor (the "first-loss protection seller") will be exposed to however many individual defaults are necessary to produce a 10 percent loss in the reference portfolio. To be more specific and simplify things further, suppose the total face value of the portfolio is $50 million and that there are 50 reference entities represented in the portfolio, each with a face value of $1 million and a zero recovery rate. As shown in Table 10.1, given the assumed recovery rate and the absence of counterparty credit risk, it would take 5 defaults in the portfolio before the bank actually becomes exposed to credit risk.

In exchange for the protection provided, the protection buyer agrees to make periodic premium payments to the protection seller, much like in a single-name credit default swap. The premium payments made by the protection buyer amount to

premium payment = (PDS premium) × (size of the first-loss piece)

TABLE 10.1
Loss Associated with 5 Defaults in the Bank's Portfolio
($ Millions)

Initial value of the portfolio	$50
Value after 5 defaults[a]	$50 − 5 × $1 = $45
Percent default-related loss	10 percent

[a]Assuming no deterioration in the credit quality of remaining solvent entities in the portfolio and no change in market interest rates.

where the portfolio default swap (PDS) premium is usually quoted in terms of basis points per annum. For instance, assume that the PDS premium in the above example is set at 100 basis points and that payments will be made annually (in more realistic cases, the payments are more likely to be made quarterly). Even though the protection seller is initially exposed to defaults by any of the 50 entities in the portfolio—a total notional amount of $50 million—the protection sold will cover a maximum of 5 defaults. Thus, the annual premium payments received by the protection seller will be $50,000 or 100 basis points times $5 million.

What happens when defaults take place? As with a single-name credit default swap, and assuming that the contract calls for cash settlement upon default events, the protection seller will pay the difference between the par and recovery values of each defaulted asset, provided, of course, these payments do not exceed the original size of the first-loss piece.

Note that, as defaults occur, the size of the first-loss piece is reduced accordingly. For instance, carrying on with the numerical example, if the protection seller has already paid $1 million as a result of the loss incurred with the first default, the future payments in the event of additional defaults are now capped at $4 million. It is common for the premium payment made by the protection buyer to be adjusted to reflect the new size of the first-loss piece. Given the PDS premium of 100 basis points, the new annual premium after the first default becomes $40,000 (= 100 b.p. × $4 mil.).

The process of paying for defaults and resetting the premium continues until the payments made by the protection seller max out, in which case the contract with the first-loss protection seller is terminated. At that point, the size of the first-loss piece, as well as the premium paid by the protection buyer, would have reached zero.

We have thus far focused on a first-loss contract, but the structure of, say, a second-loss contract is entirely analogous. For instance, suppose the bank had bought protection in an additional portfolio default swap, one where the protection seller would cover all default-related losses beyond the first $5 million. This protection seller is essentially long the second-loss piece of the portfolio. The second-loss protection seller will start covering default-related losses once the payments made by first-loss protection seller are maxed out. (If the bank had chosen not to enter into this second contract, its position would be akin that being long the second-loss piece.)

10.2   Common Uses

From the perspective of investors, portfolio default swaps allow one to take a substantially leveraged exposure to credit risk—and thus earn a higher premium—with only limited downside risk. In the above example, the first-loss protection seller was exposed to defaults in the entire loan portfolio of $50 million, but the maximum loss was capped at $5 million. At the same time, less aggressive investors might be attracted to the relative safety of higher-order-loss products, such as the second-loss piece, which will only sustain losses after the protection provided by the entire first-loss piece is exhausted.

Portfolio default swaps are attractive to protection buyers because they allow the transfer of a substantial share of the credit risk of a portfolio through a single transaction, as opposed to a large number of individual transactions. In addition, similar to basket swaps, a portfolio default swap can be a cost effective way of obtaining partial protection against default-related losses in one's portfolio.

Lastly, we should note an important general use of portfolio default swaps. As we shall see in Chapter 14, they are the basic building blocks for synthetic collateralized debt obligations, which make up a rapidly growing sector of the credit derivatives market.

10.3   Valuation Considerations

Issues of counterparty credit risk aside, portfolio default swaps cannot increase or reduce the overall degree of credit risk in the reference portfolio. What portfolio default swaps do is redistribute the total credit risk of the portfolio among different investors—e.g., first-, second-, and third-loss protection sellers.

Intuitively, it is straightforward to see that the premium on the first-loss piece depends importantly on how much of the total credit risk of the portfolio is borne out by the first-loss protection sellers. To illustrate this point we start by looking at a highly artificial but instructive example. Consider the case where the hypothetical portfolio examined in Section 10.1 is made up of five reference entities that are rated well below investment grade and

45 entities that are very highly rated.[1] Under these circumstances, most of the credit risk of the portfolio resides in the five lowly rated entities. Now let us go back to Table 10.1, which illustrates a scenario where five of the reference entities in the portfolio default while the swap is still in force. Given what we have just assumed about the composition of the portfolio, the chances that such a scenario come to unfold are likely high. At the same time, the probability of any losses beyond 10 percent of the portfolio would be rather small. What we have here then is a situation where the first-loss protection sellers end up absorbing most of the credit risk of the portfolio. What do they get in return? They are compensated in the form of a high first-loss premium. Looking beyond the first-loss piece, the likelihood that second-loss protection sellers will ever have to cover a default-related loss in the portfolio is small in this particular example, and so would be the second-loss premium.

10.3.1   A First Look at the Loss Distribution Function

In the above example, we considered a portfolio with very particular characteristics—a few very risky assets combined with lots of very highly rated assets. We used that example to discuss a situation with one specific feature: very high odds of losses of up to 10 percent of the initial par value of the portfolio and very low odds of losses beyond 10 percent. In effect, what we did was consider a particular loss distribution function for the portfolio. The loss distribution function is a key concept when it comes to valuing a portfolio default swap. Intuitively, it tells us the probabilities associated with different percentage losses in the portfolio.

Figure 10.2 shows loss distributions for two hypothetical portfolios. To highlight the importance of the loss distribution in the pricing of port-folio default swaps, both distributions correspond to portfolios with the same expected loss of 5 percent. Assuming a first-loss piece of 10 percent, the loss distribution of portfolio A (shown as the solid line) is such that it is nearly certain that virtually all the losses will be borne out by the first-loss investors: The figure shows a probability of nearly 100 percent of losses less than or equal to the first-loss piece and tiny probabilities of larger losses.

In contrast, the loss distribution of portfolio B (the dashed line) shows a much higher probability of total losses in the portfolio exceeding 10 percent, suggesting the total credit risk associated with portfolio B is more widely spread between first- and second-loss protection sellers.[2] In terms of the pricing implications for portfolio default swaps written on these portfolios,

---

[1] Assume further that the default correlation between the lowly and highly rated assets is zero.

[2] Given the loss distributions depicted in Figure 10.2, the probability of losses greater than 10 percent in each portfolio, which corresponds to the sum of the probabilities

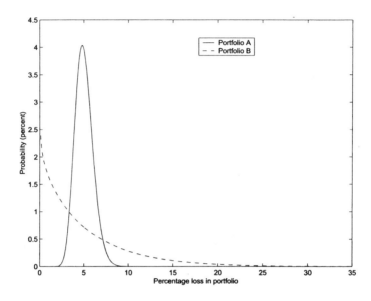

FIGURE 10.2. Loss Distributions for Two Portfolios, Each With an Expected
Loss of 5 Percent

one would expect that while first-loss protection sellers would receive most
of the credit risk premium associated with portfolio A, they would have to
share more of that premium with second-loss protection sellers in portfolio
B, despite the fact that the two portfolios have identical expected losses.

What are the main factors that determine whether the loss distribution
of actual portfolios will look more like that of portfolio A or that of portfolio B? We have thus far relied on a case that highlights how the credit
quality of the individual reference entities in the portfolio can affect the
loss distribution. In more realistic examples, however, it will not generally
be the case that the reference entities in the portfolio can be so neatly
assigned to nearly opposite ends of the credit quality spectrum. Indeed, in
many instances, the portfolio may well be composed of debt instruments
issued by entities with similar credit quality. What would determine the
shape of the loss distribution in such instances? To put it differently, how
much of the total credit risk in the portfolio is being shifted, say, to the
first-loss protection sellers? To answer these questions, we need to revisit a
theme first introduced in Chapter 9: default correlation.

---

associated with losses larger than 10 percent, is virtually zero for portfolio A and about
14 percent for portfolio B. We will examine loss distributions more closely in Part IV.

10.3.2 Loss Distribution and Default Correlation

Let us again go back to the example discussed in Section 10.1—a portfolio composed of 50 reference names, each with a $1 million notional amount and a zero recovery rate—but this time we will assume that all of the entities represented in the portfolio have the same credit quality. In particular, suppose that each of the reference entities has a risk-neutral default probability of 6 percent. We also continue to consider two portfolio default swaps written on the portfolio, one with a first-loss piece of 10 percent and the other with a second-loss piece that encompasses the remaining losses in the portfolio.

We will consider first the case of very high default correlation among the 50 names in the portfolio. In this case, as we argued in Chapter 9, the reference entities in the portfolio tend to default or survive together. As a result, the portfolio behaves more like one single asset. Let us assume the polar case of perfect default correlation. What is the expected loss in the portfolio? Note that there are only two possible outcomes in this case, either all entities represented in the portfolio default together or they all survive. Thus, with 6 percent probability all reference entities default, resulting in a total loss of $50 million, and with 94 percent probability there are no losses. The expected loss in the portfolio is

$$.06 \times \$50 \text{ million} + .94 \times \$0 = \$3 \text{ million}$$

which results in an expected loss of 6 percent for the entire portfolio.

What is the expected loss in the first-loss piece? With 6 percent probability the entire first-loss piece is wiped out; with 94 percent probability it remains intact. The expected loss in this piece is

$$.06 \times \$5 \text{ million} + .94 \times \$0 = \$0.3 \text{ million}$$

which amounts to an expected loss of 6 percent of the first-loss piece.

How about the expected loss in the second-loss piece? If all firms in the portfolio default, second-loss investors absorb the residual loss of $45 million, which corresponds to an expected loss of $2.7 million:

$$.06 \times \$45 \text{ million} + .94 \times \$0 = \$2.7 \text{ million}$$

or 6 percent of the second-loss piece. Thus, with perfect default correlation, the first- and second-loss investors in this example should, in principle, earn the same protection premium, although, naturally, the premium payments will be scaled to the sizes of the first- and second-loss pieces.

To illustrate the effect of default correlations on expected returns on the first- and second-loss pieces we now examine another limiting case, one with zero default correlation. The computation of expected losses for the first- and second-loss investors in this case is a bit more involved than that for the case of perfect default correlation.

Whereas in the perfect correlation case there were only two possible default outcomes, either all firms default together or all survive, we now have 51 possible default outcomes (no defaults, one default, two defaults, ..., 50 defaults), each with a different probability attached to it. This may sound complicated, but, with zero default correlation it is not hard to show that the expected loss of the first-loss investors will amount to approximately \$2.88 million, or about 57.5 percent of the first-loss piece, and that of the second-loss investors will be about \$0.12 million or approximately 0.27 percent of the second-loss piece.[3]

Naturally, with zero default correlation, first-loss investors in this example will only risk losing over half of the first-loss piece if the premium that they receive from the protection buyer is sufficiently high. As for the second-loss investors, because their expected loss is very small, the second-loss premium will be very low.

Table 10.2 summarizes the main results obtained thus far regarding the two alternative default correlation scenarios just discussed. The table shows that the expected loss of the second-loss investors goes from 0.27 percent in the case of zero correlation to 6 percent in the case of perfect correlation. As more of the credit risk in the portfolio is transferred to the second-loss investors in the perfect-correlation case, the premium that they receive should also increase. The reverse happens, of course, to the first-loss investors. Their expected loss falls from 57.61 percent in the case of zero default correlation to 6 percent in the case of maximum default correlation,

---

[3]One way to arrive at these results for the expected losses of the two classes of investors under the assumption of uncorrelated defaults is to make use of binomial distribution. In particular, let $q(i)$ denote the probability that there will be i defaults in the portfolio within the next 12 months. Under the binomial distribution, the current example is such that

$$q(i) = \frac{50!}{i!(50-i)!}.06^i.94^{50-i}$$

and we can, for instance, write the expected loss of first loss-investors as

$$\sum_{i=0}^{50} q(i)\mathrm{Min}[L(i), 5]$$

where $L(i)$ is the total loss, in \$ millions, in the portfolio when there are i defaults, and the notation $\mathrm{Min}[L(i), 5]$ indicates that the first-loss investors' loss is capped at \$5 million in this case. The expected losses of the overall portfolio and of second-loss investors can be computed in an analogous way.

We will get back to the binomial distribution and the modeling of expected portfolio losses in Part IV of this book. Some background on the binomial distribution is provided in Appendix B.

TABLE 10.2
Loss Distribution and Default Correlation

	zero correlation	perfect correlation
Expected loss in portfolio[a]	6 percent ($3 million)	6 percent ($3 million)
Expected loss of first-loss investors	57.61 percent ($2.88 million)	6 percent ($0.3 million)
Expected loss of second-loss investors	0.27 percent ($0.12 million)	6 percent ($2.7 million)

[a]Size of portfolio: $50 million. Sizes of first- and second-loss pieces are $5 million and $45 million, respectively.

and the premium that they receive is reduced accordingly to reflect that the total risk of the portfolio is now more evenly distributed between the first- and second-loss pieces.[4]

For the more realistic cases of intermediate degrees of default correlation, the expected losses of the first- and second-loss investors fall somewhere in between the two polar cases shown in Table 10.2. In general, as we shall see in greater detail in Part IV, as the extent of default correlation in the portfolio increases, more of the total credit risk embedded in the portfolio is shared with the second-loss piece, which, as in the example just examined, will then earn a higher protection premium than in instances of lower default correlation. At the same time, as less of the total risk in the portfolio is borne out by the first-loss protection sellers alone, the premium that they earn decreases as default correlation rises.

In terms of the loss distribution, Table 10.2 suggests that, other things being equal, portfolios with higher default correlations have higher probabilities of larger losses than portfolios with lower default correlations. Intuitively, as default correlations increase, so does the likelihood that the reference entities represented in the portfolio will default together, leading to a greater chance of larger default-related losses in the overall portfolio.

---

[4]With nonzero recovery rates, the first- and second-loss investors will not generally earn the same premiums in the case of perfect default correlation. For instance, with a 50 percent recovery rate, the second-loss investors' expected loss would be

$$.06 \times \$(25 - 5) \text{ million} + .94 \times \$0 = \$1.2 \text{ million}$$

which amounts to about 2.7 percent of the second-loss piece.

10.4   Variations on the Basic Structure

Before we move on, we should note that the terms of portfolio default swap agreements are less standardized than, say, those of single-name credit default swaps. Thus, although the example discussed above was meant to be illustrative of the basic portfolio default swap structure, one is bound to find actual contracts that will differ in one or more dimensions from the example provided.

Variations around the example examined in this chapter include physical settlement upon default, immediate vs. deferred default settlement, the timing and manner of resetting the premium, and the definition of credit events. Also, in many situations where the protection buyer is a bank, the bank retains a small first-loss piece and enters into various portfolio default swaps (e.g., second-, third-, and fourth-loss products) with investors, either directly or through an intermediary bank.

One last point: In the examples explored in this chapter, the reference portfolio was often described as a collection of loans or bonds held by the institution seeking to buy protection in the portfolio default swap. We could just as well have described the reference portfolio as a collection of individual credit default swaps in which the institution sold protection. In this case, the institution uses one or more portfolio default swaps to transfer at least some of the credit risk acquired via the single-name credit default swaps.

11

Principal-Protected Structures

Principal-protected structures are coupon-paying financial products that guarantee the return of one's initial investment at the maturity of the structure, regardless of the performance of the underlying (reference) assets. The coupon payments themselves are stopped in the event of default by the reference entity. Principal-protected structures can be thought of as a form of a funded credit derivative.

11.1 How Does It Work?

It may be useful to start by reminding ourselves about the mechanics of traditional (nonprincipal-protected) debt instruments. For instance, assuming a fixed-rate bond is valued at par, an investor in that security hands over the face value of the bond to the issuer and, in exchange, the issuer promises to return the full par amount of the note to the investor at the maturity date of the note and to make intervening coupon payments until that date. Should the issuer run into financial difficulties and default on its debt obligations, however, the investor loses both its initial investment (or part of it in the case of a nonzero recovery rate) and any remaining future coupon payments that would otherwise be made by the note.

We shall focus on single-name principal-protected notes (PPNs), the simplest form of a principal-protected structure. Such notes have some similarities with traditional fixed-rate bonds, but there are a few key differences. As with the bond in the previous paragraph, PPNs are funded instruments, generally sold at par, that promise regular coupon payments at prespecified dates and the return of principal at the maturity date of the note. Unlike traditional debt instruments, however, PPNs are generally issued by highly rated third parties, rather than by the reference entities themselves. In that regard, a PPN is very much like a credit-linked note, in that its cash flows are contingent on default events by a reference entity.[1] Where a PPN differs both from traditional bonds and simple credit-linked notes is in the event of default by the reference entity. Upon default, typical bonds and CLNs terminate with investors getting only their corresponding recovery values. With PPNs, the stream of future coupon payments terminates, but the PPN does not. In particular, the repayment of the par value of the PPN at its maturity date is unaffected by the reference entity's default.

Table 11.1 uses a simple numerical example to illustrate the main features of PPNs, and how they compare to par bonds (and, implicitly, to typical CLNs). The table shows the cash flows of two instruments: a four-year fixed-rate bond issued by XYZ Corp. and a four-year PPN that references XYZ Corp., issued by a highly rated financial institution.[2] Both instruments are assumed to pay coupons annually and are initially valued at par ($100). The bond pays a coupon of 9 percent, and the PPN's coupon is 6.8 percent.[3] If XYZ does not default during the four-year period covered by the notes, the holders of the bond and the PPN receive the cash flows shown in the upper half of the table, the only difference between them being the size of their respective coupons.

The lower panel of Table 11.1 shows the cash flows of the bond and the PPN in the event of default by XYZ Corp. at year 2, immediately after the coupon payments are made. We assume a recovery rate of 50 percent. The bond terminates with the investor's position valued at $59, the coupon payment of $9 just received plus the recovery value of $50. The PPN lives on, but makes no further coupon payments; it terminates only at its original maturity date, when it pays out its par value of $100.

We mentioned above that principal-protected structures are generally issued by highly rated entities. In addition, it is not uncommon for the principal guarantee to be collateralized. The main idea, of course, is to minimize the PPN investor's exposure to any credit risk associated with the PPN issuer.

---

[1] Credit-linked notes were introduced in Chapter 1 and are discussed further in Chapter 12.

[2] Many of the assumptions made in this example can be easily relaxed without loss of generality. For instance, as we shall see later in this chapter, to value a PPN we need not have a fixed-rate note with the same maturity as the PPN.

[3] Why does the PPN have a lower coupon than the bond? The investor essentially has to forego some yield in order to obtain the principal-protection feature.

TABLE 11.1

Cash Flows of a PPN and a Par Bond[a]

(Assuming that the PPN references the bond issuer)

Years from now	Fixed-rate bond	Principal-protected note
(1)	(2)	(3)
A. Assuming no default by the reference entity		
0	−100	−100
1	9	6.8
2	9	6.8
3	9	6.8
4	109	106.8
B. Assuming default by the reference entity at year 2^b		
0	−100	−100
1	9	6.8
2	59	6.8
3	0	0
4	0	100

[a] From the investor's perspective. Par value = $100; recovery rate = 50 percent.
[b] Assuming default occurs immediately after the coupons are paid at year 2.

11.2 Common Uses

PPNs appeal to investors seeking some exposure to credit risk, but who want to protect their initial investment. As such, PPNs can be used to make sub-investment-grade debt instruments appealing to conservative investors.

As the example in Table 11.1 illustrated, investors may have to give up a substantial portion of the credit spread associated with the reference entity in order to obtain the principal-protection feature. As a result, a PPN that references a highly rated entity would have very limited interest to some investors as its yield would be very low. On the other hand, conservative investors might welcome the additional safety that a PPN would provide even to investment-grade instruments.

11.3 Valuation Considerations

For valuation purposes, it is helpful to decompose a PPN into two components, the protected principal and the (unprotected) stream of coupon payments.

$$\text{PPN} = \text{protected principal} + \text{stream of coupon payments}$$

For simplicity, we start by assuming that counterparty credit risk is completely dealt with via full collateralization and other credit enhancement mechanisms so that the PPN buyer has no credit risk exposure to the PPN issuer. This implies that we can think of the protected principal as being akin to a riskless zero-coupon bond that has the same par value and maturity date as the PPN.

As for the stream of coupon payments, it can be characterized as a risky annuity that makes payments that are equal to the PPN's coupon and on the same dates as the PPN. We have thus decomposed the PPN into two simpler assets

$$\text{PPN} = \text{Riskless zero-coupon bond} + \text{Risky annuity}$$

where the payments made by the annuity are contingent on the reference entity remaining solvent. Indeed, using now familiar terminology, the zero-coupon bond and the annuity constitute the replicating portfolio for this PPN, and, as a result, valuing a PPN is the same as determining the market prices of the bond and the annuity.

Valuing the zero-coupon bond is straightforward, especially if one is willing to assume that it involves no credit risk. In practice, one might want to discount the repayment of principal based on the discount curve of the PPN issuer. For instance, if that issuer is a large highly rated bank, one might want to derive a zero-coupon curve from short-term LIBOR and interest rate swap rates, which embed the average credit quality of the large banks that are most active in the interbank loan and interest rate swap markets. If the PPN matures N years from today, the value of the corresponding zero-coupon bond can be written as:

$$V^{ZCB}(0, N) = D^*(0, N)F \tag{11.1}$$

where, using the same notation introduced in Chapter 5, $D^*(0, N)$ denotes a discount factor derived from the LIBOR/swap curve, and F is the face value of the PPN.

The future payments of the risky annuity, which are contingent on the financial health of the reference entity, should be more heavily discounted than the principal payment if the reference entity has a credit quality lower than that of participants in the LIBOR market. Let $D(0, j)$, $j = 1$ to N, correspond to the discount factors derived from the reference entity's yield curve. The value of the risky annuity can be written as

$$V^A(0, N) = \sum_{j=1}^{N} D(0, j)CPPN \tag{11.2}$$

where $CPPN$ is the coupon payment made by the PPN.

Given the above equations, we can write an expression for the market price of a PPN:

$$V^{PPN}(0, N) = D^*(0, N)F + \sum_{j=1}^{N} D(0, j)CPPN \tag{11.3}$$

PPNs are typically issued at their par value so pricing a brand new PPN amounts to finding the value of $CPPN$ that makes $V^{PPN}(0, N)$ in (11.3) equal to F.

Equation (11.3) tells us that the basic ingredients for pricing a new PPN are the zero-coupon bond prices that correspond to the credit quality of the PPN issuer and the reference entity. These are typically not directly observable in the marketplace, but they can be inferred from related market quotes such as the LIBOR/swap curve and CDS spreads.[4] As an example, suppose those quotes give you the zero-coupon bond prices shown in Table 11.2. If you use these numbers in equation (11.3), you will find that

TABLE 11.2
Zero-Coupon Bond Prices Used in PPN Valuation[a]

Maturity (years)	"Riskless" bonds	Reference entity's bonds
(1)	(2)	(3)
1	0.943396226	0.895426927
2	0.88999644	0.801789381
3	0.839619283	0.717943802
4	0.792093663	0.642866212

[a]Based on an assumption of flat riskless and risky yield curves. The riskless rate is set at 6 percent, and the reference entity's risk spread and recovery rate are assumed to be 300 bps and 50 percent, respectively. Face value of the bonds = $1.

---

[4]In Appendix A, we show how to derive zero-coupon bond prices from observed prices of coupon-paying bonds.

the PPN coupon that is consistent with the PPN being valued at par is 6.80 percent, the same coupon shown in Table 11.1. Indeed, the numbers in that table correspond to the zero-coupon bond prices shown in Table 11.2, and we can now verify that the PPN described in that example was indeed valued at par.

11.4   Variations on the Basic Structure

We have thus far limited ourselves to the simplest type of principal-protected structure. Other more complex structures do exist and are not uncommon, such as principal-protected structures that reference more than one entity or that pay floating coupons. One straightforward extension of the setup analyzed in this chapter are PPNs that offer only partial principal protection and thus provide a higher yield to investors. For instance, the PPN may guarantee only 50 percent of the investor's original principal in the event of default by the reference entity. The main points highlighted in the preceding sections are generally applicable to these and other variations of the basic principal-protected structure.

12

Credit-Linked Notes

Credit-linked notes are essentially securities structured to mimic closely, in funded form, the cash flows of a credit derivative. Credit-linked notes have a dual nature. On the one hand, they are analogous to traditional coupon-paying notes and bonds in that they are securities that can be bought and sold in the open market and that promise the return of principal at maturity. On the other hand, they can be thought of as a derivative on a derivative, as a credit-linked note's cash flow is tied to an underlying derivative contract.

Credit-linked notes play an important role in the credit derivatives market as they have helped expand the range of market participants. In particular, some participants are attracted to the funded nature of a CLN, either because of their greater familiarity with coupon-bearing notes or because they are prevented from investing in unfunded derivatives contracts by regulatory or internal restrictions.

12.1   How Does It Work?

To illustrate the basic workings of a CLN, we will go back to one of the simplest credit derivatives, the credit default swap (Chapter 6). Consider an asset manager who is seeking exposure to a given reference entity but who wants that exposure to be in funded form. A credit derivatives dealer may buy protection against default by that reference entity in a vanilla credit default swap and essentially securitize that contract, passing the resulting

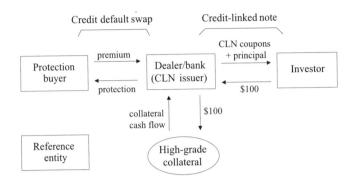

FIGURE 12.1. Diagram of a Simple Credit-Linked Note

cash flows to the asset manager, who ultimately buys the newly created securities. Alternatively, the dealer may sell protection against default by the reference entity to a special purpose vehicle, which then issues the notes to the investor.[1]

Figure 12.1 uses the example just discussed to illustrate the mechanics of a dealer-issued CLN. Imagine that the asset manager (the investor) wants to invest $100 million in the reference entity's debt. The dealer sells to another party $100 million worth of protection in a CDS contract that references that entity. At the same time, the dealer issues $100 million of notes to the asset manager, where the notes will pay a predetermined spread over LIBOR for as long as the reference entity does not trigger the underlying credit default swap.

The spread over LIBOR paid by the note may differ from the premium paid under the CDS owing to administrative costs incurred by the dealer and counterparty credit risk considerations. Here it is important to note that, even if the whole CDS premiums were passed along to the investors, they would fall short of what the investor would consider an "adequate" coupon for the CLN. (Recall that the CLN is a funded instrument, but the CDS is not—see Chapter 6.) To make up for this shortfall, the dealer may invest the proceeds of the note sale in high-grade securities and use the income generated by these securities, along with the CDS premiums, to fund the coupons owed to the investor. These high-grade securities may also be used as collateral against the dealer's obligations under the PPN.

At the maturity date of the CLN, assuming the underlying CDS was not triggered, the dealer pays out the last coupon and returns the investor's

---

[1]Special purpose vehicles are discussed in the next chapter. They are essentially entities with high credit ratings created specifically to issue CLNs and other securitized products.

initial investment ($100 million in this case) and both the CDS and CLN are terminated. Indeed, from the investor's perspective, the whole arrangement is very much akin to investing in a debt instrument issued by the reference entity, although, as we shall discuss later in this chapter, CLNs involve certain risks that are not present in traditional notes.

In the event of default by the reference entity, the investor bears the full brunt of the loss. Suppose that the recovery rate associated with the reference entity is 30 percent, and that a credit event does take place. The dealer pays its CDS counterparty the difference between the notional amount of the contract and the recovery value, $70 million, and the CLN is terminated with the asset manager receiving only $30 million of the $100 million that it had originally invested. Here again the cash flows to the investor mimic those of a traditional note issued by the reference entity.

12.2 Common Uses

We have mentioned already the most obvious applications for credit-linked notes. They allow the cash flows of derivatives instruments to be "repackaged" into securities that can be bought and sold in the market place. This is especially useful for certain classes of institutional investors, such as some mutual funds, that are precluded from taking sizable positions in unfunded derivatives contracts. These investors would otherwise be shut out of the credit derivatives market, and thus credit-linked notes play an important role in diversifying the market's investor base.

Investors who do not have master credit derivatives agreements with dealers are attracted to credit-linked notes because they generally require less documentation and lower setup costs than outright credit derivatives contracts. In addition, credit-linked notes can be tailored to meet specific needs of investors. For instance, they can be used to securitize the risk exposures in portfolio default swaps, thereby broadening the pool of potential first-loss investors. Lastly, credit-linked notes can be rated at the request of individual institutional investors.

Credit-linked notes can help increase the liquidity of certain otherwise illiquid assets or even create a market for assets that would otherwise not exist in tradable form. For instance, CLNs that reference a pool of bank loans can be traded in the open market without restrictions, whereas actual sales of the loans might be subject to restrictions and notification or approval by the borrowers.

Bankers/dealers too find value in the issuance of credit-linked notes, over and above the revenue that they generate. For instance, CLNs provide dealers with an additional vehicle to hedge their exposures in other credit derivatives positions.

12.3   Valuation Considerations

As general rule, the single most important risk exposure in a CLN is, naturally, the credit risk associated with the reference entity. CLN spreads are often wider than the spreads associated with the corresponding reference entities, however, although the issuer may reduce the spread paid under the CLN to cover its administrative costs.

The higher CLN spread reflects the investor's exposure to the counterparty credit risk associated with the CLN issuer; the investor would not be exposed to such a risk if buying a note issued directly by the reference entity. Counterparty credit risk is more important for CLNs issued out of a bank or dealer, rather than from a highly rated special purpose vehicle, which tend to make more widespread use of collateral arrangements, as we shall see in the next chapter.

12.4   Variations on the Basic Structure

There are at least as many types, if not more, of CLNs as there are credit derivatives. For instance, while the example discussed in this chapter focused on a CDS-based credit-linked note, earlier CLNs were actually set up to securitize asset swaps (Chapter 5). In addition, the principal-protected notes discussed in Chapter 11 are, in essence, a member of the CLN family.

Credit-linked notes are common features of complex structured products such as synthetic CDOs. Indeed, the cash flows of synthetic CDOs are commonly channeled to investors in the form of coupon and principal payments made by specific CLNs.

13

Repackaging Vehicles

Repackaging vehicles are special-purpose trusts or companies typically associated with banks and derivatives dealers. In the credit derivatives market, they are often counterparties in contracts that are subsequently securitized and sold off to investors. In this chapter, we will temporarily deviate from the stated goal of this book, which is to discuss specific types of credit derivatives, and take a closer look at this important aspect of many credit derivatives contracts. Repackaging vehicles are commonly backed by high-grade collateral and thus tend to be highly rated themselves in order to minimize investors' concerns about counterparty credit risk. The main buyers of structured products issued by repackaging vehicles are insurance companies, asset managers, banks, and other institutional investors.

Repackaging vehicles are important issuers of credit-linked notes and play a central role in the synthetic CDO structure (Chapter 14). In this chapter we go over the basics of repackaging vehicles, also called special-purpose vehicles (SPVs), focusing on their applications to credit-linked notes, which were discussed in Chapter 12.[1]

13.1 How Does It Work?

Repackaging vehicles are trusts or companies sponsored by individual institutions, but their legal structure is such that they are "bankruptcy-remote" to the sponsoring entity, meaning that a default by the sponsoring entity does not result in a default by the repackaging vehicle. As a result, investors

---

[1] Das (2000)[18] discusses repackaging vehicles in greater detail.

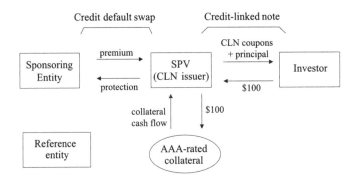

FIGURE 13.1. Diagram of a Simple SPV Structure

who buy, say, credit-linked notes issued by a repackaging vehicle are not directly subject to the credit risk associated with the sponsoring entity.

In the credit derivatives context, the purpose of the vehicle is to "repackage" the cash flows and risk characteristics of derivatives contracts into coupon and principal payments made by notes that can be bought and sold in the marketplace.[2] Figure 13.1 illustrates the basic workings of a repackaging vehicle. Consider a hypothetical situation where an investment bank (the sponsoring entity) has identified strong investor demand for, say, floating-rate notes issued by a given reference entity (XYZ Corp.). But suppose that entity has issued mostly fixed-rate liabilities. If the investors are unwilling, or unable, to enter into an asset swap with the bank, the bank can essentially use a combination of credit default swap and SPV technology to financial-engineer a note that will mimic the cash flows and risk characteristics sought by the investors.

Here is how it could work. The bank enters into a credit default swap with a repackaging vehicle especially created for the purposes of this transaction—hence the name special purpose vehicle. The bank buys protection against default by XYZ in a contract with a notional amount of, say, $100 million, which would correspond to the exposure desired by the investors.[3] At the same time, the SPV issues notes to the investors in the amount of $100 million and uses the proceeds of the note sales to buy highly rated securities. Those securities will serve as collateral for the par value of the notes, which, absent a default by XYZ Corp., will be paid

---

[2] This is similar to what was achieved in the case of a dealer-issued credit-linked note example examined in Chapter 12, but there are some important differences as we shall discuss in the next section.

[3] An alternative arrangement would be for the bank to sell an asset swap to the SPV and have the SPV securitize the asset swap, selling the notes to the investors.

to investors at the maturity of the notes. In many instances, the collateral bought by SPVs is actually selected by the investors. Along with the protection premium that the SPV receives from the sponsoring bank, the coupons paid by the collateral serve as a funding source for the coupons promised by the notes and for covering the SPV's administrative costs.[4]

From the investors' perspective, the notes bought from the SPV are very close to traditional notes sold in the capital market. For as long as the reference entity remains solvent, the investor will collect the notes' coupon payments from the SPV until the maturity date. In the event of default by the reference entity, the SPV liquidates the collateral to fund the protection payment owed to the dealer, and the notes are terminated with the residual proceeds of the collateral liquidation being transferred to the investors.

13.2   Why Use Repackaging Vehicles?

In Chapter 12 we discussed the basic structure of a simple credit-linked note issued directly by a derivatives dealer and noted that dealer banks are common issuers of such notes. Indeed, a quick look at Figures 12.1 and 13.1 will reveal remarkable similarities between the bank- and SPV-issued structures, and all of the common uses for credit-linked notes, outlined in Section 12.2, also apply to typical SPV-based structures in the credit derivatives market. The question then becomes: Why the need for repackaging vehicles in the credit derivatives market when the dealers themselves can, and do, issue credit-linked notes directly?

One rationale for the widespread use of SPVs relates to the issue of counterparty credit risk. With a bank-issued CLN, the investor is exposed to the credit risk associated both with the reference entity and the bank. In particular, if the bank defaults on its obligations, the investor may end up losing part or all of the principal and future coupon payments associated with the note even if the reference entity has not defaulted. In contrast, because the SPV is bankruptcy-remote to the sponsoring bank and is fully backed by high-grade collateral, the investor has a potentially much smaller exposure to counterparty credit risk.

Of course there are ways to mitigate the investor's exposure to counterparty credit risk in bank-issued structured notes. For instance, the bank may pledge the proceeds of the note sales as collateral. Still, counterparty credit risk considerations aside, there are other powerful factors behind the popularity of SPV-based structures. In particular, SPVs allow for greater flexibility to suit the particular needs of individual institutional investors

---

[4] Note that the sponsoring bank need not hold any debt instruments of the reference entity. Effectively, in the example in Figure 13.1, the bank has a short position on the credit quality of the reference entity.

when it comes to tax and regulatory issues. Indeed, SPVs are typically setup in jurisdictions that offer favorable tax and regulatory treatment such as, in the US, the states of Delaware and New York, and, elsewhere, in jurisdictions that include the Cayman Islands, Jersey, and Luxembourg.

Most of the examples provided above feature a bank as the SPV sponsor and an investor who buys SPV-issued notes. But one should be aware that the investor may just as well be, and in many cases is, another bank. For instance, AZZ Bank may be unwilling to do a total return swap directly with XYZ Bank, but it may feel comfortable doing that same swap with a AAA-rated SPV sponsored by AZZ Bank.

13.3   Valuation Considerations

Not surprisingly, the credit quality of the reference entity and, in the case of multiple reference entities, the default correlation of the entities loom large in the valuation of SPV-based credit derivatives. In addition, the credit quality of the SPV's collateral and of the credit derivative counterparty (the sponsoring bank) are also factored into the coupons paid by the SPV as funds received both from the sponsoring bank and the collateral pool may be used to fund the SPV's obligations.

SPV-based structures are often rated by the major credit-rating agencies. The factors mentioned above are key determinants of the credit rating of a given structure. In addition, the legal structure of the SPV, such as the way that multiple-issuance SPVs segregate collateral pools (discussed below), is also a factor in the risk profile and consequent credit rating of repackaging vehicles.

13.4   Variations on the Basic Structure

In the simple example illustrated in Figure 13.1, the repackaging vehicle was created specifically for the purposes of issuing the credit-linked notes sought by the investors. While this arrangement has the advantage that the investors are the sole claimants to the SPV's collateral (provided, of course, that the reference entity does not default) a drawback is that such "single-purpose SPVs" may be more costly than SPVs that issue more than one type of security, so-called multiple-issuance structures.

Multiple-issuance SPVs can be more cost effective than single-purpose SPVs in that their associated administrative and setup costs can be spread out among a larger number of issues. The legal structure of such vehicles is such that, even though the multiple-issuance SPV is a single entity, each note series issued by the entity has its own separate collateral pool.

As a result, investors only have recourse to the specific pool backing the notes that they hold. Assuming these non-recourse stipulations (often termed firewalls) are fully effective, defaults in one collateral pool do not affect the recourse rights of investors in notes backed by other pools, and investors in defaulted pools have no claim to assets held as collateral for other notes.

An alternative form of multiple-issuance repackaging vehicles are the so-called "umbrella" programs, whereby a separate legal entity is created for each issue, but each individual entity is based on the same master legal framework. Umbrella programs tend to provide a more effective segregation of collateral pools than other multiple-issuance vehicles while being more cost effective than single-purpose SPVs.

A particular type of repackaging vehicle that grew in popularity in the late 1990s and early 2000s, when insurers and reinsurers became increasingly active in the credit derivatives market, is the so-called "transformer." Transformers are essentially captive insurance companies established by banks/dealers for the purpose of converting a pure credit derivatives contract into an insurance contract. Transformers owe their existence to the fact that many jurisdictions place regulatory constraints on the ability of insurance companies to enter into derivatives contracts, which effectively prevent insurers from selling protection in simple CDSs. Thus, a transformer is set up in a jurisdiction where such regulatory barriers are not in place, such as in Bermuda. For instance, the transformer can, on one hand, sell protection in a CDS contract with a bank/dealer and, on the other hand, enter into a largely offsetting credit insurance contract with an insurance company that would otherwise be barred from the credit derivatives market.

14
Synthetic CDOs

Synthetic collateralized debt obligations are structured financial products that closely mimic the risk and cash flow characteristics of traditional (cash-funded) collateralized debt obligations. This "mimicking" is done through the use of credit derivatives, such as credit default swaps and portfolio default swaps, and that is why synthetic CDOs are part of any broad discussion of credit derivatives.

To explain synthetic CDOs, we first go over the general nature of the instruments they are designed to mimic, and thus we start this chapter with a brief overview of traditional CDOs. As we shall see, these are instruments that allow one to redistribute the credit risk in a given portfolio into tranches with different risk characteristics and, in the process, meet the risk appetites of different investors.

14.1 Traditional CDOs

The basic idea behind traditional CDOs is quite simple and can be illustrated with a nonfinancial example. Imagine a small number of water reservoirs located on the slope of a mountain. The reservoirs are emptied and then refilled at the beginning of each month. When each reservoir is filled to its capacity, the water in it cascades into the one just below, and in this way a single water source can in principle refill all reservoirs simply by feeding the pool at the highest elevation. We say in principle because this assumes that the source has enough water to fill all reservoirs to capacity, otherwise one or more reservoirs down the mountain may be left empty or only partially filled.

What do cascading water reservoirs have to do with collateralized debt obligations? Replace the monthly water replenishments with the monthly or quarterly cash flows generated by a portfolio of, say, business loans and think of the individual reservoirs as investors with different claims on these payments, and you arrive at the main idea behind a CDO. The reservoirs at higher elevations, which are the ones to be replenished first, correspond to investors with most senior claims on the cash flows of the portfolio—they are first in line to collect their share of the "water." The reservoirs in lower elevations, which receive their water allotments only after the reservoirs up the mountain have received their full due, are analogous to investors with junior (subordinated) claims to the cash flows of the portfolio. The reservoir at the foot of the mountain is akin to a first-loss investor: Should the water source come short of its promised amount, the lowest reservoir will be the first to dry up.

To sum up, collateralized debt obligations are essentially securities with different levels of seniority and with interest and principal payments that are backed by the cash flows of an underlying portfolio of debt instruments. When the debt instruments are loans, the CDO is often called a CLO— a collateralized loan obligation—if they are bonds, the CDO becomes a CBO—a collateralized bond obligation.

14.1.1   How Does It Work?

Let us look at a very simple and stylized CDO structure, represented schematically in Figure 14.1.[1] Consider a CDO issuer with a portfolio of loans with a total face value of, say, $100 million. (As noted above, we could call this a CLO, but we will stick to the more general terminology to emphasize that this example would work just as well with a CBO.) To fund the purchase of the loan portfolio, the issuer sells debt obligations (notes) to investors. The stream of payments promised by these notes is, in turn, backed by the cash flows generated by the loan portfolio. The figure depicts the relatively common case where the CDO issuer is a special purpose vehicle (Chapter 13).

Suppose both the loans that make up the collateral and the resulting notes make monthly payments. Each month, the issuer (the SPV) receives

---

[1] The CDO structure examined here is used to highlight only the basic features of CDOs. More complex structures are not uncommon. For instance, many CDOs allow for the addition, removal, and substitution of assets in the collateral pool—so-called ramp-ups, removals, and replenishments—during the life of the structure. In addition, the basic waterfall structure described above is often complicated by "coverage tests," a topic that is briefly discussed in Chapter 21. Goodman and Fabozzi (2002)[34] discuss CDO structures in some detail.

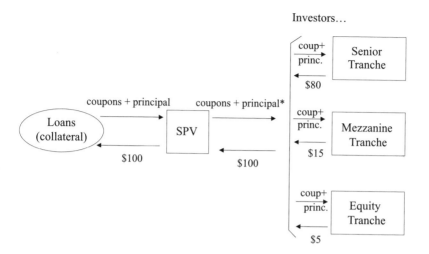

* Net of administrative costs, $ amounts are in millions

FIGURE 14.1. Diagram of a Simple CDO

the payments due on the loans and passes them through to the investors who bought the notes (net of any administrative charges). Again, a key aspect of a CDO is that the notes have different coupons to reflect various levels of seniority and risk. In particular, in each month, any income paid by the underlying loans is used first to meet payments owed to the holders of the most senior notes. Once, the holders of those notes are paid, investors in the second most senior notes are paid up, and this process continues until the holders of the most junior notes receive their share of the portfolio's cash flow. (This is the cascading pool structure that we described above.)

The payments owed to the various notes are such that, in the absence of default in the underlying loans, the net monthly cash flow generated by the loans is just enough to pay all investors, from the most senior to the most junior. In the event of default in one or more of the loans in the portfolio, however, the holders of the most junior notes will receive less than their total payment due, which implies that their "coupon + principal" cash flow shown in Figure 14.1 is essentially a residual amount after more senior investors and administrative fees are paid. Naturally, because the most junior investors are long the first-loss piece of the CDO, their expected return is higher than the expected returns that correspond to the more senior notes in the structure.

In the parlance of the CDO world, each level of seniority of the notes issued under the CDO is called a tranche. CDO tranches are typically rated by major credit rating agencies—such as Moody's, Standard and Poor's, and FitchRatings. In the case of a CDO with, say, four levels of seniority, one typically refers to the first-loss notes as the equity tranche, to the second- and third-loss notes as the subordinated mezzanine and senior mezzanine tranches, respectively, and to the most senior notes as, simply, the senior tranche. In the example depicted in Figure 14.1, the CDO involved three tranches: an equity tranche with a total par value of $5 million, a mezzanine tranche initially valued at $15 million, and a senior tranche with notes with a total face value of $80 million.

In many instances, the institution that accumulated the loans that make up the collateral held by the SPV buys back at least part of the equity tranche. This is done for a number of reasons. For instance, the high degree of credit risk associated with certain first-loss pieces may make them harder to sell in the open market. In addition, by staying on as a first-loss investor, the institution may hope to address potential CDO investors' concerns about moral hazard and adverse selection problems.

To understand the moral hazard problem associated with CDOs, consider the example of a commercial bank that intends to securitize the business loans on its books. One manifestation of the moral hazard problem is the concern that the bank may make riskier loans than otherwise if it knows that it can then transfer all of the associated credit risk to CDO investors. The adverse selection problem is related to the notion that, relative to investors, the bank may have an informational advantage when it comes to evaluating the reference entities represented in its own portfolio. As a result, investors may become concerned about the so-called "lemon" phenomenon, or the possibility that they may end up buying debt securities that reference entities with particular problems and risks that are known only by the bank. By becoming a first-loss investor in the CDO, the bank in this example hopes to dispel or at least mitigate such worries.

14.1.2   Common Uses: Balance-sheet and Arbitrage CDOs

CDOs have a wide range of applications in the financial markets and tend to be classified according to the ultimate goals of their sponsors. For instance, from the perspective of a commercial bank, CDOs make it possible to transfer a large portfolio of loans off the bank's balance sheet in a single transaction with a repackaging vehicle. Such CDOs are commonly called balance-sheet CDOs, and, indeed, historically, banks' desire to free up regulatory capital through balance-sheet CDOs was an important driver of CDO market activity in the 1990s. The banks would sell the assets to sponsored SPVs, which would then securitize them and place them with institutional investors, as broadly outlined in Figure 14.1.

In recent years, a substantial share of CDO issuance has been driven not so much by banks' balance-sheet management needs, but by investor demands for leveraged credit risk exposures.[2] These CDOs are often referred to as arbitrage CDOs in that the institutions behind the issuance are, for instance, attempting to enhance their return on the underlying assets by becoming first-loss (equity) investors in the newly created structures. Most of these arbitrage CDOs are actively managed and thus the CDO investors are exposed both to credit risk and to the particular trading strategy followed by the CDO manager. Insurance companies, asset managers, and some banks are among the main equity investors in arbitrage CDOs.

Over and above their general application to balance-sheet management and return enhancement, CDOs can be used to create some liquidity in what would otherwise be essentially illiquid assets. For instance, many bank loans are inherently illiquid, in part because each sale may require approval by the borrower. Once those loans are securitized, however, their underlying risk characteristics become more tradable as the SPV-issued notes are bought and sold in the marketplace. In addition, as noted, the CDO structure allows, through the tranching process, the creation of new assets with specific profiles that may better match the individual needs and risk tolerances of institutional investors.

14.1.3   Valuation Considerations

Three main factors enter into the pricing of the various tranches of a CDO: the degree of default correlation among the debt instruments in the collateral pool, the credit quality of the individual debt instruments, and the tranching structure of the CDO. These are essentially the same factors that we discussed in Chapters 9 and 10, where we examined key multi-name credit derivatives. In addition, and quite naturally, these are some of the main variables taken into account by the major credit-rating agencies when assessing the risk embedded in individual CDO structures. We will see more about CDO valuation in Part IV of this book.

14.2   Synthetic Securitization

Having reviewed the basics of traditional CDOs, understanding the mechanics of synthetic CDOs becomes relatively straightforward, especially if one is already familiar with portfolio default swaps (Chapter 10). Figure 14.2 illustrates a simple synthetic balance-sheet CDO structure. The figure shows a commercial bank (labeled sponsoring bank) with a loan

---

[2] Similar to first-loss investors in baskets and portfolio default swaps (Chapters 9 and 10), equity investors in CDOs are exposed to the credit risk in the entire collateral pool even though their maximum loss is substantially smaller than the total par value of the CDO.

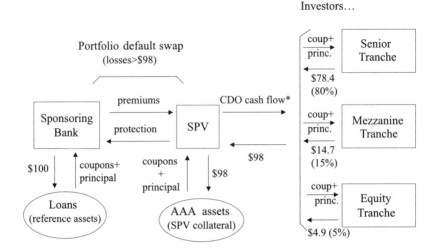

FIGURE 14.2. Diagram of a Simple Synthetic CDO

portfolio of $100 million (the reference assets). The bank wants to shed the credit risk associated with the portfolio, but, rather than selling the loans to a repackaging vehicle (labeled SPV in the figure), the bank opts for selling only the credit risk associated with the portfolio and for keeping the loans on its balance sheet.

The risk transfer is done via a portfolio default swap where the SPV is the counterparty and where the sponsoring entity buys protection against, say, any losses in excess of 2 percent of the portfolio. Alternatively, the risk transfer could be done via a series of single-name credit default swaps. (As in the case of traditional CDOs, the sponsor tends to keep a small first-loss piece, 2 percent in this case, partly in order to address investors' potential concerns about moral hazard and adverse selection problems.) The bank in Figure 14.2 makes periodic premium payments to the SPV, and the SPV promises to stand ready to step in to cover any default-related losses that exceed 2 percent of the portfolio, just as in any typical portfolio default swap agreement.

What does the SPV do next? As in the traditional CDO structure, the SPV issues notes to various classes of investors (three in the example in Figure 14.2), where each class corresponds to claims with a given level of seniority toward the SPV's cash flows. Because the portfolio default swap is an unfunded structure, however, the cash flows it generates (the protection premiums) cannot possibly fully compensate the investors both for their funding costs (the SPV-issued notes are fully funded investments) and for the credit risk embedded in the reference portfolio. To make up for this shortfall, the SPV invests the proceeds of the note sales in high-grade assets, typically AAA-rated instruments. The SPV then uses these assets both as collateral for its obligations toward the sponsoring bank and the investors and, through the income that they generate, as a funding source to supplement the coupon payments promised by the notes. The collateral is shown in the lower part of the figure.

Provided there are no defaults in the reference portfolio, the sponsoring bank keeps on making full premium payments to the SPV, which in turn uses that income, along with the cash flow generated by the AAA-rated collateral, to meet the all coupon payments owed to the note investors. At the maturity date of the CDO notes, the portfolio swap is terminated and the SPV liquidates the collateral to repay the investors' principal in full.

The CDO investors absorb all default-related losses in excess of the first-loss piece retained by the sponsoring bank, starting with the equity investors, as in a traditional CDO. Suppose, for instance that, after the bank's first-loss piece is exhausted, an additional default takes place. A common approach is for the SPV to liquidate part of its collateral in order to cover the sponsoring bank's losses and for the par value of the notes held by the equity investors to be reduced accordingly. Again, this is analogous to the portfolio default swap arrangement discussed in Chapter 10.

While Figure 14.2 shows the mechanics of a synthetic balance-sheet CDO, the structure of a synthetic arbitrage CDO would be similar. Salient differences would include the facts that the sponsoring entity could be, for instance, an asset manager, rather than the commercial bank featured in Figure 14.2, and that the SPV could potentially be selling protection to a number of buyers in the credit derivatives market, instead of just to its sponsor. Similar to the traditional CDO market, arbitrage-motivated deals have come to dominate new issuance flows in the synthetic CDO market in recent years.

14.2.1 Common Uses: Why Go Synthetic?

A powerful rationale for using synthetic, as opposed to traditional, CDOs relates to the fact that the latter does not require the sponsoring bank in a balance-sheet CDO to sell any of the loans in the reference portfolio or, especially in the case of arbitrage CDOs, the SPV to source loans and securities in various markets. To take on the sponsoring bank's perspective, as we have argued before in this book, selling loans can be both potentially problematic for maintaining bank relationships and costly in terms of the legal steps involved in the borrower approval and notification process. The situation here is entirely analogous to an example, discussed in Section 3.1, involving single-name credit default swaps and loan sales, except that now we are dealing with a potentially large number of reference entities in one single transaction: Synthetic CDOs allow a bank to sell anonymously the credit risk associated with the loans held on its books. Through the synthetic CDO, the bank essentially securitizes the credit risk in the portfolio, whereas through a traditional CDO both the credit risk and the loans are securitized.

Another rationale for using synthetic CDOs stems from banks' hedging needs regarding potential exposures through undrawn credit facilities, such as back-up lines of credit offered to investment-grade entities that issue commercial paper (CP). For instance, XYZ Corp. may have an option to borrow $100 million from AZZ Bank in case it is unable to roll over its CP obligations. Should XYZ run into unexpected difficulties that lead it to draw down on the credit facility, it may well be too late (or too expensive) for AZZ Bank to hedge its XYZ exposure. Thus, the bank has a $100 million exposure to XYZ that does not quite fit the most common form of the traditional CDO model. Instead, the bank could decide to take preemptive measures and, for instance, refashion a synthetic CDO to include a $100 million notional exposure to XYZ Corp.[3]

14.2.2   Valuation Considerations for Synthetic CDOs

Valuation considerations are similar to those involving traditional CDOs. Default correlation, the credit quality of the individual entities represented in the reference portfolio, and the details of the tranching structure are important factors—see Chapter 21. In addition, the legal structure of the SPV, as well as the credit quality of the SPV's collateral and of the sponsoring bank may also play a role. Regarding the latter two factors, their importance stems from the fact that the SPV depends on the incomes generated by the collateral and on the premiums paid by the sponsoring bank to fund the cash flows owed to the note investors. Similar to traditional CDOs, the tranches of synthetic CDOs can be, and typically are, rated by the major credit-rating agencies.

14.2.3   Variations on the Basic Structure

Synthetic CDOs are commonly structured to require even less securitization than the example shown in Figure 14.2. One such structure, motivated by an example provided by O'Kane (2001)[63], is shown in Figure 14.3. In this example, the sponsoring bank enters into two separate portfolio

---

[3] Obviously, a synthetic CDO is not the only alternative available to the bank. Protection bought through a single-name CDS written on XYZ Corp. would be another possibility.

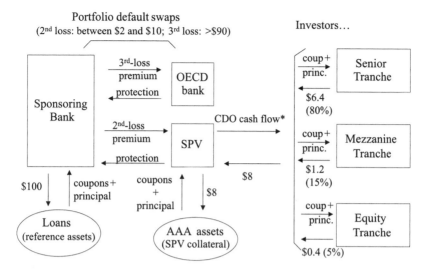

Portfolio default swaps
(2nd loss: between $2 and $10; 3rd loss: >$90)

* Net of administrative costs, $ amounts are in millions

FIGURE 14.3. Diagram of a Variation on the Simple Synthetic CDO Structure

default swaps: a second-loss contract with the SPV, covering losses between 2 percent and 10 percent of the portfolio, and a third-loss contract with an OECD bank covering any losses in excess of 10 percent. Only the contract with the SPV is securitized and sold off into different tranches to investors following the same pattern described in the discussion of Figure 14.2. In this particular example, the bank obtained substantial credit protection while securitizing only 8 percent of the total portfolio.

An alternative synthetic CDO structure to the one illustrated in Figures 14.2 and 14.3 is the unfunded synthetic CDO, where investors put up no cash at the inception of the transaction and, similar to a single-name credit default swap, receive only the premiums passed through by the SPV. In this case, there is no SPV collateral involved and an investor would only be called upon to make a payment under the terms of the contract if and when default-related losses in the underlying portfolio fall within the range covered by his or her tranche. Such a structure is akin to a collection of portfolio default swaps written on the reference portfolio, with each swap corresponding to a different tranche of the synthetic CDO.

Before we end this chapter, we should once again note that, while the examples discussed in this chapter centered on CDOs that referenced pools of loans, CDOs are also commonly set up to reference bond portfolios.

Part III

Introduction to Credit Modeling I: Single-Name Defaults

15

Valuing Defaultable Bonds

Before we start exploring specific models for pricing credit derivatives, we will pause to introduce some notation and, in the process, review a few important concepts. Those familiar with risk-neutral probabilities and the risk-neutral valuation approach, two of the most important topics discussed in this chapter, may still want to at least glance through the next few pages to familiarize themselves with the notation that will be used throughout this part of the book.

In this chapter we shall assume that riskless interest rates are deterministic. This is done for expositional purposes only so we can avoid certain technical details related to the discussion of the risk-neutral valuation in Section 15.2.[1] Stochastic interest rates are discussed in Chapter 17.

15.1 Zero-coupon Bonds

Let $Z(t, T)$ denote today's (time-t) price of a riskless zero-coupon bond that pays out \$1 at a future time T. If $R(t, T)$ is the continuously compounded

---

[1] In this non-technical overview of the valuation of defaultable bonds, we make no formal distinction between so-called risk-neutral and forward-risk-neutral probabilities. Indeed, when riskless interest rates are deterministic, these two probability measures coincide. Readers interested in pursuing these technical details further could consult Neftci (2002)[62] and Baxter and Rennie (2001)[6] for very accessible discussions of the main issues involved. More mathematically oriented readers may also be interested in the discussion in Bjork (1998)[7].

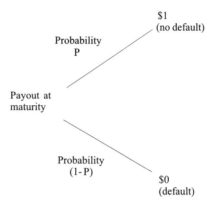

Note: P is the actual probability of no default.

FIGURE 15.1. Payout Scenarios for a Zero-Recovery Zero-Coupon Bond

yield to maturity on this bond, we have[2]

$$Z(t,T) = e^{-R(t,T)(T-t)} \qquad (15.1)$$

We can think of $Z(t,T)$ as reflecting the time-value of money, or today's (time-t) value of $1 that will be received for sure at time T. Note that, for positive interest rates, even though the terminal payout of this bond is never in question, its value today is only a fraction of that payout, i.e., $Z(t,T) < 1$.

Now consider another bond with the same maturity and face value as the above riskless security, but this bond is subject to default risk. In particular assume that there is a nonzero probability that the bond issuer will default, in which case the bond will have a recovery value of $0. As shown in Figure 15.1, this bond has two possible cash flows associated with it: At time T, it will either pay $1 (no default) or nothing (default). We shall assume that the actual probability of no default by this issuer at time T, conditional on information available at time t, is $P(t,T)$, which is also called the survival probability of the issuer. (Needless to say, this probability is also conditional on the issuer not having defaulted by time t.)

---

[2]Up until now, we have been working on discretely compounded yields—see, e.g., Chapter 4—a concept with which most people tend to be familiar. Many of the credit risk models considered in this part of the book, however, are cast in terms of continuously compounded yields, and hence our switch to continuous compounding. The relationship between discretely and continuously compounded yields is reviewed in Appendix A, where we also discuss basic concepts related to bond yields and bond prices.

From the perspective of time t, it is useful to think of this risky bond as a lottery that, at time T, will pay either \$1, with probability $P(t,T)$, or \$0, with probability $1 - P(t,T)$. Let $Z_0^d(T,T)$ be the risky bond's payout at time T.[3] While this amount is unknown at time t, its expected value can be computed based on knowledge of $P(t,T)$. Suppose that the expected payout of the bond/lottery is Y, i.e.,

$$Y \equiv E_t\left[Z_0^d(T,T)\right] = P(t,T) \times 1 + [1 - P(t,T)] \times 0 = P(t,T) \quad (15.2)$$

where $E_t[.]$ denotes an expectation formed on the basis of information available at time t, given the survival probability $P(t,T)$.

15.2   Risk-neutral Valuation and Probability

How do we compute the present value of this bond/lottery? First, as with the riskless bond, there is the time-value of money. The payout of the lottery, if any, will only be made at the future date T, and a dollar tomorrow is less valuable than a dollar today. Second, and unlike the riskless bond, there is a chance that the lottery may not pay out at all (the bond issuer may default). As a result, one may want to discount the promised payment further when assessing the current value of the bond. There are two equivalent ways of thinking about this discounting. One can apply a higher discount rate to the promised payment of \$1,

$$Z_0^d(t,T) = e^{-[R(t,T)+S(t,T)](T-t)} = Z(t,T)e^{-S(t,T)(T-t)} \quad (15.3)$$

where, for $S(t,T) > 0$, the promised payout of the risky bond is now discounted based on the higher rate $R(t,T) + S(t,T)$.

Alternatively, one can think of the artificial "probability" $Q(t,T)$—also conditional on information available at time t—which is such that the risk-free rate can be relied upon to discount the defaultable bond's expected future payment:

$$Z_0^d(t,T) = e^{-R(t,T)(T-t)}\left[Q(t,T) \times 1 + (1 - Q(t,T)) \times 0\right]$$
$$= Z(t,T)Q(t,T) \quad (15.4)$$

where $1 - Q(t,T)$ is the "probability" attached to a default by the bond issuer, as shown in Figure 15.2.

---

[3] Note that $Z_0^d(t,T)$, the time-t price of the zero-recovery, zero-coupon defaultable bond that matures at time T, corresponds to the variable $D(t,T)$, which we introduced in Chapter 4. We use this new notation in this part of the book because it is more commonly used in the modeling literature.

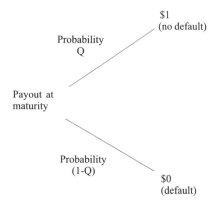

Note: Q is the risk-neutral probability of no default, not necessarily equal to P.

FIGURE 15.2. Payout Scenarios for a Zero-Recovery Zero-Coupon Bond

Note that default probability $1 - Q(t,T)$ in equation (15.4)—or the probability that the lottery will not pay out—will generally not coincide with the actual default probability $1 - P(t,T)$ featured in equation (15.2). Why? Because investors may be risk averse. Here is how we will characterize a risk averse investor. Suppose the investor is given two alternative investment opportunities at time t: (i) a promise to receive Y dollars for sure at time T and (ii) a chance to enter into the above lottery, which, based on the actual default probability $1 - P(t,T)$, has an expected payout of Y. For the purposes of this book, we will say that, if the investor is risk averse, he or she will choose the "sure thing," rather than take the risk associated with the lottery.[4]

Now note that the time-t value of a promise to pay Y dollars for sure at time T is simply $Z(t,T)Y$. The time-t value of the lottery can be thought of as the time-t price of a zero-recovery zero-coupon bond with a face value of $1 and an actual probability of default $1 - P(t,T)$. This is simply $Z_0^d(t,T)$. Thus, if the marketplace is composed mainly of risk averse investors, the former (the "sure thing") will be more valued than the latter (the lottery):

$$Z(t,T)Y > Z_0^d(t,T) \qquad (15.5)$$

Using (15.2) and (15.4), we can rewrite the above as

$$Z(t,T)P(t,T) > Z(t,T)Q(t,T) \qquad (15.6)$$

---

[4] Formal definitions of risk aversion can be found in most financial economics textbooks, such as LeRoy and Werner (2001)[54] and Huang and Litzenberger (1988)[40].

which implies that $P(t,T) > Q(t,T)$. This is a key result that bears repeating,

$$\text{Risk aversion} => Z(t,T)Y > Z_0^d(t,T) => P(t,T) > Q(t,T) \qquad (15.7)$$

In words, when investors are risk averse, the actual survival probability used in the valuation of a risky bond—equation (15.4)—is higher than the artificial survival probability associated with the bond.

What if investors are risk neutral? In the context of this book, we shall say that an investor is risk neutral if he or she is indifferent between the riskfree promise of a payout of Y at time T and a risky bond/lottery with an expected payout of Y, also to be made at time T. Thus, in a market composed of risk-neutral investors, the prices of the riskfree promise and the lottery should be the same

$$\text{Risk neutrality} => Z(t,T)Y = Z_0^d(t,T) => P(t,T) = Q(t,T) \qquad (15.8)$$

and again using equations (15.2) and (15.4) we arrive at the result that, when investors are risk neutral, the probabilities that are used in the valuation of the risky bond in equation (15.4) are indeed the actual probabilities associated with default events related to the bond issuer.[5]

15.2.1 Risk-neutral Probabilities

Note that the artificial probabilities used in equation (15.4) were such that investors would be willing to discount the uncertain payout of the risky bond at the riskless rate. As we saw in the previous section, this is essentially what a risk-neutral investor would do. Consider the case of risk-averse investors. Intuitively, what we did was ask ourselves the following question: By how much do we have to inflate the default probability $1-P(t,T)$ so that a risk-averse investor would be willing to behave as if she were risk neutral? The resulting artificial default probability $1-Q(t,T)$ is commonly called the risk-neutral probability of default, which will only coincide with the actual probability of default if the world were populated by risk-neutral investors.

Let $\tilde{E}_t\left[Z_0^d(T,T)\right]$ denote the expected payout of the risky bond, computed on the basis of the risk-neutral probabilities $Q(t,T)$ and $1-Q(t,T)$ and of information available as of time t, i.e.,

$$\tilde{E}_t\left[Z_0^d(T,T)\right] = Q(t,T) \times 1 + [1 - Q(t,T)] \times 0 = Q(t,T)$$

We will define τ as the default time, unknown at time t, of the bond issuer. If τ is independent of the riskfree rate embedded in $Z(t,T)$, which

---

[5] We have left out the case of risk-loving investors. These are the ones who would value the lottery more highly than the sure thing, which would imply that $P(t,T) < Q(t,T)$.

is clearly the case thus far given that we are assuming that the riskless rate is deterministic, the risk-neutral valuation formula for this bond, essentially given by equation (15.4), can then be written as[6]

$$Z_0^d(t,T) = Z(t,T)\tilde{E}_t\left[Z_0^d(T,T)\right] \qquad (15.9)$$

The above equation is a very important result, and we will come back to it in many instances throughout the remainder of this book. We can simplify this basic result further in the context of zero-recovery bonds. In particular, when $R(t,T)$ and τ are independent, and going back to equation (15.4), we can write

Price of zero-recovery zero-coupon risky bond

equals

price of comparable riskless bond

times

risk-neutral survival probability of risky bond issuer

where a comparable riskless bond is one with the same maturity date and face value as the risky bond, and the survival probability, $Q(t,T)$, refers to the risky-neutral probability of no default by the risky bond issuer by the maturity date of the bond, T.[7]

15.3 Coupon-paying Bonds

Thus far we have limited ourselves to zero-coupon bonds. Extending the above results to coupon-bearing bonds is relatively straightforward.

---

[6]For models that allow riskless rates to be stochastic, the simplifying assumption of independence between riskless interest rates and the default process may be a more reasonable approximation for highly rated entities than for lower-rated ones, at least as far as results based on empirical (as opposed to risk-neutral) probabilities are concerned. For instance, Duffee (1998)[21] and Collin-Dufresne, Goldstein, and Martin (2001)[14] found only a relatively weak relationship between changes in US Treasury yields and changes in credit spreads, but the sensitivity of spreads to interest rates was reported to increase with decreases in credit quality.

[7]An alternative way to write the valuation formula for a risky zero-coupon bond is to make use of the indicator function $1_{\{\tau>T\}}$, which is one if the time of default, τ, falls beyond the end of the horizon, T, and zero otherwise. Using this notation:

$$Z_0^d(t,T) = Z(t,T)\tilde{E}_t\left[1_{\{\tau>T\}}\right]$$

In particular, one can think of a coupon-paying bond as a portfolio of zero-coupon bonds. To see this, consider the case of a newly issued two-year defaultable bond that makes coupon payments annually and that promises the full repayment of its face value at maturity. Assume a fixed coupon rate of C, a face value of \$1, and a zero recovery rate. If the bond issuer does not default over the next 2 years, it will pay C in one year and $1 + C$ two years from now.

Note that this coupon-paying bond is equivalent to a portfolio with two zero-coupon bonds, one that matures in one year and has a face value of C and the other maturing in two years with a face value of $1 + C$. Thus, as we discussed in Chapter 1, if we know the price of this replicating portfolio of zero-coupon bonds, we know the price of the coupon-paying bond. Using notation consistent with that introduced in the previous section we can write the time-t value, $V^B(t, t + 2)$, of this two-year bond as

$$V^B(t, t + 2) = Z_0^d(t, t + 1)C + Z_0^d(t, t + 2)(1 + C) \qquad (15.10)$$

where t denotes the current year, and $t + 1$ and $t + 2$ are dates one and two years from today, respectively.

Here we can invoke the risk-neutral valuation formula discussed in Section 15.2 and write

$$V^B(t, t + 2) = Z(t, t + 1)Q(t, t + 1)C + Z(t, t + 2)Q(t, t + 2)(1 + C) \qquad (15.11)$$

where $Q(t, t + i)$ is the risk-neutral probability, as seen at time t, that the bond issuer will not default by time $t + i$, or the bond issuer's survival probability through time $t + i$.

We can generalize the above results to a coupon-bearing defaultable bond that matures at some future date T_N, has a face value of F, and makes coupon payments CF on dates $T_1, T_2, \ldots, T_N$. The value of such a bond at time t, $t < T_1$, is

$$V^B(t, T_N) = \left[\sum_{i=1}^{N} Z(t, T_i)Q(t, T_i)C + Z(t, T_N)Q(t, T_N) \right] F \qquad (15.12)$$

and we can now see that the discount factors $D(t, T_i)$ used, for instance, in Chapters 4 and 5, were essentially given by the product of the corresponding "riskless discount factor," $Z(t, T_i)$, and the survival probability associated with bond issuer, $Q(t, T_i)$.

15.4   Nonzero Recovery

We can bring the framework outlined in the chapter a bit closer to reality by considering the case of coupon-bearing bonds that are subject to default risk but that have a nonzero recovery value upon default. Let X, $0 \leq X < 1$, denote the recovery value of the bond. To avoid unnecessary complications at this point, assume that X is nonrandom and that the bond holder receives X on the coupon payment date that immediately follows a default.[8]

Let Prob_t[default between T_{i-1} and T_i] denote the (risk-neutral) probability of a default occurring between coupon payment dates T_{i-1} and T_i, based on all information available at time t. Intuitively, it is not hard to see that this probability should be equal to the probability of surviving through time T_{i-1} minus the probability of surviving through T_i:

$$\text{Prob}_t[\text{default between } T_{i-1} \text{ and } T_i] = Q(t, T_{i-1}) - Q(t, T_i) \quad (15.13)$$

For instance, if the probability of surviving through T_{i-1} is 50 percent and the probability of surviving through T_i is 47 percent, then there is a 3 percent probability that the bond issuer will default between T_{i-1} and T_i, where, for the reminder of this chapter, all references to probabilities are made in the risk-neutral sense.

Should the bond issuer default between T_{i-1} and T_i, the bond holder will receive X at time T_i. What is the time-t value of the recovery payment received on that date? We can think of this payment as the present discounted value of a zero-coupon bond that pays X at time T_i with probability $[Q(t, T_{i-1}) - Q(t, T_i)]$ and zero otherwise. Using the risk-neutral valuation framework, the value of such a hypothetical bond would be

$$Z(t, T_i)[Q(t, T_{i-1}) - Q(t, T_i)]X$$

which is the present discounted value of the recovery payment associated with a default between times T_{i-1} and T_i.

For a nonzero recovery bond with N payment dates, there are N possible dates for the recovery payment X to take place, each corresponding to a different default scenario. For instance, if the bond issuer defaults between T_2 and T_3, the bond holder receives X at time T_3, which, in the absence of uncertainty, has a present value of $Z(t, T_3)X$ at time t. If, instead, a default were to occur at a later period, say between T_7 and T_8, the time-t value of the bond's recovery value would be $Z(t, T_8)X$ in a world without uncertainty. As a result, once uncertainty is factored back into the computation, one can think of today's (time t) value of the bond's recovery

---

[8]See Arvanitis and Gregory (2001)[2] for the more general case where the recovery payment occurs immediately upon default.

payment as a weighted sum of all the recovery payments associated with all possible default scenarios, where the weights are given by the risk-neutral probabilities of each scenario actually taking place:

$$V^{REC}(t) = \sum_{i=1}^{N} Z(t,T_i)[Q(t,T_{i-1}) - Q(t,T_i)]X \tag{15.14}$$

Given (15.14), writing down an expression for the total value of the bond is relatively simple. This is just the sum of the present discounted values of the bond's coupon and principal payments, equation (15.12), and the bond's recovery payment:

$$V^B(t,T_N) = \left[\sum_{i=1}^{N} Z(t,T_i)Q(t,T_i)C + Z(t,T_N)Q(t,T_N) \right] F$$

$$+ \sum_{i=1}^{N} Z(t,T_i)[Q(t,T_{i-1}) - Q(t,T_i)]X \tag{15.15}$$

Upon closer inspection, one can see in equation (15.15) that the market value of a coupon-bearing defaultable bond is simply the probability-weighted sum of the present values of all possible cash flows associated with the bond.

15.5   Risky Bond Spreads

The price of a risky bond is often communicated in the marketplace in terms of the spread between the bond's yield and some benchmark yield, such as a swap rate or the yield on a government security with comparable maturity. For instance, a newly issued ten-year corporate bond in the United States might be said to be trading at, say, 156 basis points over the yield on the most-recently issued ten-year US Treasury note.

Our intuition should tell us that the yield spread on a given risky bond should be closely related to how the probability of default associated with the issuer of that bond compares to the default probability, if any, associated with the benchmark bond. Indeed, as noted in Section 15.2, one can think of the pricing of a risky bond as the process of finding the spread $S(t,T)$ over the riskless rate so that the bond's promised future cash flow is appropriately discounted to reflect both the time-value of money and the credit risk embedded in the bond. In particular, bringing together equations (15.3) and (15.4), we obtain

$$Z_0^d(t,T) = e^{-R(t,T)(T-t)}Q(t,T) = e^{-[R(t,T)+S(t,T)](T-t)} \tag{15.16}$$

Equation (15.16) leads to a simple relation between the yield spread and the (risk-neutral) probability of no default associated with a zero-coupon, zero-recovery risky bond:

$$Q(t,T) = e^{-S(t,T)(T-t)} \tag{15.17}$$

and the reader can verify that, for values of $S(t,T)$ that are not too high, $1 - Q(t,T)$ and $S(t,T)$ will be approximately equal when the period under consideration is one year $(T-t = 1)$. More generally, the annualized default probability $\frac{1-Q(t,T)}{T-t}$ is approximately equal to the risky bond spread $S(t,T)$ when $S(t,T)$ is not too large.[9]

It is relatively straightforward to examine the relationship between yield spreads and default probabilities in coupon-bearing bonds and in bonds with nonzero recovery values. For instance, in the case of a one-year zero-coupon bond, $T-t = 1$, with a recovery value X, equation (15.4) becomes

$$Z^d(t,t+1) = Z(t,t+1)\left[Q(t,t+1) + (1 - Q(t,t+1))X\right] \tag{15.18}$$

where we dropped the 0 subscript on $Z_0^d(.)$ to indicate that this is a nonzero recovery bond.

Combining (15.18) with (15.3) leads to

$$1 - Q(t,t+1) = \frac{1 - e^{-S(t,t+1)}}{1 - X} \tag{15.19}$$

And, for $S(t,t+1)$ not too large, it can be seen that

$$1 - Q(t,t+1) \approx \frac{S(t,t+1)}{1 - X} \tag{15.20}$$

15.6   Recovery Rates

Thus far we have taken the recovery value of the bond, denoted above as X, to be a nonrandom parameter in the basic bond valuation expression

---

[9] If we had cast our default probabilities in a continuous-time framework, we would have found that the risk spread and the annualized risk-neutral default probability are one and the same in the case of no recovery value. To see this, consider the above example where one is interested in the probability of default between today's date, t, and some future date T. If λdt denotes the default probability over a short time period $[t, t + dt]$, assuming that no default has occurred before t, it can be shown that the probability of no default occurring between t and T tends to $e^{-\lambda(T-t)}$ as dt becomes infinitesimally small, assuming that λ is constant for this issuer between t and T. Thus, the default probability over the period becomes $1 - e^{-\lambda(T-t)}$, leading to the result that $S(t,T) = \lambda$. We will examine this continuous-time case in greater detail in Chapter 17.

TABLE 15.1
Historical Recovery Value Statistics (1970–1999)[a]

Seniority/ security	Min	1st quartile	Median	Mean	3rd quartile	Max	Std dev
Sr. sec. loans	15.00	60.00	75.00	69.91	88.00	98.00	23.47
Eq. trust bds	8.00	26.25	70.63	59.96	85.00	103.00	31.08
Sr. sec. bds	7.50	31.00	53.00	52.31	65.25	125.00	25.15
Sr. unsec. bds	0.50	30.75	48.00	48.84	67.00	122.60	25.01
Sr. sub. bds	0.50	21.34	35.50	39.46	53.47	123.00	24.59
Sub. bds	1.00	19.62	30.00	33.17	42.94	99.13	20.78
Jr. sub. bds	3.63	11.38	16.25	19.69	24.00	50.00	13.85
Pref. stocks	0.05	5.03	9.13	11.06	12.91	49.50	9.09

Source: Moody's Investors Service
[a]Prices of defaulted instruments approximately one month after default, expressed as a percent of the instrument's par value. Abbreviations: Eq. = equipment, Sr. = senior, sec. = secured, sub. = subordinated, Jr. = junior, pref. = preferred, bds = bonds.

in equation (15.15). Yet, the recovery value of a defaultable bond is an important source of uncertainty in the valuation process. Predicting recovery rates—the recovery value expressed as a percentage of the par value of the bond—is particularly difficult in light of the relative sparseness of the underlying default data: Despite the large number of corporate defaults in the early 2000s, defaults are still relatively rare events, which makes it harder to conduct statistical analysis and develop models of recovery values. Thus, practical applications of credit risk models often involve experimentation with a range of recovery values and reliance on the credit analyst's judgment regarding the recovery rates corresponding to particular debtors, as opposed to heavy reliance on pure statistical models of recovery.[10]

As shown in Table 15.1, extracted from Keenan, Hamilton, and Berthault (2000)[49], the data that do exist on recovery rates suggest that they can vary substantially both across and within levels of seniority and security. For instance, the table shows that, while the mean recovery rate for senior unsecured bonds over the 1970–1999 period was 48.84 percent, the corresponding standard deviation was 25.01 percent, and actual recovery rates ranged from 0.5 percent to 122.6 percent just within this level of seniority. (Recall that senior unsecured debt instruments are often specified

---

[10]In Chapter 17 we briefly review the recovery assumptions embedded in the main types of credit risk models.

as deliverable instruments in physically settled credit default swaps—see Chapter 6.)

The table also shows the outer limits of the central 50 percent of observations on recovery rates for each of the security/seniority classes—the columns labeled first and third quartiles. Again focusing on the case of senior unsecured bonds, we see that these central observations involve recovery rates ranging from 30.75 percent to 67 percent. In part, variations in recovery rates reflect differences in the capital structures of defaulting firms—e.g. public vs. private debt composition (Hamilton and Carty (1999)[38])—and the fact that recovery rates seem to have a noticeable cyclical component—they tend to be higher during good economic times and low during lean times. Nonetheless, these factors explain only a portion of the observed variation in recovery rates. The one pattern that does show through strongly in the data is that recovery rates tend to be monotonically increasing with the level of seniority and security of the debt instrument.

16

The Credit Curve

We saw in Chapter 15 that risk-neutral survival probabilities are key elements in the pricing of financial market instruments that involve credit risk. For instance, we showed that the fair market price of a defaultable bond that makes payments at the future dates T_i and T_{i+1} depends importantly on the risk-neutral probabilities $Q(t, T_i)$ and $Q(t, T_{i+1})$ that the bond issuer will not default by T_i and T_{i+1}, respectively, where these probabilities are conditional on all information available at time t and, naturally, on the issuer having survived through time t.[1] More generally, for any given issuer or reference entity, one can imagine an entire term structure of survival probabilities, which is one way of thinking of the credit curve. In simpler words, the credit curve is the relationship that tells us the risk-neutral survival probabilities of a given reference entity over various time horizons.

One can derive risk-neutral survival probabilities from the prices of liquid credit market instruments and then use such probabilities to price other, less liquid or more complex, instruments. In this chapter we describe a relatively straightforward framework for inferring survival probabilities from quoted credit default swap (CDS) premiums. We focus on three progressively simpler methods: one that can handle any shape of the term structure of CDS premiums, one built on the assumption of a flat term structure of CDS premiums, and one based on a simple rule of thumb for quick, back-of-the-envelope calculations for highly rated reference entities.

---

[1] Unless otherwise stated, all probabilities conditional on information available at time t will henceforth also be conditional on the issuer having survived through time t.

Armed with the CDS-implied credit curve for two hypothetical reference entities, Sections 16.2 and 16.3 use a simple illustrative framework to go over two practical applications. In Section 16.2 we illustrate how to mark to market an existing credit default swap position. In Section 16.3 we revisit the problem of valuing a principal-protected note (PPN), which was the subject of Chapter 11. In particular, we describe how to price a PPN based on premiums quoted in the CDS market. Section 16.4 highlights some of the limitations of the simplified methodology described in this chapter.

16.1   CDS-implied Credit Curves

Consider a CDS with a notional amount of $1, written at time t on a given reference entity, and with premium payment dates at $[T_1, T_2, \ldots, T_n]$. Let S_n be the corresponding annualized CDS premium. For simplicity, assume that, in the event of default, the protection seller will pay $1 - X$ at the premium payment date immediately following the default, where X, $0 \le X < 1$, is the recovery rate. To keep things even simpler, we will ignore the question of accrued premiums, or the fact that the protection buyer would be paying any premium accrued between the last payment date and the date of default.[2]

As seen in Chapter 6, we can think of a CDS as having two "legs": The premium leg is made up of the periodic payments made by the protection buyer; the protection leg is the default-contingent payment made by the protection seller. Given the discussion in Chapter 15, assuming that, based on risk-neutral probabilities, the occurrence of defaults is independent of the riskfree interest rate embedded in the prices of riskless bonds, the present discounted value of the premium leg can be written as:

$$\text{PV(premiums)}_t = \sum_{j=1}^{n} Z(t, T_j) Q(t, T_j) \delta_j S_n \qquad (16.1)$$

---

[2] This simplifying assumption of no accrued premiums is relatively innocuous for highly rated reference entities, but can have more significant effects for riskier entities. Typically, one addresses the issue of accrued premiums by adding half an accrual period to the premium leg of the swap, which amounts to assuming that, should a default occur, it will on average take place midway through the period. In this case, equation (16.1) would become

$$\text{PV(premiums)}_t = \sum_{j=1}^{n} Z(t, T_j) Q(t, T_j) \delta_j S_n + \sum_{j=1}^{n} Z(t, T_j) \text{Prob}_t[T_{j-1} < \tau \le T_j] \frac{\delta_j S_n}{2}$$

where τ is the time of default, and $\text{Prob}_t[.]$ denotes a risk-neutral probability conditional on all information available at time t.

where $Z(t, T_j)$ is the time-t price of a riskless zero-coupon bond that matures at T_j with a face value of \$1; $Q(t, T_j)$ is the reference entity's survival probability through time T_j, or the risk-neutral probability that the reference entity will not have defaulted by T_j; and δ_j is the accrual factor for the jth premium payment (the number of days between the $(j-1)$th and jth premium payment dates divided by the number of days in the year, based on the appropriate day-count convention).

Equation (16.1) shows that there are two elements to discounting future premiums. The logic here is similar to that in Chapter 15. When computing the present value of a future payment, first, there is the time-value of money, captured by $Z(t, T_j)$, and, second, one must take account of the fact that a future premium due, say, at T_j will only be received if the reference entity has not defaulted by then, and, conditional on all information available at time t, the risk-neutral probability of that happening is $Q(t, T_j)$.[3]

The present value of the protection leg can be written in a similar way:

$$\mathrm{PV(protection)}_t = \sum_{j=1}^{n} Z(t, T_j)\mathrm{Prob}_t[T_{j-1} < \tau \leq T_j](1 - X) \qquad (16.2)$$

where τ is the time of default, and $\mathrm{Prob}_t[T_{j-1} < \tau \leq T_j]$ denotes the probability, conditional on information available at time t, that the reference entity will default between T_{j-1} and T_j. The intuition behind (16.2) is clear: One does not know whether and when a default will occur, but there is some probability $\mathrm{Prob}_t[T_{j-1} < \tau \leq T_j]$ that the reference entity will default during the interval $[T_{j-1}, T_j]$, in which case the protection seller would have to pay $1 - X$ at T_j, which is worth $Z(t, T_j)(1 - X)$ in today's dollars. As a result, the present value of the protection leg of the CDS is the probability-weighted sum of all possible default scenarios.

From Chapter 15, equation (15.13), we know that we can rewrite (16.2) as

$$\mathrm{PV(protection)}_t = \sum_{j=1}^{n} Z(t, T_j)[Q(t, T_{j-1}) - Q(t, T_j)](1 - X) \qquad (16.3)$$

16.1.1 Implied Survival Probabilities

It typically costs nothing to enter into a standard CDS so it must be that S_n is such that the expected present discounted value of the premiums paid by the protection buyer equals the expected present discounted value

---

[3] In this part of the book we sidestep the issue of counterparty credit risk, or the fact that the protection seller may default on its obligations under the CDS agreement. We will revisit this issue in Part IV.

of the protection payment made by protection seller. We can then equate the expressions in (16.1) and (16.3) and solve for the probabilities $Q(t, T_j)$. In particular, after some manipulation, we can write:

$$Q(t, T_n) = \frac{\sum_{j=1}^{n-1} Z(t, T_j)[LQ(t, T_{j-1}) - (L + \delta_j S_n)Q(t, T_j)]}{Z(t, T_n)(L + \delta_n S_n)}$$

$$+ \frac{Q(t, T_{n-1})L}{(L + \delta_n S_n)} \tag{16.4}$$

where $L \equiv (1 - X)$.

Suppose now that you observe CDS premium quotes for a reference entity covering all dates involved in the above expression, i.e., the markets tell you the vector $[S_1, S_2, \ldots, S_n]$.[4] From (16.4), and for a given recovery rate, X, it can be shown that

$$Q(t, T_1) = \frac{L}{L + \delta_1 S_1}$$

and the other survival probabilities can be computed recursively. For instance, given the value for $Q(t, T_1)$ implied by S_1, as well as the term structure of riskless discount rates, $Z(t, T_i)$,

$$Q(t, T_2) = \frac{Z(t, T_1)[L - (L + \delta_1 S_2)Q(t, T_1)]}{Z(t, T_2)(L + \delta_2 S_2)} + \frac{Q(t, T_1)L}{(L + \delta_2 S_2)}$$

Of course, given the survival probabilities $Q(t, T_n)$, $n = 1, 2, \ldots$, we can compute probabilities of default within specific horizons. For instance, the probability of default before period T_n is trivially given by $1 - Q(t, T_n)$.

At this point we should make one additional remark about the above method for computing survival probabilities from quoted credit default swap premiums. Note that the expression for the survival probabilities involves the riskfree discount factors $Z(t, T_i)$, for $i = 1, 2, \ldots, n$, which are meant to represent only the time value of money. In practice, however, these discount factors are often derived from the term structure of LIBOR and swap rates, which corresponds to the funding costs of the main participants

---

[4]In a more realistic situation, the observed CDS premiums may not exactly correspond to the ones in expression (16.4). For instance, premiums may be quoted only for contracts maturing at dates T_1, T_3, T_5, etc. In practice, what one can do in these cases is to use interpolation methods to obtain premiums for the desired maturities from the ones actually seen in the marketplace. Interpolation methods are widely used in the context of yield curve modeling. See, e.g., the book by James and Webber (2000)[44] and the several references therein.

of the credit default swap market.[5] This is consistent with the practice of interpreting CDS premiums and asset swap spreads as being roughly analogous to the yield spread of a risky floater issued by the reference entity over a floater that pays out LIBOR flat (see Chapter 6).

16.1.2   Examples

We shall illustrate the derivation of CDS-implied default probabilities using two numerical examples. Figure 16.1 shows the term structure of CDS

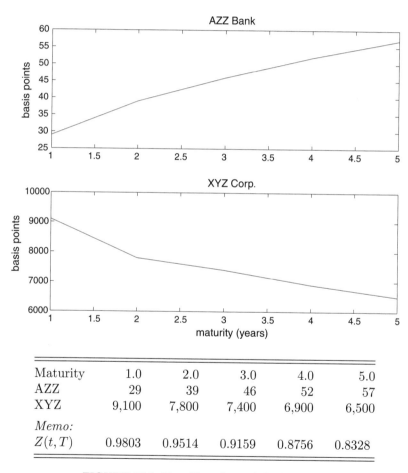

Maturity	1.0	2.0	3.0	4.0	5.0
AZZ	29	39	46	52	57
XYZ	9,100	7,800	7,400	6,900	6,500
Memo:					
$Z(t,T)$	0.9803	0.9514	0.9159	0.8756	0.8328

FIGURE 16.1. Two Hypothetical CDS Curves

---

[5]Hull (2003)[41] describes a simple approach for obtaining zero-coupon bond prices, $Z(t,T_i)$, from yields on coupon-paying riskless bonds. See also Appendix A in this book.

TABLE 16.1
Implied Survival Probabilities over Various Time Horizons
(percent)

Horizon	AZZ Bank	XYZ Corp.
One year	99.42	49.72
Two years	98.45	30.60
Three years	97.26	18.87
Four years	95.88	14.10
Five years	94.37	11.52

Note. Assumed recovery rates: AZZ Bank, 50 percent; XYZ Corp., 10 percent.

premiums for two hypothetical reference entities at opposite ends of the credit spectrum: AZZ Bank, which is assumed to be a highly rated institution, and XYZ Corp., a corporation that is seen as very likely to default in the near term.

For simplicity, we assume that the premiums in both agreements are paid once a year ($\delta_j = 1$ for all j). As can be seen in the figure, while the five-year CDS premium for AZZ Bank is under 60 basis points, that for XYZ Corp. is assumed to be 6,500 basis points. Also noteworthy is the pronounced negative slope of the XYZ Corp. curve, which is typical of companies perceived to have a high likelihood of default. The quotes plotted are shown in the table at the bottom of the figure so that the reader can verify the calculations that follow.

Table 16.1 shows implied survival probabilities for AZZ Bank and XYZ Corp. over the next five years, computed as in equation (16.4) and based on zero-coupon bond prices shown in the memo line in the table at the bottom of Figure 16.1. Judged from the perspective of CDS market participants, the risk-neutral odds that XYZ Corp. will still be around in one year's time are about even, whereas the corresponding risk-neutral probability for AZZ Bank is nearly 100 percent. Over the five-year horizon, the survival probabilities fall to almost 95 percent for AZZ Bank and 11.5 percent for XYZ Corp.

As indicated in the footnote in the table, these calculations assume recovery rates of 50 percent and 10 percent for AZZ Bank and XYZ Corp., respectively. We will examine how the results would differ under different recovery rates in what follows.

16.1.3 Flat CDS Curve Assumption

The calculation of implied survival probabilities simplifies substantially if one is willing to assume a flat CDS curve. In particular, the survival

TABLE 16.2
Implied Survival Probabilities over Various Time Horizons
under Flat CDS Curve Assumption
(percent)

Horizon	AZZ Bank	XYZ Corp.
One year	98.87	58.06
Two years	97.76	33.71
Three years	96.66	19.58
Four years	95.57	11.37
Five years	94.49	6.60

Note. Assumed recovery rates: AZZ Bank, 50 percent; XYZ
Corp., 10 percent.

probability $Q(t, T_n)$ reduces to $Q(t, T_1)^n$. (The reader can verify this by
going back to the derivation of $Q(t, T_2)$ in Section 16.1.1.)

As can be seen in Table 16.2, despite the fact that the "true" curves for
AZZ Bank and XYZ Corp. are non-flat, the flat curve assumption generates
survival probabilities that are not too far off the ones shown in Table 16.1.
The calculations in Table 16.2 assume that the credit curves of AZZ Bank
and XYZ Corp. are flat at their respective five-year CDS premium levels
and thus the survival probabilities for XYZ Corp., which has the steepest
CDS curve, are affected the most by the flat curve assumption.

16.1.4   A Simple Rule of Thumb

From the calculations done above, and assuming flat CDS curves with
premiums equal to the five-year quotes shown in Figure 16.1, we have that
the probability of default by T_1 is

$$1 - Q(t, T_1) = 1 - \frac{1 - X}{1 - X + S_5} \approx \frac{S_5}{1 - X} \qquad (16.5)$$

and thus we can approximately think of the CDS premium as a measure
of the probability of default over the next year under the assumption of
no recovery. Close inspection of equation (16.5), however, shows that the
goodness of this approximation hinges on S_5 being small enough, a topic
that we also discussed in the context of equation (15.20). Indeed, while this
rule of thumb would place the probability of default by AZZ Bank within
the next year at 1.14 percent, which is close to the number based on the flat
credit curve assumption, the corresponding number for XYZ Corp. would
be about 72 percent, compared to 42 percent in the flat curve scenario.

TABLE 16.3
Implied Survival Probabilities for AZZ Bank over Various Time
Horizons and under Alternative Recovery Rate Assumptions
(percent)

Horizon	$X = 0.20$	$X = 0.50$	$X = 0.65$
One year	99.64	99.42	99.18
Two years	99.03	98.45	97.80
Three years	98.28	97.26	96.12
Four years	97.40	95.88	94.17
Five years	96.44	94.37	92.06

16.1.5   Sensitivity to Recovery Rate Assumptions

Table 16.3 shows how the survival probabilities for AZZ Bank are affected
by alternative recovery rate assumptions. Because there is great uncertainty
surrounding actual recovery rates in the event of default, implied survival
probabilities are sometimes best reported in terms of ranges corresponding
to alternative values of the recovery rate. The differences in the results
reported in the table would be more dramatic for lower-rated reference
entities.

16.2   Marking to Market a CDS Position

Although a credit default swap agreement typically has zero market value
at its inception, that generally does not remain true throughout the life
of the agreement, especially as the credit quality of the reference entity
may change. Marking a CDS position to market is the act of determining
today's value of a CDS agreement that was entered into at some time in
the past.

One can use equations (16.1) and (16.3) to write an explicit expression
for the value of a CDS contract to a protection buyer:

$$V^{CDS}(t, T_n) = \sum_{j=1}^{n} Z(t, T_j)[Q(t, T_{j-1}) - Q(t, T_j)](1 - X)$$

$$- \sum_{j=1}^{n} Z(t, T_j)Q(t, T_j)\delta_j S_n$$

$$= \sum_{j=1}^{n} Z(t, T_j)\{[Q(t, T_{j-1}) - Q(t, T_j)](1 - X) - Q(t, T_j)\delta_j S_n\}$$

$$(16.6)$$

where the first term to the right of the first equal sign is simply the expected present value of the protection payment that the seller has committed to make in the event of a default by the reference entity, and the second term is the expected present value of the stream of future premium payments owed under the contract. The value of the contract to the protection seller is simply the negative of this expression.

Consider now a credit default swap that was written on XYZ Corp.—one of the hypothetical reference entities examined in the previous section. The contract was entered into exactly one year ago with an original maturity of five years. Today's CDS quotes for XYZ Corp. are shown in the table at the bottom of Figure 16.1. Let us imagine that XYZ Corp. was perceived to have a substantially more favorable profit outlook one year ago (and hence higher survival probabilities) than today. As a result, we assume that the CDS premium that was written into the year-old contract is 500 basis points, as opposed to the 6,500 basis points demanded by protection sellers today.

Given the significant deterioration in the prospects for XYZ Corp., the protection seller in the year-old contract is collecting a premium that is well below the going market rate. This contract then has negative market value to the seller of protection. The protection buyer, on the other hand, is holding a contract with positive market value as she is paying only 500 basis points per year per dollar of notional amount while a brand new contract with the same remaining maturity would command an annual premium of 6,900 basis points per dollar of notional amount.

How can we value the year-old contract? One approach is simply to derive the survival probabilities $Q(.)$ implied by the current CDS premiums for XYZ Corp. (as we did in Section 16.1) and to put them into equation (16.6), along with the riskfree discount factors, the assumed recovery rate, and the premium written into the contract. A simpler approach is to think of the problem of valuing the year-old contract as that of computing its "replacement cost." In particular, how much would it cost to replace the year-old contract, which now has a remaining maturity of four years, with a brand new four-year contract? To put it simply,

$$\text{replacement cost} = \text{value of new contract} - \text{value of old contract} \quad (16.7)$$

where, given that the value of the new contract is zero by construction, the replacement cost of the old contract is simply the negative of its market value. The values of the old and new contracts—denoted below as V_t^{old} and V_t^{new}—can be written as

$$V_t^{old} = \sum_{j=1}^{4} Z(t, T_j)\{[Q(t, T_{j-1}) - Q(t, T_j)](1 - X) - Q(t, T_j)\delta_j S_o\}$$

$$(16.8)$$

$$V_t^{new} = \sum_{j=1}^{4} Z(t, T_j)\{[Q(t, T_{j-1}) - Q(t, T_j)](1 - X) - Q(t, T_j)\delta_j S_n\}$$

(16.9)

where S_o and S_n are the premiums written into the old and new contracts, respectively.

Substituting equations (16.8) and (16.9) into (16.7) we arrive at the result that we can write the market value of the year-old contract as a function of the difference between the premium written in that contract and the four-year premium currently quoted in the marketplace:

$$V_t^{old} = \sum_{j=1}^{4} Z(t, T_j)Q(t, T_j)\delta_j[S_n - S_o]$$

(16.10)

which is a simpler expression than (16.6).

To sum up, to mark to market an existing CDS position one can rely on current CDS premiums to obtain implied survival probabilities, as described in Section 16.1, and use either (16.6) or (16.10) to determine the market value of the position. Either way, the year-old CDS contract written on XYZ Corp. with an original maturity of five years would now be worth 68.8 cents per dollar of notional amount to the protection buyer or about $6.9 million for a contract with a notional amount of $10 million![6]

16.3 Valuing a Principal-protected Note

Credit default swaps have become so liquid for certain reference entities that prices quoted in the CDS market are often used as the basis for valuing other credit-based instruments that reference those entities. In this section we illustrate how this can be done when valuing a principal-protected note (PPN), a credit market instrument that we discussed in Chapter 11. We will continue to work with the two examples introduced in Section 16.1.

As we saw in Chapter 11, a PPN is a coupon-paying note written on a particular reference entity and sold to an investor by a highly rated third party. In its simplest form, the note guarantees the return of its face value at its maturity date, even if the reference entity has defaulted in its obligations by then. The coupon payments themselves are stopped in the

---

[6]Note that, in the example considered here, S_o is the premium written into the year-old contract and S_n is the going premium for a four-year CDS contract written on XYZ Corp. (6,900 basis points, according to the table in Figure 16.1).

event of default by the reference entity. In Chapter 11 we examined a fixed-coupon PPN and showed that one can think of it as a portfolio consisting of a riskless zero-coupon bond and a risky annuity that pays a fixed coupon

$$\text{PPN} = \text{Riskless zero-coupon bond} + \text{Risky annuity} \qquad (16.11)$$

where the payments made by the annuity are contingent on the reference entity remaining solvent during the life of the PPN.

In practice, the price of the embedded riskless zero-coupon bond may be derived directly from the swap curve, which incorporates the credit quality of the AA-rated entities that are major sellers of PPNs. Valuing the above described PPN then essentially means determining the coupon that will be paid by the risky annuity. To see this, we can go back to equation (11.3) and recast it in terms of the notation introduced in Chapter 15.

$$V^{PPN}(t, T_n) = \left[Z(t, T_n) + \sum_{j=1}^{n} Z(t, T_j)Q(t, T_j)\delta_j RPPN \right] F \qquad (16.12)$$

where t and T_n are, respectively, today's date and the maturity date of the PPN, and the vector $[T_1, T_2, \ldots, T_n]$ contains the coupon payment dates of the PPN in the case of no default by the reference entity. F is the face value of the PPN, and $RPPN$ is its coupon rate. Two key points are worth emphasizing here about equation (16.12): $Z(t, T_n)$ corresponds to the credit quality of the PPN issuer (or a riskfree rate if the issuer poses no counterparty credit risk) and $Q(t, T_j)$ corresponds to the survival probabilities of the reference entity (*not* the PPN issuer).

PPNs are typically issued at their par value so pricing a brand new PPN amounts to finding the value of $RPPN$ that makes $V^{PPN}(t, T_n)$ in (16.12) equal to F. This is simply

$$RPPN = \frac{1 - Z(t, T_n)}{\sum_{j=1}^{n} Z(t, T_j)Q(t, T_j)\delta_j} \qquad (16.13)$$

16.3.1 Examples

Suppose we want to price a family of PPNs written on the hypothetical reference entities introduced at the beginning of this chapter. (Each "family" references only a single reference entity.) For simplicity, we assume that the notes pay coupons annually and that no accrued interest is paid in the event of default by the reference entity.

The table in the bottom of Figure 16.1 has all the information we need to conduct the valuation exercise just described. In particular, using the

TABLE 16.4
CDS-implied Coupons on
Principal-protected Notes

Maturity (years)	AZZ Bank (percent)	XYZ Corp.
1	2.02	4.04
2	2.54	6.24
3	3.00	8.84
4	3.41	11.57
5	3.78	14.28

Note. Assumed recovery rates: AZZ Bank, 50 percent; XYZ Corp., 10 percent.

method described in Section 16.1, we can rely on the CDS premiums and zero-coupon bond prices shown in that table to obtain the survival probabilities of the reference entities (Table 16.1). Armed with these probabilities, obtaining the coupons on the five-year PPNs written on AZZ Bank and XYZ Corp. is simply a matter of using the appropriate values on the right side of equation (16.13). Table 16.4 shows the resulting term structures of PPN coupons for AZZ Bank and XYZ Corp.

16.3.2   PPNs vs. Vanilla Notes

Just as we used CDS-implied survival probabilities to value PPNs of various maturities, we can obtain a CDS-implied term structure of coupons on vanilla fixed-rate notes issued by the AZZ Bank and XYZ Corp. directly. According to equation (15.15), and assuming that these notes are sold at par, the fair value of such coupons is given by

$$C = \frac{[1 - Z(t, T_n)Q(t, T_n)] - \sum_{j=1}^{n} Z(t, T_j)[Q(t, T_{j-1}) - Q(t, T_j)]X}{\sum_{j=1}^{n} Z(t, T_j)Q(t, T_j)\delta_j}$$

(16.14)

where, again, F is the par value of the notes.

Figure 16.2 shows the term structures of principal-protected and vanilla fixed-rate notes that reference AZZ Bank and XYZ Corp. As one would expect, investors have to give up some yield in order to obtain the principal-protection feature. The figure also shows that the spread between PPN and vanilla yields is wider for lower-rated entities, consistent with the intuition that principal protection is more highly valued for riskier entities than for relatively safe firms such as AZZ Bank.

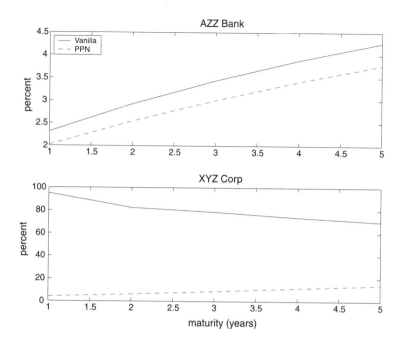

FIGURE 16.2. Implied Term Structure of Coupons on Principal-protected and
Vanilla Notes
Note. Assumed recovery rates: AZZ Bank, 50 percent; XYZ Corp.,
10 percent.

16.4   Other Applications and Some Caveats

The examples examined in this chapter illustrated several practical applications of credit curves, ranging from using CDS-implied survival probabilities to determine the fair values of coupons on principal protected
notes to marking existing CDS positions to market. Other uses include
relative-value trading, such as taking long and short positions in two
related instruments based on the view that existing discrepancies in their
valuations—as implied, say, by survival probabilities derived from CDS
quotes—will dissipate in the near future.

As we saw in Section 6.3, however, the real world rarely behaves exactly
as dictated by results reported in textbooks. Factors such as accrued
interest, liquidity, and market segmentation still very much drive wedges
between the prices of otherwise closely related credit instruments. As a
result, not only do market participants rely on more complex versions of
the simple illustrative framework described in this chapter, but they also
use their judgment and experience to assess current and prospective market
conditions when working with the credit curve of any given reference entity.

17

Main Credit Modeling Approaches

In this chapter we review and summarize the credit risk literature with a special focus on the main modeling approaches for valuing instruments subject to default risk. Section 17.1 summarizes the so-called firm value or structural approach to credit modeling, which traces its origins to the work of Black and Scholes (1973)[9] and Merton (1974)[59]. Credit models in this tradition focus on the analysis of the capital structure of individual firms in order to price their debt instruments. The discussion of the structural approach relies on some basic results regarding vanilla call and put options. Most of these results are discussed only at an intuitive level in this chapter. Readers interested in additional detail on the pricing of such options are encouraged to consult, for instance, the books by Baxter and Rennie (2001)[6] and Wilmott, Dewynne, and Howison (1999)[74], which provide excellent introductions to option pricing.

The reduced-form or default-intensity-based approach is addressed in Section 17.2, where we discuss models based on the seminal work of Jarrow and Turnbull (1995)[46]. The reduced-form approach does not directly attempt to link defaults to the capital structure of the firm. Instead, it models defaults to be exogenous stochastic events. Work in this strand of the credit risk literature is primarily interested in developing essentially statistical models for the probability of default over different time horizons.

In Section 17.3 we briefly compare the structural and reduced-form approaches, both on methodological and empirical grounds. That section also highlights the main thrust of a "hybrid" approach—motivated by the work of Duffie and Lando (2001)[23]—that incorporates elements of

both the structural and reduced-form approaches. The chapter concludes
with Section 17.4, where we outline the basic tenets of the ratings-based
approach to credit modeling.

17.1   Structural Approach

To understand the essence of the structural approach to credit modeling we
will discuss the theoretical framework first proposed by Black and Scholes
(1973)[9] and Merton (1974)[59]. Later on, we shall address some of the
most important extensions of this basic framework.

17.1.1   The Black-Scholes-Merton Model

Consider a hypothetical firm with a very simple capital structure: one zero-
coupon bond with face value K and maturity T and one equity share. In
keeping with the notation introduced in Chapter 15, let $Z^d(t, T)$ denote
the time-t price of a bond maturing at time T with a face value of \$1.
As a result, the price of the bond with face value K is $Z^d(t, T)K$. (We
are dropping the 0 subscript on $Z_0^d(t, T)$ to emphasize that this will not
generally be a zero-recovery bond.) To represent the market value of the
equity share, we shall introduce a new variable, $E(t)$, where limited liability
implies that the market value of equity cannot be negative.

The assumption of only one share and one bond is not restrictive. More
generally, one can think of K as being the total value of the firm's debt,
where all debt is in the form of zero-coupon bonds maturing at time T, and
of E as corresponding to the total value of the shares issued by the firm.

By way of the basic market value identity, which states that the market
value of the shareholder's equity is equal to the difference between the
market value of the assets and liabilities of the firm, we can write:

$$A(t) = E(t) + Z^d(t, T)K \qquad (17.1)$$

where $A(t)$ stands for the market value of the assets of the firm.

The basic idea behind the Black-Scholes-Merton (BSM) model is very
straightforward. Default is quite simply defined as a situation where, at
time T, when the firm's debt, K, becomes due, the value of the firm's
assets, $A(T)$, falls short of K:

$$\text{default} \Leftrightarrow A(T) < K \qquad (17.2)$$

Figure 17.1 illustrates the main points of the model. The figure shows the
evolution of the value of the firm over time. For as long as A remains above

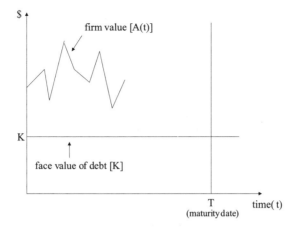

FIGURE 17.1. Simple Illustration of the Black-Scholes-Merton Model

K at T, the firm does not default. Under such circumstances, the firm's creditors receive K and the shareholders get to keep the residual $A(T) - K$. Should $A(T)$ fall short of K at time T, however, the firm defaults, with the creditors taking over the firm, receiving its full value $A(T)$, and the shareholders receiving nothing.

Thus, the debtholders either receive K or $A(T)$, whichever is lower. If we let $Z^d(T,T)K$ denote the amount that the debtholders actually receive at time T, the debtholder's payout at time T can be written as

$$Z^d(T,T)K = K - \text{Max}(K - A(T), 0) \tag{17.3}$$

As for the shareholders, they either receive $A(T) - K$ or nothing at time T. Their payoff at time T can be more succinctly written as

$$E(T) = \text{Max}(A(T) - K, 0) \tag{17.4}$$

Equations (17.2) through (17.4) summarize some of the key implications of the simple BSM framework. Examining (17.2) first, we can see that, in the context of the model, the default probability associated with this hypothetical firm is simply given by the probability that A will be lower than K at time T:

$$\text{default probability} = \text{Prob}_t[A(T) < K] \tag{17.5}$$

where, as in previous chapters, we are interested in risk-neutral probabilities. In particular, $\text{Prob}_t[.]$ denotes a risk-neutral probability conditional on all available information at t and on the firm having survived through t.

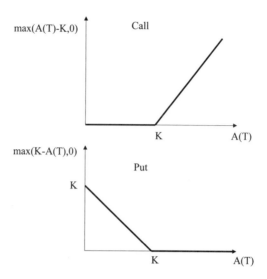

FIGURE 17.2. Payoffs of Long Positions in Vanilla Call and Put Options

In addition, from (17.2) we can also infer that the recovery value of the bond upon default is simply A:

$$\text{recovery value of defaulted bond} = A(T) \qquad (17.6)$$

which corresponds to a recovery rate in the event of default of $A(T)/K$. Thus, we have just shown how we can use this simple structural model to revisit two familiar credit concepts discussed in Chapter 15: default probabilities and recovery rates.

Turning now to equations (17.3) and (17.4), it can be shown that they lend themselves to an option-theoretic approach to the valuation of default-able bonds and equities. This is a key insight of the BSM model. For instance, upon closer inspection of $\text{Max}(K - A(T), 0)$, the last term on the right-hand side of (17.3), one can see that this corresponds to the payout of a put option written on the value of the firm's assets, where the strike price of the option is K. This is shown in the lower panel of Figure 17.2. In particular, the holder of this option would stand to gain if A were to fall below K by time T, which can be thought of as the expiration date of the option. But this expression appears with a negative sign in (17.3), which implies that, rather than being the holder of such a put, the debtholder wrote the option. Thus, one can think of the debtholder's position as being equivalent to a portfolio composed of a long position in a riskless zero-coupon bond with a face value of K and a short position in the just-described put option.

To sum up:

$$\text{defaultable bond} = \text{riskless bond} - \text{put option on } A \qquad (17.7)$$

Thus, if we let $p(T, A(T); T, K)$ denote the value of the put option at T, we can use equation (17.7) to write the following relationship between the market value of the firm's debt and that of the embedded put option:

$$Z^d(T, T)K = K - p(T, A(T); T, K) \qquad (17.8)$$

and, expressing this relationship in terms of time-t prices, we obtain:

$$Z^d(t, T)K = e^{-R(t,T)(T-t)}K - p(t, A(t); T, K)$$
$$= Z(t, T)K - p(t, A(t); T, K) \qquad (17.9)$$

which is an expression for the price of a defaultable bond under the BSM model.[1]

We have just shown that the debtholders' position is equivalent to being long a riskless bond and short a put option written on the value of the firm. But who bought this put option? The shareholders implicitly did. To see this first note that a quick look at (17.4) will reveal that what we have on the right-hand side of that equation is essentially the payout of a call option written on A, struck at K (see the upper panel of Figure 17.2). Thus

$$\text{equity share} = \text{call option on } A \qquad (17.10)$$

But now note that the payout of that call can be rewritten as:

$$E(T) = \text{Max}(A(T) - K, 0) = A(T) - K + \text{Max}(K - A(T), 0)$$

Thus, in the absence of arbitrage opportunities, for any $t < T$ we can write:

$$E(t) = A(t) - e^{-R(t,T)(T-t)}K + p(t, A(t); T, K) \qquad (17.11)$$

which establishes that the shareholders' position can also be thought of as including a long position on a put option written on the value of the firm, a put that they implicitly bought from the bondholders.[2]

---

[1] As discussed in Chapter 15, $R(t, T)$ is the time-t yield to maturity on a riskless zero-coupon bond that will mature at time T with a face value of $1.

[2] Readers familiar with basic option pricing theory will recognize equation (17.11) as the so-called put-call parity condition, which can be shown to be true regardless of

To derive model-implied risk spreads, recall that the yield to maturity, $R^d(t, T)$, on the zero-coupon bond issued by the firm is such that

$$Z^d(t, T) = e^{-R^d(t,T)(T-t)}$$

Thus:

$$R^d(t, T) = -\frac{1}{T-t} \log \left[Z^d(t, T) \right] \qquad (17.12)$$

and the credit spread is trivially given by $R^d(t, T) - R(t, T)$.

Equation (17.9) implies that the higher the value of the put option implicitly sold by the bondholder to the shareholder, the wider the gap between the prices of the defaultable and riskfree bonds and, equivalently, the wider the corresponding credit spread. In terms of risk-neutral probabilities, a high value of $p(.)$ suggests that the put option is more likely to be exercised than otherwise, which, in this context, amounts to saying that the firm is more likely to default. Thus, according to this model, issuers of defaultable bonds pay yields that are higher than those on otherwise comparable riskless bonds because such issuers are implicitly buying a put option on the value of their firms, and the value of that option is higher the lower is the credit quality of the firm.

17.1.2   Solving the Black-Scholes-Merton Model

Thus far we have discussed a few key results based on the Black-Scholes-Merton framework, but we have not actually solved the model. For instance, we have used the model to argue that the bondholder is essentially short a put option on the value of the firm, but we have not derived the price of this option or shown explicitly how that price, and thus the firm's credit spread, relates to the capital structure of the firm. Indeed, up until now all of the results we have derived—default probabilities, recovery value, risky bond prices and spreads, etc.—depend importantly on A, the value of the firm, but the evolution of A itself has not yet been addressed.

A central assumption in the BSM framework is that, based on actual (not necessarily risk-neutral) probabilities, $A(t)$ evolves continuously over time following a geometric Brownian motion:

$$\frac{dA(t)}{A(t)} = \mu dt + \sigma dW(t) \qquad (17.13)$$

---

how we model the evolution of A—see, for instance, Wilmott, Howison, and Dewynne (1999)[74].

where $dW(t)$ is an infinitesimal increment in a standard Brownian motion, and μ and σ are constants that primarily determine the average (trend) rate of growth and the volatility of $A(t)$, respectively.[3]

It can be shown that (17.13) implies that the firm value is lognormally distributed, which greatly simplifies the derivation of explicit formulas for all the quantities discussed in the previous section. For instance, the well-known Black-Scholes formula for the price of a put option, which is derived under the assumption of lognormality of the price of the underlying, is given by[4]

$$p(t, A(t); T, K, \sigma) = Ke^{-r(T-t)}N(-d_2) - A(t)N(-d_1) \qquad (17.14)$$

with

$$d_1 \equiv \frac{\log(A(t)/K) + (r + \sigma^2/2)(T-t)}{\sigma\sqrt{T-t}} \qquad (17.15)$$

$$d_2 \equiv d_1 - \sigma\sqrt{T-t} \qquad (17.16)$$

where, for simplicity, we have assumed that the term structure of riskless interest rates is flat and constant, i.e.,

$$R(t, T) = r \ \text{ for all } t \text{ and } T$$

where r is the instantaneous riskless rate of interest.[5]

It can be shown that the price of the put option, and consequently the firm's credit spread, is increasing in

$$\frac{e^{-r(T-t)}K}{A(t)}$$

---

[3] Intuitively, the reader who is not familiar with continuous time processes can think of (17.13) loosely as the continuous time analog of the following discrete process:

$$\frac{A_{t+\delta t} - A_t}{A_t} = \mu \delta t + \sigma \epsilon_{t+\delta t}$$

where ϵ is a zero-mean normally distributed variable with variance δt. This naive discretization of (17.13) is not exact, however, and is featured in this footnote only as a reference point to the novice reader. Hull (2003)[41] and Mikosch (1999)[60] provide accessible discussions of continuous-time results that are central to the pricing of options.

[4] Textbook-like derivations of the Black-Scholes formula abound. See, for instance, Baxter and Rennie (2001)[6] and Wilmott et al. (1999)[74]. Appendix B provides a brief summary of the lognormal distribution.

[5] Appendix A contains a discussion of basic concepts in bond math.

which can be interpreted as the firm's leverage ratio. This is consistent with one's intuition, in that more highly leveraged firms tend to face wider credit spreads.

17.1.3 Practical Implementation of the Model

Armed with the theoretical results discussed thus far, one might now be eager to use the model with real data. It turns out, however, that taking the model to the data is generally not a trivial matter. For instance, in the real world, a firm's liabilities are not just made up by zero-coupon bonds. In addition, balance-sheet information can sometimes be noisy indicators of the true state of the firm, a phenomenon that became patently clear with the events surrounding the Enron and WorldCom corporations in 2001 and 2002 in the United States.[6]

It should also be noted that the very same variable that plays a central role in the BSM model, the value of the firm (A), is not observed in practice. Thus, even for a hypothetical firm with the simple debt structure assumed in the basic BSM model, one is still presented with data challenges. What one does observe are daily fluctuations in share prices of the firm and the book value of the firm's liabilities (typically at a quarterly frequency). As the number of shares outstanding for a given firm is commonly a known quantity, one can then estimate the market capitalization of the firm or the value of its equity. Given estimates of the equity value, as well as the model-implied result that this value should be equal to the price of a call option on the value of the firm, one can back out the implied values of A and σ for a given assumption for the stochastic process for the value of the firm.[7]

17.1.4 Extensions and Empirical Validation

Major contributions to the structural approach to credit risk modeling include the treatment of coupon-bearing bonds—Geske (1977)[30] and Geske and Johnson (1984)[31]—and the incorporation of stochastic riskless rates into the framework—Shimko, Tejima, and van Deventer (1993)[72].

The BSM framework has also been extended into the class of so-called "first-passage" models, which include the work of Black and Cox (1976)[10], Leland (1994)[53], Longstaff and Schwartz (1995)[56], and others. These models address one limitation of the original BSM framework, which only

---

[6] Even in the absence of accounting fraud, corporate balance sheets may not reveal the entire state of a firm. For instance, "balance-sheet noise" may be introduced by ambiguities in certain accounting definitions.

[7] Backing out $A(t)$ from equity prices involves some technical steps that go beyond the scope of this introductory book. For more on this see, e.g., Duffie and Singleton (2003)[25].

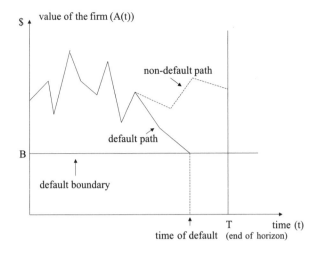

FIGURE 17.3. A Simple First-passage Model

allows for defaults to occur at the maturity date of the underlying debt. In addition, they allow for a more general treatment of the default boundary, which no longer necessarily corresponds to the face value of the firm's debt. For instance, Leland (1994)[53] models the default boundary as being the outcome of equity holders' efforts to maximize the value of their stake in the firm.

Some of the basic features of first-passage models are illustrated in Figure 17.3. Defaults are now assumed to occur at the first time that the value of the firm, $A(t)$, crosses the "default boundary," B. In contrast, in the basic characterization of the BSM framework, a default, if any, could only occur at the maturity date of the firm's debt. Figure 17.3 depicts two possible paths for $A(t)$, one where $A(t)$ never falls to B before the end of the time horizon, T—labeled a non-default path—and one where $A(t)$ crosses the boundary—labeled a default path. We will review a simple first-passage model in the next section.

A well-known offshoot of the BSM framework is the commercially available KMV model, an analytical tool provided by Moody's KMV. This model uses a large proprietary database of defaults to compute default probabilities for individual issuers—see Crosbie (2002)[16]. Similar to the simple BSM setup, the KMV model looks at equity market volatility and prices to infer the volatility and level of the firm's value, which provide a measure of the distance to default—or how far, in terms of standard deviations σ of its value A, the firm is from its default boundary K in Figure 17.1. Using proprietary methods, Moody's KMV then translates the distance from default into "expected default frequencies," which is how

Moody's KMV calls its estimator of default probabilities over a one-year horizon.

The empirical evidence on structural models is not conclusive and has focused on a model's implications for both the shape of the credit spread curve and its level. For instance, Jones, Mason, and Rosenfeld (1984)[48] reported that the BSM model tended to overprice corporate bonds (under-predict credit spreads), but Delianedis and Geske (1998)[20] found that BSM-style models have predictive power for rating migrations and defaults. The lack of consensus among empirical researchers reflects both the fact that there are different types of structural models—some have more plausible empirical implications than others—as well as data problems, such as the relative illiquidity of many corporate bonds, which makes it harder to obtain meaningful market quotes.

Intuitively, the empirical finding that the BSM framework has a tendency to generate credit spreads that are too low relative to observed spreads, especially at the short end of the credit spread curve, can be thought of as stemming from a feature that is at the very core of many structural models. In particular, the traditional forms of both the basic BSM and first-passage models assume that the value of the firm evolves as in equation (17.13), which, from a technical standpoint, implies that $A(t)$ has continuous trajectories and is thus not subject to jumps. As a result, if the value of the firm is sufficiently above the default barrier, the probability that it will suddenly touch the barrier over the very near term is virtually zero and very small for short maturities, regardless of the creditworthiness of the firm. Hence, the likelihood of a near-term default by a firm that is not in financial distress is virtually zero, and so is the firm's near-term credit spread implied by the model. Indeed, regarding the shape of the credit spread curve for a firm that is not in financial distress, traditional structural models tend to suggest that the curve starts at or near zero at the very short end and then typically roughly follows a hump-shaped pattern as the horizon under consideration is lengthened. In contrast, empirical studies suggest that short-term spreads are generally a fair amount above zero, and that it is not at all uncommon for credit spread curves to be flat or even downward sloping.[8]

One extension to the basic BSM model that was largely motivated by the desire to generate a better fit between model-implied and observed credit spread curves is the work of Zhou (1997)[76]. Zhou assumed that the dynamics of the value of the firm has two components: a continuous component that is similar to that assumed in the traditional BSM and first-passage models, and a discontinuous "jump" component, which, as the name suggests, allows the value of the firm to change suddenly and

---

[8] See, for instance, Fons (1994)[29] and Sarig and Warga (1989)[69].

unexpectedly by a sizable amount. Because of the possibility that a jump may occur at any time, so-called jump-diffusion models do not necessarily have the property that near-term credit spreads are implausibly low. Indeed, credit spread curves implied by such models can have a variety of shapes, including upward-sloping, hump-shaped, and inverted.

17.1.5   Credit Default Swap Valuation

We will use a simple extension of the basic BSM model, a first-passage model with a fixed default boundary, to illustrate the pricing of a credit default swap in the context of the structural approach to credit modeling. As noted above, some of the key features of the model can be seen in Figure 17.3.

We continue to assume that, in terms of actual probabilities, the value of the firm, $A(t)$, evolves according to (17.13) and that the riskless yield curve is constant and flat at r. In the context of this simple model, the firm is assumed to default the moment that its value touches the default boundary B.

Our interest is in computing the risk-neutral probability $Q(t,T)$, conditional on all information available at time t and no default at that time, that the firm will not default by a given future date T, where T may denote, for example, the horizon over which one is exposed to the firm. Thus, we can then write:

$$Q(t,T) \equiv \text{Prob}_t\{A(s) > B \text{ for all } s \in (t,T)\} \tag{17.17}$$

where the notation $s \in (t,T]$ denotes all values of s that are greater than t and less than or equal to T.

Given the assumed process for the evolution of $A(t)$—equation (17.13)— there is a readily available formula for $Q(t,T)$—see, e.g., Musiela and Rutkowski (1998)[61]:[9]

$$Q(t,T) = N\left(\frac{b(t) + (r - \sigma^2/2)(T-t)}{\sigma\sqrt{T-t}}\right)$$

$$- e^{\frac{2(r-\sigma^2/2)}{\sigma^2}b(t)} N\left(\frac{-b(t) + (r - \sigma^2/2)(T-t)}{\sigma\sqrt{T-t}}\right) \tag{17.18}$$

---

[9] Alternatively, a crude approach for computing $Q(t,T)$ would involve simulating a large number of risk-neutral paths for $A(t)$ and counting the number of paths where A breached the default boundary. This so-called Monte Carlo simulation method can be time consuming, however, and is best reserved for first-passage problems that do not have an easily obtainable analytical solution.

where $b(t) \equiv \log(A(t)/B)$ and $N(.)$ is the cumulative standard normal distribution.[10]

We are now ready to use the model to price a vanilla credit default swap written on the firm depicted in Figure 17.3. As we saw in Chapter 6, pricing a credit default swap means determining the premium S that will be paid periodically by the protection buyer. Taking S initially as given, we first compute the time-t value of the "premium" and "protection" legs of a contract with maturity at T. For simplicity, assume that the premium is paid continuously and that the contract has a notional amount of \$1. As a result, the present value of the premium leg is

$$\eta(t) = \int_t^T SZ(t,v)Q(t,v)dv \qquad (17.19)$$

which can be thought of as the continuous-time analog of (16.1).

To value the protection leg, we note that it is equivalent to a contingent claim that pays $(1 - X)$ at the time of default, provided default happens before T, where X is the recovery rate of the deliverable obligation(s) of the reference entity. The value of such a claim is given by the continuous-time analog of equation (16.3). Letting $\theta(t)$ denote the value of the protection leg, we can write

$$\theta(t) = (1 - X) \int_t^T Z(t,v)[-dQ(t,v)] \qquad (17.20)$$

A default swap typically has zero market value at its inception, and thus pricing such a contract is equivalent to finding the value of S that makes the two legs of the swap have equal value. This is given by

$$S = \frac{(1 - X) \int_t^T Z(t,v)[-dQ(t,v)]}{\int_t^T Z(t,v)Q(t,v)dv} \qquad (17.21)$$

Following Pan (2001)[65], if we now define the annualized probability of default as

$$\hat{h}(t,T) = \frac{-\log(Q(t,T))}{T - t}$$

---

[10] The normal and lognormal distributions are briefly discussed in Appendix B.

and if we assume that $\hat{h}(t, T) \approx \bar{h}$ for all t and T, i.e., $\hat{h}$ is approximately constant as t and T vary, we obtain[11]

$$S \approx \frac{(1 - X) \int_t^T Z(t, v) e^{-\bar{h}(v-t)} \bar{h} \, dv}{\int_t^T Z(t, v) e^{-\bar{h}(v-t)} \, dv} = (1 - X)\bar{h} \qquad (17.22)$$

which gives us the intuitive (and, by now, familiar) result that the credit default swap premium is closely connected to the recovery rate and the annualized probability of default associated with the reference entity. Thus, starting from a model for the evolution of the asset value of the firm, we were able to price a credit default swap agreement written on that firm.

17.2   Reduced-form Approach

Rather than tying defaults explicitly to the "fundamentals" of a firm, such as its stock market capitalization and leverage ratio, the reduced-form approach takes defaults to be exogenous events that occur at unknown times. Let τ denote the time of default, which, of course, is a stochastic variable. A central focus of the reduced-form approach is to propose a model that assigns probabilities to different outcomes involving τ. For instance, conditional on all information available at time t and given no default at that time, one might want to know the (risk-neutral) probability that a given reference entity will not default within the next year. Continuing to use the notation introduced earlier in this book, this probability can be written as

$$Q(t, T) \equiv \text{Prob}_t[\tau > T | \tau > t] \qquad (17.23)$$

where time T in this specific example is exactly one year from today, i.e., $T - 1 = 1$ year.

As we saw in the previous section, structural models also allow for the time of default to be stochastic, but in those models τ is determined endogenously by the evolution of the value of the firm, $A(t)$. In contrast, in reduced-form models, the stochastic properties of τ are specified as an exogenous process that is not directly related to the balance sheet of the firm.

17.2.1   Overview of Some Important Concepts

Before we go on to describe the basic features of the reduced-form approach, we should stop to introduce some additional notation and review a few key

---

[11] If $\hat{h}(t, T)$ is constant, the expression in (17.22) becomes an equality.

concepts. We shall focus primarily on extending the risk-neutral valuation approach to the case of stochastic interest rates and on the notion of forward default probabilities.

17.2.1.1   Stochastic Interest Rates

Up until now we have been taking the riskless interest rate r to be time invariant. We will now start relaxing this assumption in order gradually to bring the modeling framework a bit closer to the real world. In particular, let us allow the riskless rate to vary deterministically from month to month, but, for now, we will continue to insist on time-invariant rates within the month. Consider an investor who puts \$1 in a riskless bank account that pays interest on a continuously compounding basis. At the end of the first month the investor will have $e^{r(1)(t_1-t_0)}$ in the bank, where $r(1)$ is the riskless rate prevailing that month, expressed on an annual basis, and t_1-t_0 is the fraction of a year represented by the first month. Carrying on with this exercise, and assuming no withdrawals, after two months the investor's bank account balance will be

$$e^{r(1)(t_1-t_0)}e^{r(2)(t_2-t_1)} = e^{r(1)(t_1-t_0)+r(2)(t_2-t_1)}$$

where $r(2)$ is the rate applied to the second month and $(t_2 - t_1)$ is defined as above. Generalizing, after n months, the account balance will be

$$e^{\sum_{i=1}^{n} r(i)(t_i-t_{i-1})}$$

If instead of allowing the riskless rate to vary only from month to month, we had allowed for perfectly predictable daily changes in r, the above scheme would still work, with $r(i)$ being redefined to mean the interest rate corresponding to day i and $(t_i - t_{i-1})$ representing the fraction of the year represented by the ith day. If we shorten the period over which r is allowed to vary to the point where $(t_i - t_{i-1})$ becomes infinitesimally small, the value of the bank account between the current instant in time $t_0 = t$ and some future instant $t_n = T$ becomes

$$e^{\int_t^T r(v)dv}$$

where dv is the length of the infinitesimally small time interval.

Recall that the expression above is the time-T value of a \$1 deposit made at time t. It is easy to see then that the time-t value of a dollar received at time T would be given by

$$\beta(T) \equiv e^{-\int_t^T r(v)dv} \tag{17.24}$$

and we arrive at the well-known result that, in a world with deterministic interest rates, the price of a riskless zero-coupon bond that matures at time T is simply given by $\beta(T)$.

With stochastic interest rates, the discount factor can no longer be defined as above because the future values of r are not known. Instead, the price of a zero-coupon bond that pays out \$1 at T can be shown to be the expected value of (17.24):

$$Z(t,T) = \tilde{E}_t \left[e^{-\int_t^T r(v)dv} \right] \tag{17.25}$$

where $\tilde{E}_t[.]$ denotes the expected value of "." based on information available at time t, computed using risk-neutral probabilities.[12]

17.2.1.2 Forward Default Probabilities

Given (17.23), it is straightforward to see that the time-t probability of default before time U, $U > t$, is given by

$$1 - Q(t,U) \equiv \text{Prob}_t[\tau \leq U | \tau > t] \tag{17.26}$$

We can also write down the probability of default between future times T and U, as seen from time t, for $t < T < U$. As discussed in Chapter 15, this is simply the probability of surviving through time T minus the survival probability through time U:

$$\text{Prob}_t[T < \tau < U | \tau > t] = \text{Prob}_t[\tau > T | \tau > t] - \text{Prob}_t[\tau > U | \tau > t]$$
$$= Q(t,T) - Q(t,U) \tag{17.27}$$

Equation (17.27) is an expression for the unconditional forward probability of default associated with this firm. We say unconditional because we are making no explicit particular stipulations about what will happen between today, time t, and time T. We are still assuming, however, that there is no default today and that we are using all information available at time t.

One might be interested in the probability, conditional on all available time-t information, that the firm will survive through some future time U, given that it has survived through an earlier future time T, but having no other time-T information about either the state of the firm or

---

[12] See Neftci (2002)[62] for additional non-technical insights into risk-neutral probabilities and the derivation of an explicit expression for (17.25). Bjork (1998)[7] provides further details.

of the economy. This is the conditional forward probability of survival, $\text{Prob}_t[\tau > U | \tau > T]$. By the Bayes rule, we can write[13]

$$\text{Prob}_t[\tau > U | \tau > T] = \frac{\text{Prob}_t[\tau > U | \tau > t]}{\text{Prob}_t[\tau > T | \tau > t]} = \frac{Q(t, U)}{Q(t, T)} \qquad (17.28)$$

and hence the forward conditional probability of default regarding the future time period $[T, U]$ is given by

$$\text{Prob}_t[\tau \leq U | \tau > T] = 1 - \text{Prob}_t[\tau > U | \tau > T]$$

$$= -\frac{Q(t, U) - Q(t, T)}{Q(t, T)} \qquad (17.29)$$

17.2.1.3   Forward Default Rates

We can now introduce a key concept in the context of reduced-form models, the default rate $H(t, T)$, defined as the risk-neutral default probability associated with a given horizon divided by the length of the horizon[14]

$$H(t, T) \equiv \frac{\text{Prob}_t[\tau \leq T | \tau > t]}{T - t} = \frac{1 - Q(t, T)}{T - t} \qquad (17.30)$$

The forward default rate, as seen at time t, that corresponds to the future period $[T, U]$ is analogously defined as

$$H(t, T, U) \equiv \frac{\text{Prob}_t[\tau \leq U | \tau > T]}{U - T} = -\frac{Q(t, U) - Q(t, T)}{U - T} \frac{1}{Q(t, T)} \qquad (17.31)$$

If we now let $U \equiv T + \Delta T$, we can define the time-t instantaneous forward default rate as:

$$h(t, T) \equiv \lim_{\Delta T \to 0} H(t, T, T + \Delta T) \qquad (17.32)$$

---

[13] The Bayes rule simply says that, given two events A and B, and denoting $\text{Prob}[A\&B]$ as the probability that both A and B occur, one can write

$$\text{Prob}[A\&B] = \text{Prob}[A]\text{Prob}[B|A]$$

where $\text{Prob}[A]$ is the unconditional probability that A will take place and $\text{Prob}[B|A]$ is the probability of B occurring given that A has taken place.

In the context of (17.28), we can think of event A as the event defined as $\tau > T$, B as $\tau > U$, and, given $U > T$, $A\&B$ corresponds to $\tau > U$. (To be sure, all of the corresponding probabilities would have to be defined as being conditional on information available at time t, as well as on survival through that time.)

[14] Unless otherwise indicated, all probabilities discussed in this chapter are risk-neutral probabilities.

and it is not difficult to see that

$$h(t,T) = -\frac{\partial Q(t,T)}{\partial T}\frac{1}{Q(t,T)} \qquad (17.33)$$

To see how we arrived at (17.33), recall that (17.31) implies that

$$h(t,T) \equiv \left[\lim_{\Delta T \to 0} -\frac{[Q(t,T+\Delta T) - Q(t,T)]}{\Delta T}\right]\frac{1}{Q(t,T)} \qquad (17.34)$$

but, assuming that certain technical conditions on $Q(.)$ are satisfied, the expression within the square brackets is nothing more than the definition of the negative of the derivative of $Q(t,T)$ with respect to T.

Equation (17.33) is probably the single most important preliminary result derived so far in Section 17.2. In particular, integrating both sides of (17.33) from T to U, we obtain

$$e^{-\int_T^U h(t,v)dv} = \frac{Q(t,U)}{Q(t,T)} = \text{Prob}_t[\tau > U | \tau > T] \qquad (17.35)$$

where the last equality results from (17.28).

Equation (17.35) is the forward survival probability associated with the future period $[T, U]$, given survival through time T and conditional on all available time-t information. Indeed, we can now express default and survival probabilities over any horizon for a given entity simply on the basis of the instantaneous forward default rate $h(t, s)$.[15] For instance, the time-t probability that the firm will survive through time U is

$$\text{Prob}_t[\tau > U | \tau > t] = Q(t,U) = e^{-\int_t^U h(t,v)dv} \qquad (17.36)$$

For $t = T$, we can rewrite (17.34) as

$$h(t,t) \equiv \lim_{\Delta t \to 0} -\frac{[Q(t,t+\Delta t) - Q(t,t)]}{\Delta t}\frac{1}{Q(t,t)} \qquad (17.37)$$

but, by definition, $Q(t,t) = 1$, and thus, for infinitesimally small dt,

$$\text{Prob}_t[\tau \le t + dt | \tau > t] = h(t,t)dt \qquad (17.38)$$

---

[15] Readers familiar with yield curve models will notice the analogy between the concept of instantaneous forward interest rates and that of instantaneous forward default rates, especially regarding their relationship to zero-coupon bond prices and survival probabilities, respectively. (Appendix A provides a brief overview of instantaneous forward interest rates.)

which, in words, is the time-t instantaneous probability of default, assuming no default at t. Thus, for small time intervals Δt, the probability of default between t and $t + \Delta t$, given no default by t, is approximately equal to $h(t, t)\Delta t$.[16]

17.2.2   Default Intensity

In the context of most reduced-form models, the random nature of defaults is typically characterized in terms of the first "arrival" of a Poisson process. In particular, for a given reference entity, if we assume that defaults arrive (occur) randomly at the mean risk-neutral rate of λ per year, the time-t risk-neutral probability of no default by time T can be written as[17]

$$Q(t, T) = e^{-\lambda(T-t)} \tag{17.39}$$

provided λ is time invariant and, of course, given no default by time t. In the credit risk literature λ is commonly called the intensity of default or the hazard rate.

If λ is not constant over time, but varies deterministically, we can follow the same logic discussed in Section 17.2.1 to show that if λ changes continuously over infinitesimally small time intervals we can write

$$Q(t, T) = e^{-\int_t^T \lambda(v)dv} \tag{17.40}$$

and thus, as suggested by a comparison between (17.40) and (17.36), with deterministic λ, the terms default intensity and forward default rate can essentially be used interchangeably.

---

[16] Given the definition of derivative in classic calculus:

$$\frac{\partial Q(t, T)}{\partial T} \equiv \lim_{dt \to 0} -\frac{[Q(t, T + dt) - Q(t, T)]}{dt}$$

we can write

$$Q(t, T + dt) \approx Q(t, T) + \frac{\partial Q(t, T)}{\partial T}dt = Q(t, T)[1 - h(t, T)dt]$$

For $T = t$, and given that $Q(t, t) = 1$, we can write:

$$1 - Q(t, t + dt) \approx h(t, t)dt$$

which becomes an equality if $Q(t, T)$ has a derivative at $T = t$ and we let $dt \to 0$. Thus, given that $1 - Q(t, t + dt) = \text{Prob}_t[\tau \leq t + dt | \tau > t]$, we arrive at (17.38)—Neftci (2002)[62] discusses basic notions from classic calculus that are relevant for finance.

[17] For a Poisson process with a constant mean arrival rate of λ, a basic result from statistics states that the time until the "first arrival," τ, is a random variable with probability density function $\lambda e^{-\lambda \tau}$, which characterizes the exponential distribution. From this, equation (17.39) easily follows. See Appendix B for further details on the Poisson and exponential distributions.

But default intensity can vary stochastically over time in response to, say, unanticipated developments regarding the economy or the financial condition of the firm. With stochastic default intensity, it can be shown that, under some technical conditions that go beyond the scope of this book—see, for instance, Lando (1998)[51]—the expression for the time-t survival probability of a given firm can be written in a way that is entirely analogous to (17.25):

$$Q(t,T) = \tilde{E}_t \left[e^{-\int_t^T \lambda(v)dv} \right] \qquad (17.41)$$

Models where (17.41) holds are typically called doubly stochastic models of default because they assume that not only is the time of default a random variable, but so is the mean arrival rate of default at any given point in time.

A comparison between equations (17.41) and (17.36) suggests that the equality between time-t forward default rates and future values of intensity generally breaks down when λ is assumed to be stochastic. For instance, consider the value of default intensity at some future time v. That value, $\lambda(v)$, incorporates all information available at time v, including the values of any stochastic factors that may affect default intensity at time v, such as the prevailing states of the economy and of the firm at time v. In contrast, the forward default rate $h(t,v)$ can be thought of as the intensity rate for the future time v, as seen on the basis of currently available (time-t) information, and conditional on the firm surviving through time v.

Thus, whereas $\lambda(v)$ is based on all information available at time v, the only time-v information on which $h(t,v)$ is conditional is the survival of the firm through time v. Still, from the perspective of time t, it can be shown the following relationship between forward default rates and default intensity holds:

$$h(t,t) = \lambda(t) \qquad (17.42)$$

which says that when defaults occur according to a Poisson process, today's (time-t) instantaneous default rate associated with the infinitesimally small time interval $[t, t+dt]$ is simply the default intensity of the reference entity, which is assumed to be known at time t. Moreover, we can write the conditional instantaneous time-t probability of default as:

$$\text{Prob}_t[\tau \leq t + dt | \tau > t] = \lambda(t)dt \qquad (17.43)$$

Reduced-form models can essentially be characterized in terms of the particular assumptions that they make regarding how λ changes over time. Indeed, the case of constant default intensity constitutes the simplest of all reduced-form models.

A simple model that admits random variation in default intensity involves the following specification for the evolution of λ:

$$d\lambda(t) = k[\bar{\lambda} - \lambda(t)]dt + \sigma\sqrt{\lambda(t)}dW(t) \tag{17.44}$$

where $dW(t)$ is an infinitesimal increment in a standard Brownian motion.[18]

Equation (17.44) closely parallels the yield curve model proposed by Cox, Ingersoll, and Ross (1985)[15]. In words, it says that, although the default intensity associated with a given reference entity varies stochastically over time, it has a tendency to revert to its long-run mean of $\bar{\lambda}$, where k indicates the degree of mean reversion.

17.2.3   Uncertain Time of Default

The use of reduced-form models in the valuation of defaultable securities and related credit derivatives often requires the derivation of a probability distribution function for τ, the time of default. This is the function $G(s)$ such that

$$\text{Prob}[s < \tau \le s + ds] = G(s + ds) - G(s) \approx g(s)ds$$

where $g(s)$ is the probability density function (p.d.f.) of τ and the approximation error in the above equation is negligible for very small values of ds—see Grimmett and Stirzaker (1998)[36], p. 90.[19]

The probability density of default time can be thought of as the product involving the probability of no default by time s and the probability of default in the interval from s to $s + ds$ conditional on no default by time s:

$$\text{Prob}[s < \tau \le s + ds] = \text{Prob}[\tau > s] \ \ \text{Prob}[\tau \le s + ds | \tau > s]$$

which is an implication of the Bayes rule.

Conditional on all information available at time t, and given no default by time t, we can use equations (17.41) and (17.43) to write the conditional

---

[18] A discrete-time approximation helps convey some of the intuition behind equation (17.44):

$$\lambda_{t+\delta t} \approx \lambda_t + k[\bar{\lambda} - \lambda_t]\delta t + \sigma\sqrt{\lambda_t}\,\epsilon_{t+\delta t}$$

where ϵ is a normally distributed random variable with mean zero and variance δt. Thus, we can think of $\lambda_{t+\delta t}$ as a mean-reverting random variable with conditional variance $\text{var}[\lambda_{t+\delta t}|\lambda_t]$ equal to $\sigma^2\lambda_t\delta t$.

[19] $G(.)$ is the so-called cumulative distribution function of τ. Appendix B reviews key concepts surrounding cumulative distribution and probability density functions.

p.d.f. of τ as the function $g_t(s)$ such that:

$$g_t(s)ds = \text{Prob}_t[s < \tau \leq s + ds] = \tilde{E}_t\left[e^{-\int_t^s \lambda(u)du}\lambda(s)ds\right] \qquad (17.45)$$

where we are assuming that ds is infinitesimally small and that $s \geq t$.

For nonrandom intensity, we can make use of (17.40), and equation (17.45) simplifies to

$$g_t(s)ds = \text{Prob}_t[s < \tau \leq s + ds] = Q(t,s)\lambda(s)ds$$

17.2.4   Valuing Defaultable Bonds

Suppose we want to value a zero-coupon bond that pays \$1 at time T if its issuer has not defaulted by then. Otherwise the bond becomes worthless, a zero recovery rate. As in previous chapters, we let $Z_0^d(t,T)$ denote today's (time-t) price of this bond.

In Section 15.2.1, where survival probabilities and future values of the riskless rate were assumed to be known with certainty, we argued that one can write the price of a defaultable bond as the product of the bond issuer's risk-neutral survival probability and the price of a riskless zero-coupon bond with the same maturity date and face value as the defaultable bond. That result still holds when interest rates are stochastic but independent from the default intensity process, an assumption that we will maintain throughout this chapter.[20] Thus, given (17.25) and (17.41), we can write:

$$Z_0^d(t,T) = \tilde{E}_t\left[e^{-\int_t^T [r(v)+\lambda(v)]dv}\right] = Z(t,T)Q(t,T) \qquad (17.46)$$

which gives the logical result that, in the absence of default risk, the expression for $Z_0^d(t,T)$ reduces to $Z(t,T)$.

Given the above equation, it is relatively straightforward to derive the yield spread associated with this risky bond. In particular, recall from Chapter 15 that the yield to maturity of this bond is the annualized rate $R^d(t,T)$ that discounts the face value of the bond back to its market price. Thus, $R^d(t,T)$ is such that $Z_0^d(t,T) = e^{-R^d(t,T)(T-t)}$ for a bond with a face

---

[20] Two events are said to be independent if the knowledge that one has occurred does not affect one's assessment of the probability that the other will occur. Whenever we refer to independent random variables in this book, we mean independence with respect to risk-neutral probabilities. Independence is discussed further in Appendix B. We briefly discussed some empirical results regarding the relationship between defaults and riskless interest rates in Chapter 15.

value of $1. As a result,

$$R^d(t,T) = \frac{-\log(Z_0^d(t,T))}{T-t} = \frac{\int_t^T [f(t,v) + h(t,v)]dv}{T-t} \qquad (17.47)$$

where the second equality stems from equation (17.36) and from the basic result, reviewed in Appendix A, that the price of a riskless zero coupon bond can be expressed in terms of the time-t instantaneous forward riskless interest rates, $f(t,v)$, that span the remaining maturity of the bond:

$$Z(t,T) = e^{-\int_t^T f(t,v)dv}$$

The risky bond spread $S(t,T)$, defined as $R^d(t,T) - R(t,T)$, is given by

$$S(t,T) = \frac{\int_t^T h(t,v)dv}{T-t}$$

In light of (17.36), we can write

$$S(t,T) = \frac{-\log(Q(t,T))}{T-t}$$

which has the intuitive implication that the higher the risk-neutral survival probability $Q(t,T)$ of the bond issuer, the lower the corresponding risk spread.

If we assume that both r and λ are deterministic and time invariant, equation (17.46) reduces to

$$Z_0^d(t,T) = e^{-(r+\lambda)(T-t)} \qquad (17.48)$$

and it is easy to see that, with zero recovery, the spread between the yield to maturity on a defaultable bond, $r + \lambda$, over that on a riskless bond, r, is equal to the default intensity of the issuer of the defaultable bond:

$$S(t,T) = \lambda$$

17.2.4.1 Non zero Recovery

Armed with the probability distribution of default times, we can now discuss the valuation of defaultable bonds with a nonzero recovery rate. In particular, we will take advantage of the fact that such bonds can be thought of as a portfolio involving two simpler securities: an otherwise comparable zero-recovery defaultable bond and a contingent claim that pays X at the time of default, if a default occurs before the maturity date of the bond, and zero otherwise, where X is the recovery value of the original bond.

Let $\Phi(t,T)$ be the time-t price of the contingent claim just described. In order to value such a claim we rely on the continuous-time analog of the argument developed in Section 15.4 in the valuation of defaultable bonds with a nonzero recovery value. In particular $\Phi(t,T)$ is equal to the probability-weighted average of all possible recovery payment scenarios involving the bond, where the weights are given by the risk-neutral probability density function of the time of default. Thus,

$$\Phi(t,T) = X \int_t^T Z(t,v) g_t(v) dv \tag{17.49}$$

where $g_t(v) \equiv \tilde{E}_t[e^{-\int_t^v \lambda(u)du} \lambda(v)]$ is the probability density function of the default time, which we discussed in Section 17.2.3.

We are now ready to derive the valuation formula for a zero-coupon bond that has a value of X in the event of default. Given the above discussion, we can write

$$Z^d(t,T) = Z_0^d(t,T) + \Phi(t,T) \tag{17.50}$$

where the two right-hand side terms of (17.50) are given by (17.46) and (17.49), respectively.

For the simple reduced-form model that assumes that both r and λ are time invariant, the valuation formula for the defaultable zero-coupon bond with recovery value X can be shown to be:

$$Z^d(t,T) = e^{-(r+\lambda)(T-t)} + \frac{X\lambda}{r+\lambda}(1 - e^{-(r+\lambda)(T-t)}) \tag{17.51}$$

17.2.4.2 Alternative Recovery Assumptions

Thus far in the context of reduced-form models we have essentially assumed that investors recover, at the time of default, a fraction of the defaulted instrument's original face value. It should be noted, however, that this is only an assumption, and that there are alternative ways for reduced-form models to handle the valuation of bonds with nonzero recovery values.

One alternative to the framework based on immediate recovery of face value is the so-called equivalent recovery assumption. This was actually the recovery assumption made in the seminal work of Jarrow and Turnbull (1995)[46]. In the original Jarrow-Turnbull model, a defaulted security with face value \$1 is immediately replaced by X otherwise equivalent riskfree zero-coupon bonds, with $0 \leq X \leq 1$. (Obviously, $X = 1$ would constitute the case of a riskfree bond to begin with.) By "otherwise equivalent," we mean that the newly issued riskfree zero-coupon bonds will have the same maturity date and face value as the defaulted bond.

How does the valuation of defaultable bonds under the equivalent recovery assumption differ from (17.50)? The assumption that, in the event of default, the recovery payment only takes place at the original maturity of the risky bond makes this valuation exercise simpler because we no longer need to explicitly derive a p.d.f. for the time of default. To see this, note that, at the maturity date T, the bond holder will either receive the full face value of the bond ($\$1$) or the recovery value X, and the risk-neutral probabilities associated with these events are $Q(t,T)$ and $1-Q(t,T)$, respectively. Thus the risk-adjusted expected value of the bondholder's payout, based on information available at time t, is

$$Q(t,T) + [1 - Q(t,T)]X$$

and, following the logic set out in Chapter 15, the time-t value of this expected payout is:

$$Z^d(t,T) = Z(t,T)\{Q(t,T) + [1 - Q(t,T)]X\}$$

Recall that $Q(t,T)Z(t,T)$ is simply $Z_0^d(t,T)$. Thus, the bond valuation formula becomes:

$$Z^d(t,T) = Z_0^d(t,T)(1 - X) + Z(t,T)X \tag{17.52}$$

and a comparison of (17.50) and (17.52) makes it clear that one obtains different values for a defaultable bond depending on the assumed recovery scheme.

A third common recovery assumption is the fractional recovery of market value framework, proposed by Duffie and Singleton (1999)[24]. Duffie and Singleton essentially assume that upon a default at time τ the bond loses a fraction L of its market value. (This is equivalent to saying that upon default the bondholder recovers a fraction $1 - L$ of the no-default market value of the bond.) Duffie and Singleton show that, under such circumstances, the value of a defaultable zero-coupon bond would satisfy

$$Z^d(t,T) = \tilde{E}_t \left[e^{-\int_t^T [r(s)+L\lambda(s)]ds} \right] \tag{17.53}$$

which simplifies to

$$Z^d(t,T) = Z(t,T)\tilde{E}_t \left[e^{-\int_t^T L\lambda(s)ds} \right] \tag{17.54}$$

when the riskless rate process is independent of the default process.

TABLE 17.1

Effect of Alternative Recovery Assumptions on the Valuation of a Five-year
Zero-coupon Bond[a]

Recovery Assumption	Price ($)	Yield (percent)	Risk Spread (basis points)
Fractional recovery of face value	.699	7.18	218
Equivalent recovery	.676	7.83	283
Fractional recovery of market value	.664	8.20	320
No recovery	.552	13.00	800
Memo: Riskless five-year bond	.779	5.00	

[a]Based on the assumption of flat riskless curve. The riskless rate r is set at 5 percent, and the default intensity of the bond issuer is assumed to be constant at 8 percent. For the nonzero recovery rate cases, X is set at 60 percent ($L = 40$ percent). Face value of the bonds = $1.

To illustrate the effect of the recovery assumption on the valuation of a zero-coupon bond, we compare the prices of a five-year zero-coupon bond implied by equations (17.50), (17.52), and (17.54) derived from an otherwise identical reduced-form model and based on the same parameter values. Suppose, for instance, that both the riskless interest rate and default intensity are constant at 5 percent and 8 percent, respectively. Let the relevant recovery rates be 60 percent under each of the recovery rate assumptions examined.[21]

Table 17.1 shows that the recovery assumption can have a non-trivial effect on the model-implied prices and yield-to-maturities of this bond, with the latter ranging from 7.18 percent when the bond is priced under the assumption of fractional recovery of the face value of the bond to 8.20 percent under the assumption of partial recovery of the market value of the bond. The case of recovery of face value has the lowest yield given that it involves an immediate payment to the bond holder upon default, as well as a payment that represents 60 percent of the full par value of the bond. Under the equivalent recovery case, even though the recovery value still corresponds to 60 percent of the par value, that payment is effectively received in full only at the bond's original maturity date so that the investor effectively has to be compensated for this "delay" by receiving a higher yield.

The lowest bond price (highest yield) corresponds to the case involving the fractional recovery of market value. This occurs because the market

---

[21] For the recovery-of-market-value framework, we assume that L is equal to $1 - X$ or 40 percent.

value of the bond just before default can be substantially below par for a zero-coupon bond. The table also shows the price of the defaultable bond under the assumption of a zero recovery value, which corresponds to a yield of 13 percent (a spread of 800 basis points over the yield on a comparable riskfree bond, shown as a memo item).

The differences in model-implied bond prices can be significantly less dramatic than those shown in Table 17.1 for zero-coupon bonds of shorter maturity. For instance, for a one-year bond, the theoretical yields would range from 8 percent to 8.2 percent given the assumptions listed in the table's footnote. Differences in bond prices across different recovery assumptions can also be much smaller than those in the table for coupon-bearing defaultable bonds, as shown by Duffie and Singleton (1999)[24] in the context of a reduced-form model with stochastic riskfree rates and intensity.

Which recovery assumption should one favor? Each has its pros and cons, and neither has gained complete acceptance among either academics or practitioners. The assumption of fractional recovery of face value is closest to the market convention for defaulted bonds, where the obligations of a liquidated debtor tend to have the same value, assuming the same level of seniority, regardless of their maturity date. Nonetheless, as discussed by O'Kane and Schlogl (2001)[64], the recovery of face value assumption imposes upper bounds on the yields of defaultable bonds, as does the equivalent recovery assumption. The latter has the advantage of being easier to deal with analytically than the recovery of face value assumption. (This can be seen by examining how much simpler it was to arrive at (17.52) than at (17.50), which involved, for instance, the computation of the probability distribution of default times.)

From an analytical perspective, the most tractable of the recovery assumptions is likely the formulation involving fractional recovery of the market value of the bond. Indeed, this assumption has the advantage of making the valuation of defaultable bonds almost entirely analogous to that of default-free bonds. One drawback of the recovery-of-market-value assumption, however, is that one can no longer separately infer default probabilities from observed market quotes using the simple steps outlined in Chapter 16.

17.2.5   Extensions and Uses of Reduced-form Models

Most of the model-specific results derived thus far, such as the valuation formulae for defaultable zero-coupon bonds with zero recovery and with fractional recovery of face value—equations (17.48) and (17.51), respectively—came from the simple reduced-form model based on constant intensity and riskless rate of interest and nonrandom recovery rates. To be sure, these are over-simplistic assumptions, which were made solely for the sake of analytical tractability and pedagogical convenience.

Richer models do exist with various degrees of complexity, ranging from specifications with stochastic riskless rates but deterministically time-varying intensity to fully stochastic models with uncertain recovery. Examples of work in this strand of the literature include Lando (1998)[51], Duffie and Singleton (1999)[24], Jarrow and Yu (2001)[47], Madan and Unal (2000)[58], Schonbucher (1998)[70], and many others.

Reduced-form models are commonly used in practice to extract default probability information from the prices of actively traded instruments and use those probabilities to value, for instance, less liquid or more complex credit derivatives. Nonetheless, given that we essentially did this in Chapter 16 without ever having explicitly to resort to a model, one might wonder why reduced-form models would be used in this context. The answer partly resides in the fact that an important motivation for using such models relates to an assumption proposed in the simple exercise carried out in Chapter 16. There we made the assertion that default intensities were independent of the riskless interest rate process. But one might well suspect that the level of market interest rates and default probabilities are correlated, in which case a credit risk model—such as the reduced-form and structural frameworks described in the current chapter—is needed.[22] Other instances where a particular model for the forward default rate are needed include some valuation problems for derivatives involving spread optionality, some of which are discussed in Chapter 18.

17.2.6   Credit Default Swap Valuation

Models in the reduced-form tradition can be used to price both single- and multi-issuer credit derivatives. As an illustration, we will use it to value a vanilla credit default swap. As in Section 17.1.5, we will let S denote the credit default swap premium for a contract that matures at time T. For simplicity, we will continue to assume that the premium is paid continuously and that the notional amount of the contract is \$1. In addition, we will take both the riskless interest rate and default intensity to be time invariant.

In the context of the basic reduced-form model, the present value of the premium leg of the credit default swap can be written as:

$$\eta(t) = \int_t^T Se^{-(r+\lambda)(s-t)}ds = \frac{S}{r+\lambda}(1 - e^{-(r+\lambda)(T-t)}) \qquad (17.55)$$

---

[22]We discussed some empirical results on the relationship between defaults and interest rates in Chapter 15.

Notice above that, as in equation (17.48), the premium stream is discounted at the risky rate $r + \lambda$, reflecting the uncertainty surrounding the default event. (λ is the default intensity associated with the reference entity.)

To value the protection leg, we note that it is equivalent to a contingent claim that pays $(1 - X)$ in the event of default before T, where X is the recovery rate of the reference entity's defaulted liabilities. The value of such a claim is given by equation (17.49) with X replaced with $1 - X$. Letting $\theta(t)$ denote the value of the protection leg, we can write

$$\theta(t) = \frac{\lambda(1 - X)}{r + \lambda}(1 - e^{-(r+\lambda)(T-t)}) \qquad (17.56)$$

A default swap typically has zero market value when it is set up, and thus pricing such a contract is equivalent to finding the value of S that makes the two legs of the swap have equal value. This is given by

$$S = \lambda(1 - X) \qquad (17.57)$$

which gives us the result that, for a given recovery rate and constant r and λ, the credit default swap premium tells us about the default intensity of the reference entity. In other words, by assuming a value for the recovery rate, we can use the above expression and observable default swap spreads to infer the default intensity associated with the reference entity. Such a CDS-implied default intensity can then be used in the valuation of other credit derivatives instruments.

This simple CDS pricing exercise has made several restrictive assumptions, such as continuously paid premiums and constant interest rates and default intensity. As discussed in Section 17.2.4, many of these assumptions can be relaxed in order to bring the valuation exercise closer to reality.

17.3   Comparing the Two Main Approaches

There is no clear consensus in either the practitioner or academic literatures about which of the two credit risk modeling approaches—structural and reduced-form—is the most appropriate one. For instance, while the structural form approach might be said to have the advantage of relying explicitly on the fundamentals underlying a given firm—as these are reflected in the firm's balance sheet—such reliance could also be seen as a drawback. Indeed, balance sheet information tends to become available only on a quarterly basis, which could be a limitation if one is interested, for instance, in accurately marking positions to market. (Moreover, balance-sheet information can be quite noisy as the financial reporting scandals of the early 2000s painfully reminded the markets.) At the same time, reduced-form models might be of more limited value if one's interest is, for example, in assessing how a change in the capital structure of a given firm may affect its financing costs, in which case careful use of a structural model might be the most appropriate approach.

The two approaches can also be compared from a methodological perspective. For instance, those familiar with models of the term structure of interest rates tend to feel more at ease, from a purely technical standpoint, in the world of reduced-form models. Take, for instance, the relationship between the survival probability, $Q(t,T)$, and the forward default rate, $h(t,s)$,

$$Q(t,T) = e^{-\int_t^T h(t,s)ds}$$

As noted, this is similar to the mathematical relationship between zero-coupon bond prices $Z(t,T)$ and time-t instantaneous forward interest rates. Likewise, the mathematical treatment of default intensity, λ, as well as its relationship with $h()$ and $Q()$, is analogous to the links among the spot short-term interest rate, instantaneous forward interest rates, and zero-coupon bond prices. Moreover, when λ is assumed to be stochastic, many of the basic models for describing its evolution mirror common specifications developed for interest rate models, such as the well-known yield curve model of Cox, Ingersoll, and Ross (1985)[15].

While fixed-income modelers might find substantial commonality between techniques used in interest rate models and those used in the reduced-form approach, equity-minded analysts will no doubt see familiar ground in the structural approach. In addition to focusing on balance-sheet information, to which many equity analysts are already used, a centerpiece of the structural approach is the use of equity-based option theoretic results to price defaultable debt instruments.

To sum up, from a methodological perspective, the pros and cons of each approach have to be examined in the context in which the models will be used, with certain models being more naturally suited for certain applications. In addition, some analysts might be more attracted to one approach vs. the other based on how comfortable they feel with the underlying methodological framework behind each class of models.

Empirically, while structural models are appealing in that they attempt to link explicitly the likelihood of default of a given firm to its economic and financial condition, traditional forms of such models tend not to fit the data as well as reduced-form models, especially, as noted in Section 17.1.4, in relation to short-term credit spreads. Indeed, in the intensity-based framework, defaults can happen suddenly and unexpectedly without having to be presaged by observable phenomenon, such as the value of the firm approaching the default barrier in the typical BSM-style model. In this regard, what may be characterized as another class of credit risk models has emerged.

These models attempt to combine the economic/intuitive appeal of structural models with the empirical plausibility of the intensity-based approach. The model of Duffie and Lando (2001)[23] is one of the better-known works in this strand of the literature.[23]

The Duffie-Lando model can be thought of as a hybrid structural/intensity-based model because it is essentially a first-passage model that, contrary to standard structural models, also has an intensity-based interpretation. In particular, rather than being given exogenously as in the pure reduced-form approach, default intensity in the Duffie-Lando model can be calculated in terms of observable variables related to the balance-sheet fundamentals of the firm. Moreover, Duffie and Lando argue that many estimation methods used in the context of pure intensity-based models are also applicable to the hybrid framework.

Essentially, a main thrust of this hybrid approach to credit risk modeling is to assume that investors only have imperfect information about the true financial condition of the firm. For instance, investors may not know with certainty just how far the value of the firm is from its default boundary. As a result, the possibility of a default in the very near term cannot be fully discarded, and thus the pattern of short-term credit spreads generated by these models tends to be more realistic than that implied by traditional BSM-type models.[24]

17.4   Ratings-based Models

Instead of allowing for the firm to be only in one of two states—default and survival—ratings-based models allow for a variety of states, where each non-default state might correspond, for instance, to a given credit rating— such as AAA, A, BB$^+$, etc.—assigned to the firm by a major credit rating agency. Such models are not widely used for the direct pricing of vanilla credit derivatives as most such instruments do not have payouts that are ratings-dependent. Nonetheless, ratings-based models can be useful in the context of credit derivatives that involve collateral requirements that are linked to the credit rating of the counterparties.

We will not describe ratings-based models in detail in this book, but simply highlight their main features and how they relate to the models examined in previous sections. A well-known ratings-based model is that

---

[23] Other related work includes Giesecke (2001)[32] and Giesecke and Goldberg (2004)[33].

[24] Within the structural framework, Zhou's (1997)[76] jump-diffusion model, discussed in Section 17.2, constitutes an alternative approach to address the empirical implausibility of the short-term credit spreads implied by traditional structural models.

of Jarrow, Lando, and Turnbull (1997)[45]. In what follows, we limit ourselves mostly to providing a basic description of a discrete-time version
of the Jarrow-Lando-Turnbull (JLT) model. In so doing, we follow JLT
themselves, who also used a discrete-time setting to introduce their model.

Suppose that a given bond issuer can have one of $J - 1$ credit ratings,
with 1 representing the highest credit quality and $J - 1$ representing the
rating just prior to default. We will also allow for a Jth "rating," which
will correspond to default. Let $\omega_{i,j}$ represent the actual (not necessarily
risk-neutral) probability, based on all information available at time t, of
the firm migrating from a rating of i at time t to one of j at time $t+1$. For
simplicity we shall assume that these probabilities are time-invariant over
the horizon of interest, which we assume to span from time 0 to time U.
Let us define the $J \times J$ transition matrix Ω such that its (i,j)th element
is $\omega_{i,j}$:

$$
\Omega = \begin{pmatrix}
\omega_{1,1} & \omega_{1,2} & \cdots & \omega_{1,J} \\
\omega_{2,1} & \omega_{2,2} & \cdots & \omega_{2,J} \\
\cdots & \cdots & \cdots & \cdots \\
\omega_{J-1,1} & \omega_{J-1,2} & \cdots & \omega_{J-1,J} \\
0 & 0 & \cdots & 1
\end{pmatrix}
\tag{17.58}
$$

We further assume that:

$$
\omega_{i,j} \geq 0 \quad \text{for all } i, j, \, i \neq j
\tag{17.59}
$$

$$
\omega_{i,i} \equiv 1 - \sum_{j=1, j \neq i}^{J} \omega_{i,j} \quad \text{for all } i
\tag{17.60}
$$

Equation (17.60) essentially acknowledges the fact that for any given firm
rated i at time t, its time-$t + 1$ rating will have to be one of the J ratings.
In particular, the probability that the firm will retain its i rating at $t + 1$
must be one minus the sum of the probabilities associated with migration
to any one of the remaining $J - 1$ ratings.

In technical terms, the last row of Ω says that default—the Jth
"rating"—is an "absorbing state," meaning that once the firm enters into
a state of default, we assume that it will stay there with probability
$\omega_{J,J} = 1$. In corporate finance terms, the model assumes that there is
no reorganization after default.

Let $\omega_{i,j}(t, t+n)$ be the probability, conditional on information available
at time t, that the firm's rating will change from i at time t to j at time
$t+n$. If $\Omega(t, t+n)$ is the matrix such that its (i,j)th element is $\omega_{i,j}(t, t+n)$,

it can be shown that:

$$\Omega(t, t + n) = \Omega^n \tag{17.61}$$

i.e., ratings transitions are said to follow a Markovian process in that the current ratings transition matrix is assumed to contain all currently available relevant information regarding future ratings transitions.

Empirical estimates of Ω are published regularly by some of the major credit-rating agencies based on actual rating changes in the universe of firms covered by these agencies. For pricing purposes, of course, what matter are the risk-neutral transition probabilities $\tilde{\omega}_{i,j}$, rather than the empirical probabilities in Ω. JLT propose the following mapping between empirical and risk-neutral probabilities:

$$\tilde{\omega}_{i,j}(t, t + 1) = \pi_i(t)\omega_{i,j} \text{ for all } i, j, i \neq j \tag{17.62}$$

for $\pi_i(t) \geq 0$ for all i and t. Consistent with the discussion in Chapter 15, $\pi_i(t)$ can be thought of as a risk-premium-induced adjustment to the actual transition probabilities.

The risk-neutral transition probabilities are assumed to satisfy conditions analogous to those in equations (17.59) and (17.60). In addition, JLT imposed the technical condition that $\tilde{\omega}_{i,j}(t, t+1) > 0$ if and only if $\omega_{i,j} > 0$, for $0 \leq t \leq U - 1$.

Thus, we can also define the risk-neutral transition matrix $\tilde{\Omega}(t, t + n)$, and it should by now be clear that its (i, j)th entry is $\tilde{\omega}_{i,j}(t, t + n)$, which is the risk-neutral probability that the entity will migrate from a rating of i at time t to one of j at time $t + n$. If we make the simplifying assumption that both Ω and π_i are time invariant:

$$\tilde{\Omega}(t, t + n) = \tilde{\Omega}(t, t + 1)^n \tag{17.63}$$

Suppose one is interested in the risk-neutral probability, conditional on all information available at time t, that an i-rated firm will survive through some future date T. Given all the assumptions discussed thus far, this probability is simply

$$Q_i(t, T) = 1 - \tilde{\omega}_{i,J}(t, T) \tag{17.64}$$

Thus, as discussed throughout this part of the book, and assuming that riskless interest rates are independent of the stochastic process underlying the ratings transitions of the firm, the time-t price of a zero-recovery, zero-coupon bond that will mature at time T with a face value of $1 is:

$$Z_0^d(t, T; i) = Z(t, T)[1 - \tilde{\omega}_{i,J}(t, T)] \tag{17.65}$$

where we added the argument i to the zero-coupon bond price to indicate that this bond was issued by a firm that is currently rated i.

If $R^d(t, T; i)$ denotes the yield to maturity on this bond, we can use results discussed in earlier sections in this chapter to derive the credit risk spread associated with this firm. In particular,

$$R^d(t, T; i) - R(t, T) = \frac{-\log(Z_0^d(t, T; i)) + \log(Z(t, T))}{T - t}$$

$$= \frac{-\log(1 - \tilde{\omega}_{i,J}(t, T))}{T - t} \qquad (17.66)$$

where we continue to assume that $R(t, T) \equiv \frac{-\log(Z(t, T))}{T-t}$ is the yield to maturity on a riskless zero-coupon bond with the same maturity date and face value as the risky bond.

Thus far we have been using the model essentially to derive expressions for prices and spreads that we were also able to examine with the modeling approaches summarized in Sections 17.1 and 17.2. As their name suggests, however, ratings-based models are particularly suitable for analyses involving yield spreads across different ratings. For instance, the model-implied yield spread between two bonds rated i and j is

$$R^d(t, T; i) - R^d(t, T; j) = \log\left[\frac{1 - \tilde{\omega}_{j,J}(t, T)}{1 - \tilde{\omega}_{i,J}(t, T)}\right] \frac{1}{T - t} \qquad (17.67)$$

Equations (17.66) and (17.67) can be used to identify potentially profitable opportunities across different issuers with various credit ratings, by, for instance, comparing model-implied spreads to the ones observed in the market place. Alternatively, one may be interested in using equations like (17.66) and (17.67) to calibrate the model to the data in order to use the resulting risk-neutral transition probabilities to value financial instruments and contracts with ratings-dependent payoffs, such as bonds with ratings-dependent coupons and credit derivatives contracts with ratings-linked collateral requirements.

A full continuous-time version of the model described in this section is provided in the original JLT paper—Jarrow, Lando, and Turnbull (1997)[45]—which also addresses calibration-related issues. Discussing the technical details behind that version of the model, as well as model calibration and other implementation topics, is outside the scope of this book. Instead we limit ourselves to providing a very brief overview of some basic concepts that are germane to the continuous-time specification of the JLT model. In particular, in the simplest case of time-invariant risk-neutral transition probabilities, the $J \times J$ transition matrix for the continuous-time version of the model can be written as:

$$\Omega(t, T) = e^{\Lambda(T-t)} \tag{17.68}$$

where the $J \times J$ matrix Λ is typically called the generator matrix. The ith diagonal element of Λ, $\lambda_{i,i}$, can be thought of as the exit rate from the ith rating, and, for $i \neq j$, the (i,j)th element of Λ, $\lambda_{i,j}$, is the transition rate between ratings i and j. The concepts of exit and transition rates are analogous to that of default intensity, examined in Section 17.2. In this sense, one can think of the JLT model as a generalized intensity-based model, and, indeed, the JLT model is essentially an extension of the Jarrow and Turnbull (1995)[46] model.

The literature on ratings-based models is a vast one, and the uses and implications of these models go well beyond the analysis and valuation of credit derivatives. Other contributions to the literature include the work of Kijima and Komoribayashi (1998)[50], Lando and Skodeberg (2002)[52], Das and Tufano (1996)[19], and Arvanitis, Gregory, and Laurent (1999)[3]. Some structural credit risk models that are commercially available also incorporate the analysis of ratings transitions. We summarize the main features of a few well-known commercial models in Chapter 22.

18

Valuing Credit Options

Chapter 8 contained a basic discussion of the main features of spread and bond options. In this chapter we describe a relatively simple framework for valuing these instruments. We start Section 18.1 with a discussion of forward-starting credit default swaps, introducing some concepts that will come in handy in the valuation of credit default swaptions, the subject of Section 18.2. Section 18.3 generalizes the valuation approach for credit default swaptions so it can be used with other spread options. Extensions and alternatives to the simple framework described in Sections 18.2 and 18.3 are briefly discussed in Section 18.4. The valuation of bond options is sketched out in Section 18.5.

18.1 Forward-starting Contracts

At the end of Chapter 7 we briefly mentioned the forward-starting total return swap, which is a contractual commitment to enter into a total return swap at a fixed future date and at a predetermined spread. In this discussion of valuation methods for credit default swaptions and other credit options, we will meet two additional types of forward-starting contracts, the forward-starting credit default swap and forward contracts involving floaters. The aims of such contracts are self-evident; they are agreements to enter into a credit default swap and to buy and sell floaters, respectively, at future dates and at predetermined premiums (in the case of a CDS) and spreads (the forward floater contract).

As we shall see below, forward-starting credit default swaps can be thought of as the underlying "asset" in a credit default swaption, and thus it will be instructive to have a basic understanding of how they are valued before proceeding to examine the valuation of credit default swaptions. The same idea applies to forward contracts written on floaters, and so we shall examine them in some detail.

18.1.1   Valuing a Forward-starting CDS

Consider a forward-starting CDS agreement entered into at time t where one party agrees to buy protection in a CDS that will start at the future date T with a corresponding CDS premium of K, and premium payment dates $T_1, T_2, \ldots, T_n$. For simplicity, we assume that the notional amount of the CDS is \$1.

From Section 16.2, we know that the time-t market value of such an agreement to the protection buyer can be written as

$$W(t) = \sum_{j=1}^{n} Z(t, T_j)\{[Q(t, T_{j-1}) - Q(t, T_j)](1 - X) - Q(t, T_j)\delta_j K\} \quad (18.1)$$

where $Z(t, T_j)$ corresponds to the proxy for a riskfree discount factor— which, as discussed in Chapter 16, tends to be derived in practice from the LIBOR/swap curve to reflect the funding costs of the large banks that tend to be most active in the CDS market—and X and $Q(t, T_j)$ relate to, respectively, the recovery rate of the reference entity ($0 \leq X < 1$) and the risk-neutral probability that the reference entity will survive through T_j, conditional on all information available at time t. δ_j is the accrual factor for the jth premium payment (the number of days between the $(j-1)$th and jth premium payment dates divided by the number of days in the year, based on the appropriate day-count convention).

We can now introduce the notion of the forward CDS premium, which can be thought of as the value of K in (18.1) such that the forward-starting credit default swap has zero market value at time t. We shall let $S^F(t, T, T_n)$ denote the forward CDS premium, as seen at time t, for a CDS contract that will start at time T and have premium payment dates at $T_1, T_2, \ldots, T_n$. Solving (18.1) for K while requiring $W(t)$ to be zero, we can write

$$S^F(t, T, T_n) = \frac{\sum_{j=1}^{n} Z(t, T_j)[Q(t, T_{j-1}) - Q(t, T_j)](1 - X)}{\sum_{j=1}^{n} Z(t, T_j)Q(t, T_j)\delta_j} \quad (18.2)$$

and substituting this last expression into (18.1) we arrive at a convenient formula for the market value of a protection-buying position in a forward-starting credit default swap:

$$W(t) = \sum_{j=1}^{n} Z(t, T_j) Q(t, T_j) \delta_j [S^F(t, T, T_n) - K] \qquad (18.3)$$

which has the intuitive implication that the market value of a forward-starting CDS depends crucially on the difference between the corresponding forward CDS premium and the predetermined premium written into the contract.[1]

18.1.2 Other Forward-starting Structures

The valuation of other credit-related forward-starting structures, such as forward-starting asset swaps and forward contracts involving floating-rate notes, can be carried out using similar methods to the one just described for forward-starting credit default swaps. Consider, for instance, a forward contract to receive par for a floating-rate note at a future date with a prespecified spread over LIBOR. Assume, for simplicity, that the floater has a zero recovery rate. (This is a forward contract to sell a given floater for its par value at a future date at a predetermined spread.)

Recall, from Chapter 4, that the time-T market value of a just-issued par floater with a face value of \$1 and coupon payment dates $T_1, T_2, \ldots, T_n$ can be written as

$$1 = \sum_{j=1}^{n} Z_0^d(T, T_j) \delta_j [F^*(T, T_{j-1}, T_j) + s(T, T_n)] + Z_0^d(T, T_n) \qquad (18.4)$$

where $F^*(T, T_{j-1}, T_j)$ is the point on the forward LIBOR curve, as seen at time T, that corresponds to a loan lasting from the future date T_{j-1} to T_j; $s(T, T_n)$ is the par floater spread, and, to simplify the notation, $Z_0^d(T, T_j) \equiv Z(T, T_j) Q(t, T_j)$.

Likewise, for a par floater that pays LIBOR flat:

$$1 = \sum_{j=1}^{n} Z(T, T_j) \delta_j F^*(T, T_{j-1}, T_j) + Z(T, T_n) \qquad (18.5)$$

which differs from the previous equation only because of the zero spread and the choice of discount factors.

---

[1] Note the similarity between (18.3) and the expression for marking to market a CDS position in Chapter 16.

The time-t value of the latter par floater, for $t < T$, can be shown to be

$$Z(t,T) = \sum_{j=1}^{n} Z(t,T_j)\delta_j F^*(t,T_{j-1},T_j) + Z(t,T_n)$$

which can be verified given the definition of forward LIBOR (see Chapter 4):

$$F^*(t,T_{j-1},T_j) \equiv \delta_j^{-1}\left[\frac{Z(t,T_{j-1})}{Z(t,T_j)} - 1\right]$$

As for the riskier par floater, its time-t value becomes

$$Z_0^d(t,T) = \sum_{j=1}^{n} Z^d(t,T_j)[F^*(t,T_{j-1},T_j) + s^F(t,T,T_n)]\delta_j + Z_0^d(t,T_n)$$

where $s^F(t,T,T_n)$ is defined as the forward par floater spread associated with this particular issuer, as seen at time t, for future borrowing between times T and T_n.

Given the above, the task of valuing an arbitrary forward contract involving a floater that will pay a spread of say K, which is not necessarily the par spread, is relatively straightforward, and the reader can easily verify that, from the perspective of the party committed to selling the floater, the time-t value of such a contract can be written as

$$W^{FL}(t) = \sum_{j=1}^{n} Z^d(t,T_j)\delta_j[s^F(t,T,T_n) - K] + Z^d(t,T) \qquad (18.6)$$

which, again, has the simple intuition that a contract to sell a floater at a future date for par—in essence, a contract to pay a given spread starting at some future date—will have positive market value whenever the spread K written into the contract is below the corresponding forward spread associated with the issuer.

We carried out this discussion with a forward contract to sell a floater. The results would be entirely analogous for a forward-starting asset swap, and we leave this exercise to the reader.

18.2   Valuing Credit Default Swaptions

Let $W(t)$ be the time-t value, to a protection buyer, of a forward-starting credit default swap. Continuing with the same setup introduced in the previous section, the CDS will start at a future time T, with payment dates at $T_1, T_2, \ldots, T_n$, and the premium is set at K. As a result:

$$W(t) = \sum_{j=1}^{n} Z(t, T_j) Q(t, T_j) \delta_j [S^F(t, T, T_n) - K]$$

which is simply (18.3).

Consider now a European option, written at time t, to buy protection in the contract underlying the forward-starting CDS described in the previous section. At time T, the exercise date of the option, $S^F(T, T, T_n) = S(T, T_n)$, i.e., the forward premium converges to the spot premium, and the value of the default swaption will be:

$$V(T) = \text{Max}(W(T), 0) = \text{Max} \left\{ \sum_{j=1}^{n} Z_0^d(T, T_j) \delta_j [S(T, T_n) - K], 0 \right\}$$

$$(18.7)$$

Equation (18.7) tells us that the holder of this credit default swaption will exercise it only if the underlying CDS has positive market value at T, which is the case whenever the then-prevailing par CDS premium exceeds the premium written into the option (otherwise the holder would be better off paying the prevailing CDS premium, $S(T, T_n)$, in a par CDS, which has zero market value).

One can think of the term $\sum_{j=1}^{n} Z_0^d(T, T_j) \delta_j$ in equation (18.7) as an annuity factor that gives the time-T value of the entire stream of differences between the premium payments in a par CDS contract and the one specified in the default swaption. If we let $A(T, T_n)$ denote this factor, we can write the time-T value of the default swaption as

$$V(T) = \text{Max}[A(T, T_n)(S^F(T, T, T_n) - K), 0] \qquad (18.8)$$

To find the time-t value of the default swaption, it is convenient to rewrite (18.8) as

$$V(T) = A(T, T_n) \text{Max}[(S^F(T, T, T_n) - K), 0] \qquad (18.9)$$

which tells us that the time-T value of the option is simply a function of the present value of the difference between the premium payments of the two credit default swaps.

If we now recall that the time-t value of any financial asset is simply the risk-adjusted expected present value of its cash flow, we can write

$$V(t) = A(t, T) E_t^*[\text{Max}(S^F(T, T, T_n) - K, 0)] \qquad (18.10)$$

where $E_t^*[.]$ denotes the expected value of "." conditional on information available at time t, computed on the basis of probabilities that are appropriately adjusted for risk in a way that follows the spirit of the risk-neutral probabilities discussed in Chapter 15.[2]

In order to derive a pricing formula for this default swaption, we need to have an explicit assumption (a model) that describes the evolution of the forward CDS premium over time. A common assumption is to assert that $S^F(t, T, T_n)$ is lognormally distributed, which allows one to use the option pricing formula derived by Black (1976)[8].[3] If we let $\sigma(t, T, T_n)$ denote the volatility of percentage changes in $S^F(t, T, T_n)$, we can write the Black formula for a credit default swaption as:

$$V(t) = A(t, T_n)[S^F(t, T, T_n)N(d_1) - KN(d_2)] \qquad (18.11)$$

with

$$d_1 \equiv \frac{\log(S^F(t, T, T_n)/K)}{\sqrt{\sigma(T, T_n)^2(T-t)}} + .5\sigma(T, T_n)\sqrt{T-t}$$

$$d_2 \equiv \frac{\log(S^F(t, T, T_n)/K)}{\sqrt{\sigma(T, T_n)^2(T-t)}} - .5\sigma(T, T_n)\sqrt{T-t}$$

$N(.)$ is the cumulative standard normal distribution, and we made the simplifying assumption that $\sigma(t, T, T_n)$ is time-invariant.

As with vanilla calls and puts, credit default swaption prices are strictly increasing in the volatility of the relevant forward CDS premium. Other basic features of call and put options, such as put-call parity, also hold.

18.3   Valuing Other Credit Options

The valuation of other credit options, such as an option to sell the floater underlying the forward contract discussed in Section 18.2, can be carried out following essentially the same steps outlined for credit default swaptions.

---

[2] The reader with some familiarity with continuous-time finance methods may recognize the probability measure embedded in $E_t^*[.]$ as that corresponding to the so-called "annuity measure" (Hunt and Kennedy, 2000[43]). Under this probability measure, both the relative price $\frac{V(t)}{A(t, T_n)}$ and the forward par CDS premium $S^F(t, T, T_n)$ follow a random walk.

[3] The Black pricing formula is a variant of the well-known Black-Scholes formula. Black originally derived it for the pricing of options on futures contracts, but it can be shown that it applies directly to the pricing of credit default swaptions and many other related options. See Hull (2003)[41] for a textbook discussion of the Black formula.

Consider, for instance, a put option on a floater with a face value of $1. The option expires at date T and has a strike price of $1. As discussed in Chapter 8, this is basically a call option on the floater spread.

At time T, the value of the put option will be

$$V^{FL}(T) = \text{Max}(1 - W^{FL}(T), 0) \qquad (18.12)$$

i.e., the option holder will choose to sell the floater for its face value only if the market value of the floater, $W^{FL}(T)$, is less than $1.

We can use the results of Section 18.1.2 to rewrite equation (18.12) as

$$V^{FL}(T) = A(T, T_n)\text{Max}[s^F(T, T, T_n) - K, 0] \qquad (18.13)$$

and from here on one would proceed as in Section 18.2 to obtain the Black pricing formula for this call spread option.

18.4   Alternative Valuation Approaches

An implicit (but fundamental) assumption made in this chapter is that credit spreads and, thus, CDS premiums are stochastic variables. Indeed, it would make no sense to write an option on something that behaves deterministically. Going back to results derived in previous chapters, however, which suggested a close relationship between CDS premiums and the default probabilities of the reference entity, the assumption of stochastic forward CDS premiums is tantamount to admitting that default probabilities are themselves stochastic.

Indeed, an alternative approach to valuing spread and bond options is to model the stochastic behavior of default intensity directly, often jointly with the behavior of short-term interest rates, and use the resulting framework to derive the option prices of interest. As discussed by Arvanitis and Gregory (2001)[2] and Schonbucher (1999)[71], stochastic default probability models can also be used to value more complex credit options than the ones examined in this chapter, such as Bermudan options and other structures with more than one exercise date.

18.5   Valuing Bond Options

We discussed above the valuation of options written on floating-rate bonds and on credit default swaps. Similar methods apply to the valuation of options written on fixed-rate bonds. For instance, one may assume that the forward price of the bond is lognormally distributed and then use the Black formula as in Sections 18.2 and 18.3. Hull (2003)[41] provides a useful textbook discussion of the valuation of fixed-rate bond options.

Part IV

Introduction to Credit Modeling II: Portfolio Credit Risk

19

The Basics of Portfolio Credit Risk

The credit risk models we have examined thus far in this book have all focused on single default events, or on the likelihood that a given firm will default on its financial obligations within a given period of time. We shall now shift gears, so to speak, and take a quick tour of approaches and techniques that are useful for modeling credit risk in a portfolio setting. As we saw in Chapters 9, 10, and 14, two key concepts in the modeling of portfolio credit risk are default correlation and the loss distribution function. The basic model discussed in this chapter allows us to take a closer quantitative look at these concepts.

Before we proceed, however, one caveat is in order. The discussion in this part of the book only scratches the surface of what has become a large and growing technical literature on the modeling of portfolio credit risk. Our goal is only to introduce the reader to some of the main issues and challenges facing both academics and practitioners in the real world when it comes to modeling the default risk embedded in a portfolio of credit-related instruments.

19.1 Default Correlation

Intuitively, default correlation is a measure related to the likelihood that two or more reference entities will default together within a given horizon. The higher the default correlation between two firms, the higher the chances that default by one of them may be accompanied by a default by the other. Given that corporate defaults are relatively rare events, empirical measures of default correlation are not easy to come by. The available evidence suggests that default correlation tends to be higher for lower quality credits for higher borrowers, presumably because less-credit worthy firms are more sensitive to the ups and downs of the economy, and that the extent of default correlation depends on the time horizon in question (Lucas, 1995)[57]. In addition, it seems plausible that default correlation tends to be higher among firms in the same industry than among firms in different lines of business altogether, although one can imagine situations where a default by one firm strengthens the position of its main competitor, making it less likely to default.

19.1.1   Pairwise Default Correlation

From elementary statistics, we know that the correlation coefficient, ρ_{Y_1,Y_2}, involving two random variables Y_1 and Y_2 is defined as

$$\rho_{Y_1,Y_2} \equiv \frac{\text{Cov}[Y_1, Y_2]}{\sqrt{\text{Var}[Y_1]}\sqrt{\text{Var}[Y_2]}} \tag{19.1}$$

where $\text{Cov}[Y_1, Y_2]$ denotes the covariance between Y_1 and Y_2, and $\text{Var}[Y_1]$ and $\text{Var}[Y_2]$ stand for the variances of Y_1 and Y_2, respectively, all of which are defined below.

Mathematically, one can write an expression for the coefficient of default correlation for any two entities—called the pairwise default correlation—in terms of their respective default probabilities. To see this, we shall take another look at the two hypothetical entities we have been analyzing throughout this book: XYZ Corp. and AZZ Bank.

Using notation introduced earlier, we shall let ω_A and ω_X denote the (risk-neutral) default probabilities of AZZ and XYZ, respectively, over a given time horizon.[1] As for the probability that both AZZ Bank and XYZ Corp. will default together, we shall denote it as $\omega_{A\&X}$. These probabilities are represented in the diagram in Figure 19.1. The area encompassed by the rectangle in the figure represents all possible survival and default outcomes associated with AZZ and XYZ over a given time horizon. Those outcomes that involve a default by AZZ are shown within area A and those involving defaults by XYZ are represented by area X. For simplicity, we shall assume that the area of the rectangle is equal to 1 and thus we can think of the areas A and X as the probabilities that AZZ Bank and XYZ Corp. will default, respectively, within the prescribed time horizon. Furthermore, the region of overlap between areas A and X corresponds to the probability $\omega_{A\&X}$ that both AZZ Bank and XYZ Corp. will default.

---

[1] In terms of the notation used in Part III, ω_A and ω_X can be written as $1 - Q_A(t, T)$ and $1 - Q_X(t, T)$, respectively, where, for instance, $Q_A(t, T)$ is the risk-neutral probability, conditional on all information available at time t, that AZZ will survive through some future time T. As in previous chapters, we continue to denote the current time as t.

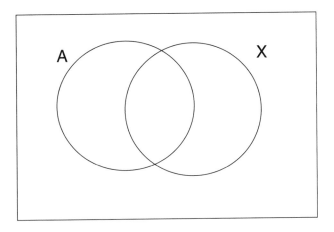

FIGURE 19.1. Diagrammatic Representation of Default Probabilities

Let us now define I_X as a random variable that takes the value of 1 in the event of default by XYZ Corp. over a given horizon and 0 otherwise. I_A is likewise defined for AZZ Bank. In technical terms, I_X and I_A are called indicator functions regarding default events by XYZ and AZZ. It is straightforward to see that the expected values of I_X and I_A are simply the associated default probabilities over the horizon of interest. For instance, given that I_A can only take two values, and relying on risk-neutral probabilities, its expected value is:

$$\tilde{E}[I_A] = \omega_A \times 1 + (1 - \omega_A) \times 0 = \omega_A \tag{19.2}$$

where $\tilde{E}[I_A]$ is the expectation of I_A, computed on the basis of risk-neutral probabilities.

Again using basic results from elementary statistics, we can also compute the variance of I_A and the covariance between I_A and I_X. The variance is

$$\text{Var}[I_A] \equiv \tilde{E}\left[(I_A - \tilde{E}[I_A])^2\right] = \omega_A(1 - \omega_A) \tag{19.3}$$

and the covariance can be written as

$$\text{Cov}[I_A, I_X] \equiv \tilde{E}\left[(I_A - \tilde{E}[I_A])(I_X - \tilde{E}[I_X])\right] = \tilde{E}[I_A I_X] - \tilde{E}[I_A]\tilde{E}[I_X]$$

But notice that $I_A I_X$ is only nonzero when both I_A and I_X are 1, and that happens with probability $\omega_{A\&X}$. Thus

$$\tilde{E}[I_A I_X] = \omega_{A\&X}$$

and we can write

$$\text{Cov}[I_A, I_X] = \omega_{A\&X} - \omega_A\omega_X \tag{19.4}$$

We can now derive an expression for the pairwise default correlation for AZZ Bank and XYZ Corp. entirely in terms of their respective default probabilities:

$$\rho_{A,X} \equiv \frac{\text{Cov}[I_A, I_X]}{\sqrt{\text{Var}[I_A]}\sqrt{\text{Var}[I_X]}} = \frac{\omega_{A\&X} - \omega_A\omega_X}{\sqrt{\omega_A(1-\omega_A)}\sqrt{\omega_X(1-\omega_X)}} \tag{19.5}$$

Equation (19.5) formalizes an intuitive and key result regarding pairwise default correlations. In particular, other things being equal, the higher the probability that any two entities will default together over the prescribed horizon—the region of overlap between areas A and X in Figure 19.1—the higher their pairwise default correlation coefficient over that horizon.[2]

It can be shown that (19.5) is such that the pairwise default correlation coefficient lies between 1 (perfect positive correlation) and -1 (perfect negative correlation). In the former case, the two entities either default or survive together; in the latter case, only one of the entities will survive through the end of the relevant horizon and a position in a bond issued by one entity can be used as a hedge against default-related losses in an otherwise comparable bond issued by the other.

The case of perfect positive correlation, $\rho_{A,X} = 1$, corresponds to a scenario where the two entities have identical default probabilities, $\omega_A = \omega_X = \bar{\omega}$, and where $\omega_{A\&X} = \bar{\omega}$. The case of perfect negative correlation corresponds to a scenario where $\omega_{A\&X}$ is zero, its lower bound, and $\omega_X = 1 - \omega_A$, i.e., there is no region of overlap between areas A and X in Figure 19.1 and area X takes up the entire portion of the rectangle that is not encompassed by area A.[3]

In addition to the two polar cases of perfect positive and negative correlation, another special case is the situation of zero default correlation between any two entities. As can be seen in equation (19.5), this corresponds to the case where $\omega_{A\&X} = \omega_A\omega_X$.

Before we proceed, we can use a variant of Figure 19.1 to verify a result advanced in Chapter 9. We claimed in that chapter that as the default

---

[2] Equation (19.5) is only one of several possible ways to define default correlation. For instance, an alternative approach would be to focus on the correlation of default times. Technically oriented readers interested in this topic may wish to consult Li (2000)[55] and Embrechts, McNeil, and Strautman (1999)[26].

[3] One way to verify that 1 is the maximum value that $\rho_{A\&X}$ can achieve is to convince yourself that $\omega_{A\&X}$ cannot be larger than $\text{Min}[\omega_A, \omega_X]$. Hint: Look at the diagram in Figure 19.1.

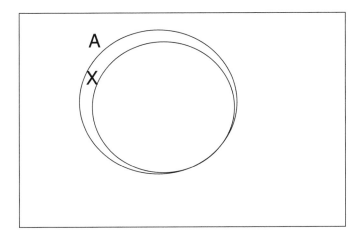

FIGURE 19.2. Diagrammatic Representation of a Case of High Default Correlation

correlation between two entities approaches 1, the probability that both entities will default over a given period approaches the default probability of the entity with the higher credit quality. This is illustrated in Figure 19.2, which shows a near complete overlap between areas A and X—or a default correlation of nearly one according to the results discussed above—but where area A is larger than area X—AZZ bank is of an inferior credit quality (greater default probability) than XYZ Corp. In the case depicted in the figure, all scenarios where XYZ Corp. defaults are also scenarios where AZZ Bank defaults. Hence the region of overlap between areas A and X is the same as area X.

19.1.2   Modeling Default Correlation

Thus far we have essentially limited ourselves to a portfolio with debt instruments issued by only two entities. How do we examine default correlation in more realistic settings, which often involve a large number of entities? We discuss below a very simple modeling framework that allows us to start tackling this issue and that should expose many of the difficulties and challenges associated with modeling portfolio credit risk.[4]

The model builds on the seminal work of Black and Scholes (1973)[9] and Merton (1974)[59], which we discussed in Part III. In particular, for a hypothetical firm i, we define default as a situation where the return R_i on

---

[4]Versions of the simple model discussed in this section can be found in Gupton, Finger, and Bhatia (1997)[37], O'Kane and Schlogl (2001)[64], Crosbie (2002)[16], and many others.

owning the firm falls below a given threshold C_i at a given date T.[5] Thus,

$$\text{Default by firm } i \text{ at time } T \iff R_i \leq C_i \qquad (19.6)$$

and the default probability associated with this firm is simply the probability that its return will fall short of C_i over the relevant time horizon.

To simplify the analysis, especially when debt instruments issued by several firms are included in the portfolio, we shall assume that the above returns have already been standardized, i.e., for each firm i in the portfolio, we express returns in terms of deviations from the sample mean and divide the result by the standard deviation of returns:

$$R_{i,t} \equiv \frac{\bar{R}_{i,t} - \mu_i}{\sigma_i}$$

where $\bar{R}_{i,t}$ are the raw ("non-standardized") returns associated with owning firm i at time t, and μ_i and σ_i are the mean and standard deviation of $\bar{R}_{i,t}$, respectively. Note that, by working with standardized returns, all the firms in the portfolio have the same expected returns and standard deviations of returns—0 and 1, respectively.

Let us now consider a portfolio that contains debt instruments issued by I different firms, where default events for each firm are defined as in equation (19.6). Two key assumptions of the model we are about to introduce are that (i) individual returns R_i are normally distributed, and (ii) returns (and thus defaults) across firms are correlated through dependence on one common factor. A straightforward corollary of the first assumption is that, for a given time horizon, the probability of default by any one single firm is given by

$$\omega_i \equiv \text{Prob[default by firm } i] = \text{Prob}[R_i \leq C_i] = N(C_i) \qquad (19.7)$$

where $N(.)$ is the cumulative distribution function of the standard normal distribution.

---

[5] Strictly speaking, R_i could be more properly called a log-return given that we implicitly define it in discrete time as

$$R_{i,t} \equiv \log(A_{i,t}) - \log(A_{i,t-1})$$

where $A_{i,t}$ is the value of firm i at time t. In the remainder of this book, however, we will economize on terminology and simply call $R_{i,t}$ the return associated with firm i.

Readers of earlier chapters will notice that we have shifted from an asset-value-based definition of default—recall, for instance, that the Black-Scholes-Merton framework discussed in Chapter 17 modeled defaults as situations where the *value* of the firm fell below some critical level—to one that is based on (log) returns. These two approaches to specifying defaults are perfectly consistent with one another: In the Black-Scholes-Merton framework, the value, A_i, of the firm was assumed to be lognormally distributed, which has the implication that log-returns are normally distributed, as assumed here.

Here we pause to note that the probabilities involved in equation (19.7)—and, indeed, throughout this part of the book—correspond to the concept of risk-neutral probabilities, which we discussed in Part III. Thus, if they are available, one can use market prices of liquid assets, such as credit default swap premiums for certain reference names, as a means of arriving at a value for ω_i and then rely on (19.7) to back out a market-implied value for C_i:

$$C_i = N^{-1}(\omega_i) \tag{19.8}$$

where $N^{-1}(.)$ is the inverse of $N(\cdot)$, or the function that determines the value of C_i in (19.7) that corresponds to a given value of ω_i.

Going back to the second assumption (correlation through dependence on a common factor), we complete the model by making the following assumption regarding the evolution of returns:

$$R_{i,t} = \beta_i \alpha_t + \sqrt{1 - \beta_i^2}\,\epsilon_{i,t} \tag{19.9}$$

for all firms in the portfolio, i.e., for $i = 1, 2, \ldots, I$.

Equation (19.9) says that individual returns, and thus the likelihood of default, depend on a factor α, which affects all entities represented in the portfolio, and on an entity-specific factor ϵ_i. For instance, the entities represented in the portfolio may all be sensitive to conditions in the overall stock market, or, alternatively, α_t may stand for the current state of the economy.

To be consistent with the definition of $R_{i,t}$ as a random variable with zero mean and unit variance, we further assume that α_t and, for all i, $\epsilon_{i,t}$ have also been standardized—they have zero mean and unit variance—and that they are independently and normally distributed.[6] We also assume that, for any two firms i and j, $\epsilon_{j,t}$ and $\epsilon_{i,t}$ are independently distributed and that α_t and $\epsilon_{i,t}$, and thus $R_{i,t}$ are serially uncorrelated, i.e.,

$$\tilde{E}[\alpha_t \alpha_{t-s}] = \tilde{E}[\epsilon_{i,t} \epsilon_{i,t-s}] = 0$$

for all nonzero values of s.[7]

---

[6] It is easy to verify that (19.9) is consistent with the assumption of zero mean and unit variance of returns. $\tilde{E}[R_{i,t}] = 0$ follows directly from the zero-mean assumption on α and ϵ_i. To see that the variance of $R_{i,t}$ remains unit, simply note that we can write it as

$$\text{Var}[R_{i,t}] = \beta_i^2 \tilde{E}[\alpha_t^2] + (1 - \beta_i^2)\tilde{E}[\epsilon_{i,t}^2] + 2\beta_i \sqrt{1 - \beta_i^2}\,\tilde{E}[\alpha_t \epsilon_{i,t}]$$

which is equal to one given the variance and independence assumptions regarding α_t and $\epsilon_{i,t}$.

[7] The concept of serial independence is discussed briefly in Appendix B.

In light of equation (19.9), we can show that β_i plays a crucial role in capturing the extent of return correlation among any two entities in the portfolio. In particular, the covariance between $R_{i,t}$ and $R_{j,t}$ can be written as

$$\text{Cov}(R_{i,t}, R_{j,t}) \equiv \tilde{E}[(R_{i,t} - \tilde{E}[R_{i,t}])(R_{j,t} - \tilde{E}[R_{j,t}])] = \beta_i \beta_j \qquad (19.10)$$

which, given the assumption of unit variances, also corresponds to the correlation between $R_{i,t}$ and $R_{j,t}$.

From a modeling standpoint, one advantage of the above framework is that, for a given value of the common factor, α, returns involving any two firms in the portfolio, and thus their respective default events, are uncorrelated.[8] To verify the conditional independence of defaults, we start by computing the conditional mean and variance of returns under the model:

$$\tilde{E}[R_{i,t}|\alpha_t] = \beta_i \alpha_t \qquad (19.11)$$

$$\text{Var}[R_{i,t}|\alpha_t] = 1 - \beta_i^2 \qquad (19.12)$$

and it is then straightforward to see that returns are indeed pairwise conditionally uncorrelated:

$$\text{Cov}[R_{i,t}, R_{j,t}|\alpha_t] = \sqrt{1 - \beta_i^2}\sqrt{1 - \beta_j^2}\,\tilde{E}[\epsilon_{i,t}\epsilon_{j,t}] = 0 \qquad (19.13)$$

where $\tilde{E}[R_{i,t}|\alpha_t]$ is the expected value of $R_{i,t}$ conditioned on the time-t value of α, and $\text{Var}[.|\alpha_t]$ and $\text{Cov}[.|\alpha_t]$ are analogously defined. Note that (19.13) follows from the fact that $\epsilon_{i,t}$ and $\epsilon_{j,t}$ are mutually independently distributed, i.e., $\tilde{E}[\epsilon_{i,t}\epsilon_{j,t}] = 0$.

We can also compute conditional default probabilities over given horizons for any firm in the portfolio. For instance, for $\alpha_T = \alpha_t$, the time-t probability that the firm will default at time T can be written as

$$\omega_i(\alpha_t) \equiv \text{Prob[default by firm } i \text{ at } T|\alpha_t] = \text{Prob}\left[\epsilon_{i,T} \leq \frac{C_i - \beta_i \alpha_t}{\sqrt{1 - \beta_i^2}}\right] \qquad (19.14)$$

which, unlike the expression for unconditional default probabilities, equation (19.7), depends importantly on β_i.

---

[8] Throughout this chapter we assume that C_i is a deterministic variable for all i.

19.1.3   Pairwise Default Correlation and "β"

We have shown that the model-implied correlation between returns on any two assets in the portfolio is:

$$\text{Cor}(R_{i,t}, R_{j,t}) = \text{Cov}(R_{i,t}, R_{j,t}) = \beta_i \beta_j \tag{19.15}$$

How does that relate to the concept of pairwise default correlation discussed in Section 19.1.1? There we saw that we can write the default correlation between any two entities i and j in the portfolio as

$$\rho_{i,j} = \frac{\omega_{i\&j} - \omega_i \omega_j}{\sqrt{\omega_i(1-\omega_i)}\sqrt{\omega_j(1-\omega_j)}} \tag{19.16}$$

where we have already seen that the model implies that the probabilities ω_i and ω_j can be written as $N(C_i)$ and $N(C_j)$, respectively. Now, $\omega_{i\&j}$ denotes the probability that both i and j will default over the time horizon of interest. In the context of the model,

$$\omega_{i\&j} \equiv \text{Prob}[R_i \leq C_i \text{ and } R_j \leq C_j] \tag{19.17}$$

but, given that R_i and R_j are individually normally distributed with correlation coefficient $\beta_i \beta_j$, they are jointly distributed according to the bivariate normal distribution. Thus,

$$\omega_{i\&j} = N_2(C_i, C_j, \beta_i \beta_j) \tag{19.18}$$

where $N_2()$ is the cumulative distribution function of the bivariate normal distribution.[9]

We can now write out the default correlation between any two entities in the portfolio entirely in terms of model parameters:

$$\rho_{i,j} = \frac{N_2(C_i, C_j, \beta_i \beta_j) - N(C_i)N(C_j)}{\sqrt{N(C_i)(1-N(C_i))}\sqrt{N(C_j)(1-N(C_j))}} \tag{19.19}$$

Equation (19.19) shows the explicit link between the return correlation parameters, β_i and β_j, and the degree of default correlation between reference entities i and j. Figure 19.3 illustrates the nature of this link for a particular parameterization of default probabilities—$\omega_i = \omega_j = .05$—and return correlations—$\beta_i = \beta_j = \beta$, and β varies from 0 to 1. The figure shows that default correlation increases monotonically with return correlation, but the relationship is very nonlinear. Given this one-to-one mapping

---

[9]See Appendix B.

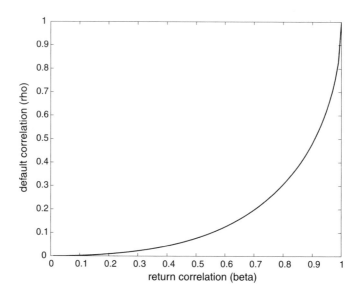

FIGURE 19.3. Return Correlation (β) and Pairwise Default Correlation

between β and $\rho_{i,j}$, we shall couch the discussion of default correlation in this part of the book mostly in terms of β. We do this simply for analytical convenience.

19.2   The Loss Distribution Function

We first met the concept of the loss distribution function in this book in Chapter 10, where we discussed portfolio default swaps. To recap, an informal definition of the loss distribution function would say that, for a given portfolio, it is the function that assigns probabilities to default-related losses of various magnitudes over a given time horizon.

We will continue to build on the simple modeling framework introduced in the previous section to take a closer look at the loss distribution function and its relation to default correlation. For convenience, however, we will make a few additional simplifying assumptions. First, we assume that the portfolio is composed of a set of homogeneous debt instruments, i.e., for all i,

$$\beta_i = \beta$$

$$C_i = C$$

Second, we assume that each entity represented in the portfolio corresponds to an equal share of the portfolio. Henceforth, we will refer to such a portfolio as an equally weighted homogeneous portfolio.

The first assumption ensures that all entities represented in the portfolio have the same default probability over the time period of interest; the second guarantees that there is a one-to-one correspondence between the number of defaults in the portfolio and the size of the percentage default-related loss in the portfolio. In particular, in a portfolio with, say, I reference entities, the probability of k defaults among the entities in the portfolio is equivalent to the probability of a $100\frac{k}{I}$ percent default-related loss in the portfolio.[10]

19.2.1 *Conditional Loss Distribution Function*

Armed with the tools developed thus far we can compute the probability distribution of default-related losses for a given value of α, which corresponds to the concept of the conditional loss distribution function. Given that, conditional on α, individual returns are independently and normally distributed, a basic result from statistics says that the number of defaults in the portfolio is binomially distributed for a given value of α.[11] Thus, if we let L denote the percentage (default-related) loss in the portfolio over, say, the next year, we can write the conditional probability of a given loss as

$$\text{Prob}\left[L = \frac{k}{I}|\alpha\right] \equiv \text{Prob}\left[k \text{ defaults}|\alpha\right] = \frac{I!}{k!(I-k)!}\omega(\alpha)^k[1-\omega(\alpha)]^{I-k} \tag{19.20}$$

where

$$\omega(\alpha) \equiv \text{Prob}\left[\epsilon_{i,t} \leq \frac{C-\beta\alpha}{\sqrt{1-\beta^2}}\right] = N\left(\frac{C-\beta\alpha}{\sqrt{1-\beta^2}}\right) \tag{19.21}$$

is the conditional probability of default of each reference entity represented in the equally weighted homogeneous portfolio.

Equation (19.20) is essentially the expression for the conditional loss distribution function implied by (19.9), applied to the case of an equally-weighted homogeneous portfolio. To highlight its dependence on the common factor, α, Figure 19.4 shows conditional loss distribution functions corresponding to a period of, say, one year for a portfolio with 20

---

[10] For added convenience, we are assuming a zero recovery rate for all entities in the portfolio.

[11] See Appendix B for an overview of the binomial distribution.

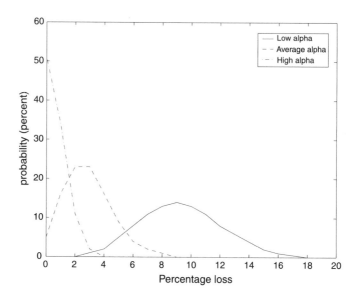

FIGURE 19.4. Conditional Loss Distribution Functions for an Equally Weighted Homogeneous Portfolio

reference entities, each with an individual default probability of 5 percent and a β of 0.5. The figure depicts three cases, one with α set at its average value of zero, and the others corresponding to α set at plus and minus one standard deviation, -1 and 1, respectively.[12]

As can be seen in Figure 19.4, the conditional loss distribution function flattens out as α declines. This is consistent with the intuition that, with positive dependence of returns on α, conditional default probabilities increase for all entities in the portfolio as α decreases. Lower values of α in this case pull individual returns closer to their default thresholds, C, increasing the likelihood of larger losses in the portfolio and thus allowing for "fatter tails" in the conditional loss distribution function.

19.2.2 Unconditional Loss Distribution Function

When pricing multi-name credit derivatives such as basket swaps and portfolio default swaps it is often the unconditional loss distribution function that will matter most. As its name suggests, this concept is not predicated on any one particular value of the common factor, α, and thus it fully

---

[12] Figure 19.4 illustrates an additional use of the modeling framework examined in this chapter, which is to assess likely losses in the portfolio under different scenarios involving the common factor, a practice commonly called scenario stress testing.

takes on board the reality that future values of α are themselves generally subject to substantial uncertainty.

In what follows we shall use the model to derive an analytical solution for the unconditional loss distribution function of a homogeneous portfolio. The technical requirements for this derivation are perhaps a bit beyond the scope of this book, but we should note that readers less interested in statistical and mathematical details may skip this subsection entirely without any fear of missing out on what is to come in the remainder of Part IV. Indeed, the main reason for obtaining an expression for the loss distribution here—equation (19.24) below—is so we can use it later on to check the accuracy of the large-portfolio approximation and simulation-based methods described in sections 19.2.3 and 19.4, respectively. It is the latter method, in particular, that will be our tool of choice throughout most of this part of the book, not just for deriving loss distribution functions, but also for valuing multi-name credit derivatives.

To derive an expression for the unconditional loss distribution, we appeal to a basic result from statistics, known as the law of iterated expectations. According to this "law," the unconditional expectation of having, say, k defaults in the portfolio is given by the probability-weighted average of conditional probabilities of having k defaults. These latter probabilities are computed over all possible values of the common factor α, and the weights are given by the probability density function of α. Thus,

$$\text{Prob}\,[k \text{ defaults }] = \int_{-\infty}^{\infty} \text{Prob}\,[k \text{ defaults }|\alpha = y]\, n(y)dy \qquad (19.22)$$

where $n(.)$ is the probability density function of the standard normal distribution.[13]

Substituting equations (19.20) and (19.21) into (19.22) we obtain the following expression for the unconditional probability of k defaults in the portfolio:

$$\text{Prob}\,[k \text{ defaults }] = \int_{-\infty}^{\infty} \frac{I!}{k!(I-k)!}\omega(y)^k(1-\omega(y))^{I-k}n(y)dy \qquad (19.23)$$

where $\omega(y) \equiv N\left(\frac{C-\beta y}{\sqrt{1-\beta^2}}\right)$, as we saw earlier.

---

[13] See Appendix B for a quick review of key results from statistics.

Given equation (19.23), the analytical solution for the loss distribution function of a homogeneous portfolio is:

$$\text{Prob}\,[l \le K] = \sum_{k=0}^{K} \int_{-\infty}^{\infty} \frac{I!}{k!(I-k)!} \omega(y)^k (1 - \omega(y))^{I-k} n(y) dy \quad (19.24)$$

where $\text{Prob}[l \le K]$ denotes the probability that the number of defaults in the portfolio will be equal to or less than K. Equation (19.24) is a somewhat cumbersome expression that can be solved, for instance, via numerical integration, provided I is not too large.

19.2.3 Large-Portfolio Approximation

As we saw in the previous section, allowing for both the common and the firm-specific factors to be fully stochastic makes the mathematical analysis of credit risk in portfolios substantially more involving than in the case of fixed values for the common factor, especially for portfolios with a large number of assets. One technique that greatly simplifies the analysis of relatively homogeneous portfolios with many assets is the so-called large-portfolio approximation method—see, for instance, Vasicek (1987)[73].[14] As the name suggests, the main thrust of this approach is to assume that the portfolio has a sufficiently large number of reference entities so that the expected fraction of entities defaulting over a given time horizon can be approximated by the corresponding individual default probabilities of the entities.[15] In terms of the conditional default probabilities derived in Section 19.2.1, this implies

$$\theta \equiv \tilde{E}[L|\alpha] \approx \omega(\alpha) \quad (19.25)$$

where θ and L are the expected and actual percentage loss in the portfolio, respectively.

Note that for any given value of θ, one can back out the implied value of α upon which the conditional expectation in (19.25) is based:

$$\alpha = \omega^{-1}(\theta) \quad (19.26)$$

where $\omega^{-1}(.)$ is the inverse function of $\omega(\alpha)$.[16]

---

[14] Our presentation of the large-portfolio approximation method partly follows O'Kane and Schlogl (2001)[64].

[15] Readers with some familiarity with statistics will recognize the (conditional) law of large numbers at work here.

[16] We will ignore the approximation error embedded in (19.25) from now on. Obviously, that error can be significant, especially for small portfolios, which, as we will see in Section 19.4, can be examined with alternative methods.

Suppose now that the actual value of α turns out to be larger than the one used in (19.25). Other things being equal, the actual percentage loss, L, will be smaller than the expected loss, θ, because, for positive β, individual returns will be farther away from the default boundary C than implicit in (19.25). Mathematically, this can be summed up as:

$$\alpha \geq \omega^{-1}(\theta) \Longleftrightarrow L \leq \theta \tag{19.27}$$

Thus, we can make the following probabilistic statement:

$$\text{Prob}[\alpha \geq \omega^{-1}(\theta)] = \text{Prob}[L \leq \theta] \tag{19.28}$$

Given that α was assumed to be normally distributed, and relying on the symmetric nature of the normal probability density function,[17]

$$\text{Prob}[\alpha \geq \omega^{-1}(\theta)] = \text{Prob}[\alpha \leq -\omega^{-1}(\theta)] = N(-\omega^{-1}(\theta))$$

Thus we arrive at the result:

$$\text{Prob}[L \leq \theta] = N(-\omega^{-1}(\theta)) \tag{19.29}$$

which is an approximate expression for the unconditional loss distribution of the large homogeneous portfolio.

To write out (19.29) explicitly in terms of the parameters of the model, note that, ignoring any errors introduced by the large portfolio approximation, equations (19.21) and (19.25) imply

$$\theta = N\left(\frac{C - \beta\alpha}{\sqrt{1 - \beta^2}}\right) \tag{19.30}$$

and thus we can write

$$\alpha = \frac{C - N^{-1}(\theta)\sqrt{1 - \beta^2}}{\beta} \tag{19.31}$$

which, together with (19.26), implies

$$\omega^{-1}(\theta) = \frac{C - N^{-1}(\theta)\sqrt{1 - \beta^2}}{\beta} \tag{19.32}$$

---

[17] By symmetry of the normal distribution we mean the fact that, for any normally distributed random variable α that has an expected value of zero,

$$\text{Prob}[\alpha \geq U] = \text{Prob}[\alpha \leq -U]$$

where U is any arbitrary real number.

and we arrive at our final expression for the (approximate) unconditional loss distribution of a large homogeneous portfolio:

$$\text{Prob}[L \leq \theta] = N(-\frac{C - N^{-1}(\theta)\sqrt{1-\beta^2}}{\beta}) \qquad (19.33)$$

19.3   Default Correlation and Loss Distribution

We are now ready to start tying together some of the different topics discussed in this chapter by examining how the probability distribution of future losses is affected by the degree of default correlation among the issuers in the portfolio. This analysis also expands on an early exercise on correlation and loss distribution, discussed in Chapter 10.

Our goal is to examine the crucial role that default correlation plays in the determination of a portfolio's loss distribution function and, as we shall see in greater detail in Chapters 20 and 21, in the valuation of multi-name credit derivatives. To highlight that role, we shall examine two large homogeneous portfolios—which we shall call portfolios A and B—that are identical in every respect, except for their extent of return, and, thus, default correlation. In particular, for a given horizon, the individual default probabilities of the entities represented in either portfolio are assumed to be 5 percent, which, following the spirit of equation (19.25), means that both portfolios have expected default-related losses of 5 percent. (For simplicity, we continue to assume zero recovery rates for all entities.) As for their degree of correlation with the common factor, we shall assume that portfolio A has a β of 0.2, and portfolio B's β is 0.5.

Figure 19.5 shows the unconditional loss distribution functions for the two portfolios described above. The loss distributions are quite different despite the fact that both portfolios have the same expected loss. In particular, the loss distribution of portfolio A (low β) shows a virtually zero probability of default-related losses amounting to more than 15 percent of the portfolio. In contrast, for portfolio B (high β), that probability is distinctively positive, although still relatively small. Portfolio B also has a higher probability of very small losses than does portfolio A, reflecting the fact that its higher correlation results in a greater tendency for its reference entities to either survive or default together. In statistical parlance, the portfolio with the greater default correlation has a loss distribution with "fatter tails," i.e., the loss distribution of portfolio B assigns greater odds to extreme events than does that of portfolio A.

From a practical perspective, the basic insights derived from the analysis of portfolios A and B are very powerful. First, the degree of default correlation in a portfolio can dramatically affect its risk characteristics. For instance, while holding a portfolio that includes a large number of issuers

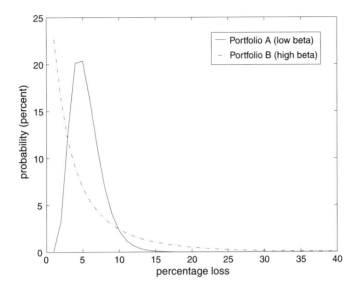

FIGURE 19.5. Unconditional Loss Distribution Functions for Two Large Homogeneous Portfolios

generally contributes to diversification across different types of risks, that diversification may be significantly reduced if the degree of default correlation among the issuers is high. Indeed, higher odds of extreme events can be thought of as reduced diversification. For instance, as we discussed in Chapter 10, in the extreme case of perfect correlation either all of the issuers in the portfolio survive or default together, which is akin to holding only one asset (no diversification).

A second basic insight from Figure 19.5 regards the valuation of credit derivatives that involve some tranching of credit risk, such as baskets and portfolio default swaps, which we will examine more fully in the next two chapters. As we saw in Chapters 9 and 10, the valuation of these derivatives can be importantly affected by the probability distribution of losses in the underlying portfolio, which, as we have just seen, depends crucially on the degree of default correlation among the entities represented in the portfolio.

19.4   Monte Carlo Simulation: Brief Overview

As an alternative to the large portfolio approximation, one can use Monte Carlo simulation methods to compute the (approximate) loss distribution function of a portfolio. In their simplest form, described below, simulation methods place less mathematical demands on the user, at the cost of longer computer running times than the version of the large portfolio method discussed in Section 19.2.[18] An advantage of simulation-based methods is that they are best applied to smaller portfolios, for which the large portfolio approximation method is less suitable. In addition, they can be easily used in the analysis of heterogeneous portfolios and in versions of the model that allow for more than one common factor.

We can use equations (19.6) and (19.9)—repeated below for convenience—to illustrate the basic principle of the Monte Carlo simulation approach:

$$\text{Default by firm } i <=> R_{i,t} \leq C_i$$

$$R_{i,t} = \beta_i \alpha_t + \left(\sqrt{1 - \beta_i^2} \right) \epsilon_{i,t}$$

where, as assumed before, α and ϵ_i are mutually independent random variables that are normally distributed with zero mean and unit variance.

The basic thrust of simulation-based methods is very straightforward. It consists of generating a large number of draws from the standard normal distribution for α and, for all i in the portfolio, for ϵ_i. For instance, for a portfolio with 20 reference entities, each draw will consist of 21 values randomly selected according to the standard normal distribution, and, for each draw, one compares the resulting return R_i for each entity to its default boundary, C_i, to determine whether or not a default has occurred. After a sufficiently large number of draws, one can count the number of defaults and estimate the probability distribution of losses as

$$\text{Prob}[j \text{ defaults}] = M_j / M$$

where M_j is the number of draws where there were j defaults in the portfolio, and M is the total number of draws.[19]

We illustrate the simple simulation-based method described above for an equally weighted homogeneous portfolio with 40 reference entities, each with a one-year individual default probability of 5 percent and a degree of correlation (β) of 0.2. The solid line in Figure 19.6 shows the corresponding loss distribution function for this portfolio, based on 500,000 draws from the standard normal distribution. To keep the analysis comparable

---

[18] Hull (2003)[41] provides an overview of simulation techniques in finance.

[19] If one is interested in the distribution of percentage losses in the portfolio, one can modify these calculations accordingly. For instance, M_j could stand for the number of draws where percentage losses in the portfolio amounted to j percent.

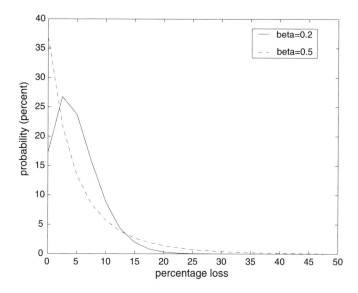

FIGURE 19.6. Unconditional Loss Distribution Functions for Smaller Portfolios (based on 500,000 simulations of the model)

to that of large portfolios, we also computed the probability loss distribution for an otherwise identical portfolio with a β of 0.5. We arrive at some of the same conclusions discussed in Section 19.3. Portfolios with a larger degree of default correlation have more probability mass at tail events than do portfolios with less correlation. Again, we see the benefits of effective diversification (less default correlation) at work.

19.4.1 How Accurate is the Simulation-Based Method?

We have mentioned some desirable features of the simulation-based method—such as ease of use and applicability to both small and heterogeneous portfolios, as well as to multifactor models—and a potential drawback—Monte Carlo simulations tend to be computer intensive. Simulation-based methods would be of limited value, however, if the resulting loss distribution function were a poor representation of the true function implied by the model—equation (19.24)—or if it took an unreasonably large number of simulations—and thus substantial computing time—for the simulation method to get it right.

Figure 19.7 takes an informal look at the accuracy of the Monte Carlo simulation approach for two portfolios that are identical in every respect

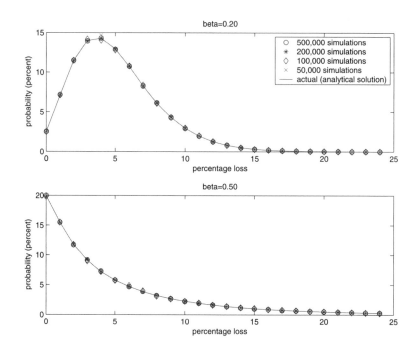

FIGURE 19.7. How Accurate is the Simulation-based Method? (Homogeneous equally weighted portfolios with 100 assets; total face value = $100,000)

except for their degree of asset correlation. In particular, each port-folio is composed of 100 assets with individual default probabilities of 5 percent and zero recovery rates. For each portfolio, the figure shows "actual" (analytical) values of the loss distribution, as well as a set of Monte-Carlo-based values. The results suggest that, even for computations involving a number of simulations as low as 50,000—which take only a few seconds to run in a well equipped laptop—the Monte Carlo method seems to do a very good job capturing both the level and the shape of the true loss distribution function.

The results in Figure 19.7 are only illustrative, however. A more formal evaluation of the Monte Carlo approach would involve examining the results of a large number of simulation exercises—for instance, running 100,000 simulations of the model 1,000 times and computing the mean and standard deviation of all 1,000 results—so that one could look at the variability of the final results. It should also be noted, that the simple simulation method described in this chapter can be improved considerably through the use of "variance-reduction" techniques, which are designed to reduce the amount of random noise that is inherent in simulation-based methods.[20]

19.4.2   Evaluating the Large-Portfolio Method

We can now compare results obtained through the large-portfolio approximation method to those generated by the simulation-based approach, which, as we have just seen, can be made very accurate. Similar to the spirit of the last subsection, one can view this exercise as a very informal evaluation of the large-portfolio approximation approach's ability to capture the main features of the loss distribution function of progressively smaller portfolios under different correlation assumptions.

Figure 19.8 summarizes the main findings. We consider several hypothetical portfolios designed along the same lines as the ones examined thus far in this chapter. The top panel shows the unconditional loss distribution

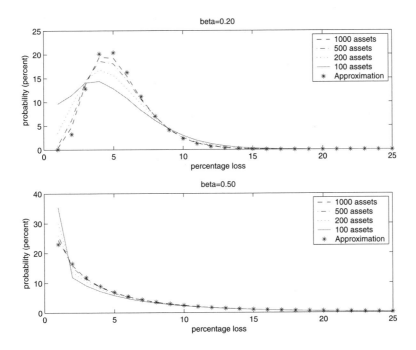

FIGURE 19.8. An Informal Evaluation of the Large-Portfolio Approximation Method

---

[20] See, for instance, Hull (2003)[41] for an overview of variance reduction techniques.

functions for four equally weighted homogeneous portfolios that are identical in every aspect, except for the number of reference entities included in the portfolio, which varies from 100 to 1,000. For all portfolios, the default probabilities of the individual entities are assumed to be 5 percent and $\beta = 0.2$. The Monte-Carlo-based results were derived based on 500,000 simulations of the model. The figure also shows the loss distribution function based on the large-portfolio approximation. Not surprisingly, the approximation works best for the largest portfolio, but it is noteworthy that even for the 200-asset portfolio, the large-portfolio approximation seems to have been able to capture the general shape and level of the loss distribution.

The lower panel of Figure 19.8 depicts results for the same cases examined in the upper panel, but we now examine scenarios with a bit more return correlation among the entities in the portfolios, $\beta = 0.5$. The results suggest that the approximation works relatively well, especially as we move away from the left end of the distribution. On the whole, the figure suggests that the large-portfolio approximation seems to work "better" for portfolios with higher correlation than for those with lower correlation. While we are being vague here about what better means in this context, our intuition would suggest that in the limit case of perfect correlation, the portfolio essentially behaves as a single asset and the loss distributions of small and large portfolios should essentially become the same.

Once again, we should emphasize that this section provides only an informal evaluation of the large-portfolio approximation approach. Our purpose here was only to provide some of the flavor of the practical and methodological issues that one is likely to face when dealing with real-world portfolios and more advanced techniques. Issues not addressed here include the fact that real-life portfolios are not strictly homogeneous, which would add another source of approximation error to the large portfolio approach.

One final point about Figure 19.8. The loss distribution functions of the various portfolios shown is remarkably similar, especially for the portfolios with more than 100 reference names, although one can see a pattern of slightly less dispersion of likely losses—more of the probability mass is in the center of the distribution—for the larger portfolios. Yet, from an investment and portfolio management perspective, it may be substantially more costly to monitor, say, a portfolio with more than 500 names, as opposed to one with 200. (Not to mention that, in most markets, one may be hard pressed to find 500+ names that fit the profile sought by the investor/manager.) One small simple lesson learned from Figure 19.8 then is that the diversification benefits, in terms of less disperse loss distributions, achieved by adding more and more names to the portfolio eventually are likely to be outweighed by the potentially higher costs of constructing and managing portfolios in which an ever larger number of entities is represented.

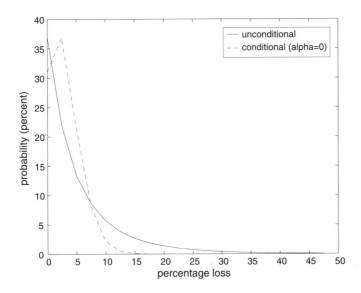

FIGURE 19.9. Conditional vs. Unconditional Loss Distribution Functions

19.5 Conditional vs. Unconditional Loss Distributions

Suppose one has a view as to where the common factor will be by a certain date and then computes the loss distribution function of a given portfolio based on that view. The resulting function is none other than the conditional loss distribution function that we discussed earlier in this chapter. Suppose, in particular, that one makes the seemingly reasonable forecast that α will be at its expected value of zero at the end of the relevant time horizon and then computes the corresponding (conditional) loss distribution of the portfolio.

How much off would one be by making risk assessments based on particular views regarding the common factor? Figure 19.9 answers this question for the portfolio described in the previous section, with β set to 0.5. It shows that conditioning the distribution of losses on the expected value of α would lead one to underestimate significantly the default risk in the portfolio, exposing the danger of what would otherwise look like a sensible assumption regarding the evolution of the common factor. More generally, ignoring the uncertainty related with future values of the common factor can lead one to understate substantially the likelihood of large losses in the portfolio.

19.6   Extensions and Alternative Approaches

We discussed a simple approach for modeling the credit risk in a portfolio and described three basic methods for deriving a portfolio's loss distribution function. The first method involved the analytical derivation of the loss distribution function. The second technique was the large-portfolio approximation motivated by the work of Vasicek (1987)[73] and others. The third was a simple simulation-based method that can also be used for small portfolios. We also highlighted the key role that default correlation plays in determining the range of likely losses that can be experienced in a portfolio.

There are several directions in which the basic model discussed in this chapter can be extended. For instance, portfolios with heterogeneous assets can be examined in a relatively straightforward manner with the help of simulation-based methods, a topic that we examine further in Chapter 20. Other extensions include allowing for defaults to take place at any time— rather than only at the maturity date of the contract—the treatment of accrued premiums, and the analysis of multi-period contracts—an issue that we address in Chapter 23.

Additional modeling approaches for examining portfolio credit risk fall along the lines of the more advanced versions of the single-default models that we studied in Part III of the book. For instance, they include both intensity- and ratings-based models. We briefly discuss examples of such models in Chapter 22.

20

Valuing Basket Default Swaps

We now start applying some of the techniques introduced in Chapter 19 to the valuation of basket default swaps, the mechanics of which we discussed in some detail in Chapter 9. We start by reviewing some of the basic ideas addressed in that chapter, which mostly centered on two-entity baskets, and then move on to the valuation of more realistic cases involving baskets with several reference entities.

20.1 Basic Features of Basket Swaps

As we saw in Chapter 9, a basket default swap is a credit derivative contract where the protection seller agrees to take on some of the credit risk in a basket (portfolio) of reference entities. For instance, in the first-to-default (FTD) basket the protection seller commits to making a payment to the protection buyer to cover the first default among the entities referenced by the basket. As with a standard credit default swap, the default-contingent payment made by the protection seller is typically equal to the face value of the defaulted asset minus its recovery value. In exchange for this kind of protection, the protection buyer makes periodic payments to the seller—the FTD premium—until the maturity date of the contract.

After payments associated with the first default in the FTD basket are settled, both parties are relieved of further obligations under the contract. Thus, assuming the protection buyer bought no additional default protection on the basket, any losses related to further defaults among the remaining reference entities in the basket will be borne out entirely by the protection buyer. Similar to other credit derivative contracts, if no default takes place during the life of the contract, the protection seller keeps on collecting the FTD premium from the buyer until the expiration of the contract.

Second- and third-to-default baskets are similarly defined. We will take a quick look at the second-to-default basket towards the end of this chapter.

20.2   Reexamining the Two-Asset FTD Basket

Continuing with a brief review of Chapter 9, we reexamine the valuation principles surrounding the simplest basket swap, one that references only two debt issuers, but we now start to incorporate some of the results discussed in Chapter 19.

For a given time horizon, say one year, let w_A and w_X denote the risk-neutral default probabilities associated with XYZ Corp. and AZZ Bank, the two reference entities included in the basket. We further assume that the default correlation between the two entities is $\rho_{A,X}$, which, as we saw in Chapter 19—equation (19.5)—can be written as

$$\rho_{A,X} = \frac{w_{A\&X} - w_A w_X}{\sqrt{w_A(1 - w_A)}\sqrt{w_X(1 - w_X)}} \tag{20.1}$$

where $w_{A\&X}$ is the probability that both XYZ and AZZ will default within a specific horizon.

Let us consider a one-year FTD basket involving only one premium payment date, at the end of the contract. The probability that the protection seller will have to make a payment under the contract is simply equal to the probability $w_{A \, or \, X}$ of at least one default in one year's time. From Chapter 9, we know:

$$w_{A \, or \, X} = w_A + w_X - w_{A\&X} \tag{20.2}$$

For simplicity, we shall assume that both reference entities have a zero recovery rate and that defaults, if any, will only take place in one-year's time. We further assume that the total notional amount of the basket is $10 million, with each reference entity accounting for exactly half of the total. Thus, the expected value of the payment made by the protection seller, denoted below as $\tilde{E}[\text{protection payment}]$, is

$$\tilde{E}[\text{protection payment}] = w_{A \, or \, X} \times \$5 \text{ million} + (1 - w_{A \, or \, X}) \times 0 \tag{20.3}$$

i.e., with probability $w_{A \, or \, X}$ the protection seller will have to pay for one default—$5 million given our assumptions—and with probability $1 - w_{A \, or \, X}$

there will be no default in the basket, in which case the protection seller will not have to make any payment.

Given that the contract typically has zero market value at its inception (no money changes hands at the inception of the basket swap), and, again, assuming a single premium payment date, at the end of the contract, it must be the case that the premium paid by the protection buyer is equal to the expected payment made by the protection seller.[1] Thus, the value of the FTD premium payment is:

$$S_{basket} = \omega_{A \; or \; X} \times \$5 \text{ million} \qquad (20.4)$$

which is customarily quoted in terms of basis points (see Section 6.1). For instance, if $\omega_{A \; or \; X}$ is equal to .01—a 1 percent probability that either one of the reference entities will default in one-year's time—then the premium for this one-year FTD basket would be 100 basis points, and the total premium paid by the protection buyer would be $50,000.

A few additional points are worth remembering about the two-asset FTD basket. First, as we have just seen, the key ingredient in the determination of the FTD premium is the probability that any one of the reference entities in the basket will default during the life of the contract. Second, that probability depends importantly on the default correlation of the two entities. Indeed, as we saw in Chapters 9 and 19 (Section 19.1.1), as we approach the polar cases of (i) perfect correlation, $\rho_{A,X} = 1$, and (ii) no correlation, $\rho_{A,X} = 0$, coupled with a sufficiently low value for the probability that both reference entities will default while the contract is in force, the FTD basket premium tends to the default probability of the weaker asset and to the sum of the default probabilities of each asset, respectively.[2]

20.3   FTD Basket with Several Reference Entities

In practice, basket swaps are generally written on more than two reference entities. The basic results derived from the two-asset case do carry over to baskets with several entities, but the valuation exercise does become a bit more involved.

20.3.1   A Simple Numerical Example

We start with a simple example that can be used to fix some important points regarding more realistic cases involving baskets with more than two

---

[1] Unless otherwise indicated, throughout most of Part IV, we shall assume that future premiums are discounted at the same rate as expected future protection payments.

[2] The reader is invited to verify this using the diagrams discussed in Section 19.1.

TABLE 20.1

Basic Valuation of Five-Asset Basket Swaps[a]

(Total notional = $50 million; individual recovery rates = 0)

Possible outcomes (No. of defaults)	Outcome probabilities (percent)	Payment by FTD protection seller[b] ($ millions)	Payment by STD protection seller[b] ($ millions)
(1)	(2)	(3)	(4)
0	90.0	0	0
1	6.0	10	0
2	3.0	10	10
3	0.5	10	10
4	0.3	10	10
5	0.2	10	10

[a]Each reference entity represents an equal portion of the portfolio ($10 million).
[b]Values shown in columns 3 and 4 are the total payments made by FTD and STD protection sellers under each possible default outcome.

reference entities. Table 20.1 shows all possible default outcomes for a one-year basket swap that references five entities, along with the risk-neutral probabilities, shown in column 2, associated with each outcome.[3] There are six such possible outcomes, ranging from no defaults to defaults by all entities referenced by the basket. For instance, there is a 90 percent probability that none of the entities referenced by the basket will default during the life of the basket and a 6 percent probability that only one of the entities will default.

We now consider a reference portfolio with the characteristics featured in Table 20.1. The total face value of the portfolio is $50 million, and each of the reference entities accounts for an equal piece, $10 million, of the portfolio. We continue to assume a zero recovery rate for all the entities referenced by the basket.

The third column in Table 20.1 shows, for each possible default outcome, the payment made by a protection seller in a first-to-default basket swap written on the portfolio. Naturally, if there are no defaults, the FTD protection seller owes nothing to the protection buyer, but if at least one of the reference entities defaults, she is liable for the entire loss associated with that asset, $10 million in this example. Note that, provided there is at least one default, the total payment made by the FTD

---

[3]Note that columns 1 and 2 essentially correspond to the loss distribution function of the portfolio.

protection seller is always $10 million as she is only liable to cover the first default.

What would be the FTD premium for this five-asset FTD basket? Following the same logic outlined in the valuation of the two-asset basket, if, as customary, the contract has zero market value at its inception, then the FTD premium owed by the protection buyer to the protection seller should be equal to the (risk-neutral) expected value of the payment made by the protection seller. Armed with the probabilities shown in Table 20.1, this expected value is $1 million:

$$\text{FTD premium} \quad = .9 \times 0 + .1 \times \$10 \text{ million} = \$1 \text{ million}$$

i.e., with probability 90 percent there is no default among the entities referenced by the basket, and the protection seller makes no payment under the contract; but with probability 10 percent there is at least one default, in which case the protection seller owes the buyer the $10 million loss associated with the first default. Thus the premium is $1 million for $10 million worth of protection, which amounts to 1,000 basis points.

The last column of Table 20.1 illustrates possible payments made by a protection seller in a second-to-default (STD) basket swap written on the portfolio. By definition, such a seller would owe nothing under the terms of the STD agreement if less than two defaults take place, but would be liable for $10 in the event of a second default, and nothing more for any additional defaults. Proceeding as with the FTD basket, one would find that the STD premium amounts to 400 basis points, considerably less than that of the FTD basket, given a much smaller probability of at least two defaults than that associated with one default.

20.3.2   A More Realistic Valuation Exercise

Table 20.1 was an illustration used to provide some intuition about the valuation of basket default swaps. In real-world situations, however, one will not be presented with the risk-neutral probabilities associated with every possible default outcome regarding the entities referenced in a basket swap. Indeed, arriving at a table such as Table 20.1 is perhaps the most crucial step in the basket swap valuation exercise. We outline below a simple method for estimating the needed default probabilities.

Consider a one-year FTD basket that references five entities, each with different, but unknown, default probabilities. As in the previous section, the total notional amount of the basket is $50 million, equally divided among the five reference entities, and all entities have a zero recovery rate. To avoid the need to model explicitly the joint probability density of default times, we follow the traditional BSM framework—see Chapter 17—and assume that defaults, if any, only occur at the maturity date of the contract,

TABLE 20.2

Reference Entities in a Hypothetical Five-Asset Basket Swap
(Total notional = $50 million; individual recovery rates = 0)

Reference entity	CDS premium (basis points)	Notional amount ($ million)
(1)	(2)	(3)
Entity #1	25	10
Entity #2	45	10
Entity #3	50	10
Entity #4	60	10
Entity #5	100	10

an assumption that also simplifies the treatment of accrued premiums.[4]
We also assume that one-year CDS contracts written on each reference
are negotiated in a liquid market, and Table 20.2 lists the corresponding
premiums.

Given the information in Table 20.2, we are then asked to value a first-
to-default basket swap written on this portfolio. To do so we shall rely
on the one-factor credit risk model discussed in Chapter 19, with a slight
modification to allow us to leave the homogeneous portfolio case that was
examined in that chapter. Namely, for each of the five entities in the basket,
we assume that their returns vary in response to a common factor, α, and
an entity-specific factor ϵ_i, where the subscript $i = 1, \ldots 5$ identifies each
reference entity. Thus, as in equation (19.9):

$$R_{i,t} = \beta_i \alpha_t + \sqrt{1 - \beta_i^2} \epsilon_{i,t} \tag{20.5}$$

where $R_{i,t}$, α, and ϵ_i have been standardized as discussed in Chapter 19,
and R_i is the return on owning reference entity i.

Recall that the model defines default as a situation where the return R_i
reaches or falls below a given threshold C_i:

$$\text{Default by entity } i \iff R_i \leq C_i \tag{20.6}$$

and thus the probability ω_i of default by entity i by the maturity date of
the contract is given by

$$\omega_i = \text{Prob}[R_i \leq C_i] = N(C_i) \tag{20.7}$$

---

[4] Chapter 17 discussed the notion of the probability density of default time in a
single-issuer context.

where $N(.)$ is the cumulative density function of the standard normal distribution.

Given that our interest lies in risk-neutral probabilities, ω_i can be obtained from the observed CDS premiums for each entity—see Chapters 6 and 16—and C_i can be computed by inverting (20.7), as discussed in Chapter 19. Lastly, to parameterize β_i, one can regress stock returns for each of the entities on the common factor α, where α could correspond, for instance, to standardized stock market returns.[5] To keep things simple, we shall assume that $\beta_i = .5$ for all companies.

We now have all ingredients necessary to run the valuation exercise. Using the simulation-based method described in Chapter 19, we obtain the results presented in Table 20.3. Such results are analogous to the information presented in Table 20.1, except that we have now derived the probabilities associated with each default outcome on the basis of market data—CDS premiums and equity returns—and of an explicit portfolio credit risk model. Carrying on with the same calculations done for Table 20.1, we arrive at the result that the FTD basket premium for this portfolio is about 265 basis points, which is well in excess of the CDS premiums for any one of the reference entities included in the basket.

TABLE 20.3
Valuation of a Five-Asset FTD Basket Swap[a]
($\beta = .5$; total notional = $50 million; individual recovery rates = 0)

Possible outcomes (No. of defaults)	Outcome probabilities (percent)	Payment by FTD protection seller[b] ($ millions)	Loss to unhedged investor ($ millions)
(1)	(2)	(3)	(4)
0	97.35	0	0
1	2.51	10	10
2	0.13	10	20
3	0.01	10	30
4	0.00	10	40
5	0.00	10	50

[a] The referenced portfolio is the one described in Table 20.2.
[b] Values shown in column 3 are the total payments made by the FTD protection seller under each possible default outcome.

---

[5] This regression-based approach is only a rough approximation, however, because the resulting correlations are computed based on estimates of actual probabilities, rather than risk-neutral probabilities.

As we discussed in Chapter 9, from the standpoint of investors (protection sellers), the FTD basket swap represents an opportunity to leverage one's credit exposure: While the protection seller is exposed to the credit risk in debt instruments that total $50 million in terms of notional amount in the example just described, the actual potential loss is limited to $10 million, all while earning a premium that corresponds to a credit quality that is well inferior to that of each individual entity referenced in the portfolio.

To conclude this subsection, we compare the expected loss of the FTD protection seller to that of an unhedged investor who owns the entire portfolio.[6] The total default-related losses experienced by such an investor under each possible default outcome are shown in the last column of Table 20.3. If we multiply each element of column 2 by its counterpart in column 4, and sum the resulting numbers across all possible default outcomes, we find that the unhedged investor faces an expected loss of about 0.56 percent of the entire portfolio, compared to an expected loss of 2.65 percent for the FTD protection seller—column 2 times column 3. Note, however, that the maximum loss of the unhedged investor is five times as much as that of the FTD protection seller. Moreover, for this particular portfolio, the expected (dollar) losses of the FTD protection seller—who is long only the first loss—and of the unhedged investor—who is long the entire portfolio—are $265,000 and $280,000, respectively.

20.4   The Second-to-Default Basket

Let us briefly revisit the second-to-default (STD) basket, which is a contract where default protection is bought and sold for the second default, and the second default only, among all the entities in a given portfolio. Column 2 in Table 20.3 has all that we need to value a STD basket written on the portfolio described in Table 20.2, once we note the fact that the potential losses of the STD protection seller are zero if the number of defaults falls below 2 and $10 million thereafter (see Table 20.1). The reader is then invited to verify that the STD premium for our hypothetical portfolio amounts to about 14 basis points. The fact that the STD premium is so low reflects the very small probabilities associated with more than one default in the overall portfolio.

---

[6] By an unhedged investor, we mean one who is holding the portfolio, but who has not hedged his or her credit risk exposure via baskets, credit default swaps, or any other hedging vehicle.

20.5 Basket Valuation and Asset Correlation

In Chapter 9, and also in Section 20.2, we used the simple two-asset basket example to suggest that default correlation can have a significant effect on the valuation of basket swaps. We can now verify this result using the more realistic basket described in Section 20.3.2. To do this we propose the following exercise: compute the one-year FTD premiums for baskets referencing 11 portfolios. The portfolios are identical to the one described in Table 20.2, except for the degree of correlation, which we vary from zero to one. We continue to assume that the premium is paid annually.

Figure 20.1 summarizes the results, which are consistent with the main conclusions drawn from the two-asset case. In particular, the figure plots one-year FTD premiums for different values of β. It shows that when $\beta = 1$, the FTD premium is equal to the default probability of the reference entity with the lowest credit quality (highest default probability), which is 1 percent or 100 basis points in this case. As for the case of no correlation, $\beta = 0$, the FTD premium is essentially equal to the sum of the CDS premiums of each individual entity referenced in the basket, or 280 basis points. As the figure shows, for intermediate values of β the FTD premium varies between these two polar cases, but the relationship between asset correlation and the FTD premium is very nonlinear.

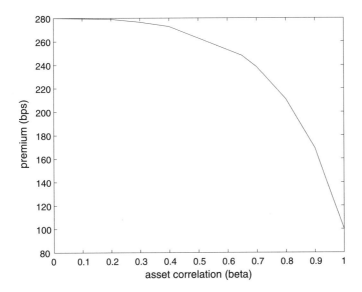

FIGURE 20.1. Asset Correlation and the FTD Premium

One practical lesson from Figure 20.1 regards the importance of trying to obtain good estimates for the degree of asset correlation in the portfolio. A large error in the estimation of β could result in a significant mispricing of the basket and, consequently, lead to a credit risk exposure that could differ substantially from the intended one. For instance, a FTD protection seller who overestimated the degree of asset correlation in the portfolio could end up charging a much lower premium than would be warranted by the risk profile of the portfolio.

20.6   Extensions and Alternative Approaches

We have mentioned already, at the end of Chapter 19, the several directions in which the simple model used here for the valuation of basket default swaps has been extended, as well as alternative modeling approaches for examining portfolio credit risk. For instance, the work of Li (2000)[55] is of particular interest in that he proposes a method that explicitly addresses issues related to the joint probability density of default times. He also illustrates an application of his method to the valuation of a basket swap.

For convenience, we have been limiting ourselves essentially to the analysis of contracts involving only one premium payment date and assets with zero recovery rates. We should note, however, that the methods described here can be extended to deal with multi-year contracts with several premium payment dates and with assets with nonzero recovery rates. Such extensions would be analogous to what we did in Part III when we went from examining zero-coupon bonds to coupon-paying bonds.

21

Valuing Portfolio Swaps and CDOs

As we discussed in Chapter 10, portfolio default swaps share many of the characteristics of basket default swaps. Some salient differences include the fact that they tend to reference a larger number of entities than do baskets and that default protection is bought and sold in terms of percentage losses in the portfolio, as opposed to with reference to the number of individual defaults. For instance, an investor might enter into a portfolio default swap where it agrees to cover the first ten percent in default-related losses in the portfolio. In exchange, the investor receives periodic payments from the protection buyer. Given these basic similarities, many methods used for the valuation of portfolio default swaps are variations of those used to value baskets.

Portfolio default swaps are important in their own right, but they are also of interest because they can be thought of as building blocks for the increasingly common synthetic CDO structure, which we discussed in Chapter 14. We conclude this chapter with a brief discussion of additional valuation issues that are relevant for the pricing of these structures.

21.1   A Simple Numerical Example

We start the discussion of valuation principles for portfolio default swaps with a simple numerical example. Similar to the analysis surrounding Table 20.1, when we examined basket swaps, the goal of this discussion is to provide some basic intuition into the valuation exercise.

TABLE 21.1

Valuation of Portfolio Default Swaps: A Simple Numerical Example

(Total notional = \$400 million; individual recovery rates = 0)

Possible outcomes (No. of defaults)	Outcome probabilities (percent)	Portfolio losses (\$ millions)	Portfolio swap losses[a]	
			first-loss (\$ millions)	second-loss (\$millions)
(1)	(2)	(3)	(4)	(5)
0	52.73	0	0	0
1	23.28	20	20	0
2	11.21	40	40	0
3	5.80	60	40	20
4	3.03	80	40	40
5	1.80	100	40	60
6	0.92	120	40	80
7	0.56	140	40	80
8	0.29	160	40	80
9	0.19	180	40	80
10	0.10	200	40	80
11	0.05	220	40	80
12	0.03	240	40	80
13	0.01	260	40	80
14	0	280	40	80
15	0	300	40	80
16	0	320	40	80
17	0	340	40	80
18	0	360	40	80
19	0	380	40	80
20	0	400	40	80

[a]Values shown in columns 4 and 5 are the total losses of FTD and STD protection sellers under each possible default outcome.

Consider a portfolio composed of bonds issued by 20 entities, all with a zero recovery rate. The first column of Table 21.1 lists all possible default outcomes associated with this portfolio over the next year, ranging from no defaults to all 20 reference entities in the portfolio defaulting together. The second column shows the corresponding risk-neutral probabilities associated with each of the 21 default outcomes.[1] As in previous chapters in this part of the book, we continue to assume that defaults, if any,

---

[1] Columns 1 and 2 together essentially correspond to the loss distribution function of this portfolio.

only occur at the maturity date of the contract, which is assumed to be one year. For instance, the second row of column 2 tells us that there is a 23.3 percent probability of the reference portfolio experiencing one default at the maturity date of the swap.

We assume that each of the entities represented in the portfolio accounts for an equal portion of the total value of the portfolio. Thus, for a portfolio that corresponds to a total notional amount of $400 million, each default results in a loss of $20 million, or 5 percent of the total. Default-related losses for each possible default outcome are shown in column 3. As a result, as we did in Chapter 20, we can multiply columns 2 and 3 on an element-by-element basis and sum the resulting numbers across all possible default outcomes to arrive at the expected (risk-adjusted) loss in the overall portfolio over the life of the contract:

$$\text{Expected loss} = \sum_{i=0}^{20} w_i l_i \tag{21.1}$$

which is roughly $20 million, or 5 percent of the portfolio's face value. (In the above expression, w_i and l_i correspond to the ith elements of the second and third columns of Table 21.1, respectively.)

Consider now a portfolio default swap written on the portfolio detailed in Table 21.1. The protection seller in this swap commits to absorb all default-related losses up to 10 percent of the notional amount of the contract, which corresponds to a maximum loss of $40 million. The possible outcomes facing such a protection seller, in terms of his losses under different default scenarios, are listed in column 4. Multiplying columns 2 and 4 and summing across all outcomes as in equation (21.1) leads to an expected loss for this investor in the order of $14.3 million, or 35.6 percent of the first-loss piece.

Assuming that the swap is fairly valued and that no money changes hands at its inception, and relying on arguments entirely analogous to the ones used in previous chapters, we then arrive at a premium of 35.63 percent, or 3,563 basis points, for this first-loss contract, i.e., the protection buyer promises to pay $14.3 million (3,563 bps × $40 million) in exchange for the protection provided by the contract.

Column 5 lists, for every possible default outcome, the total payment made by a second-loss protection seller who committed to cover all default-related losses falling between 10 and 30 percent of the portfolio. Again, multiplication and addition of columns 2 and 5 show that, on a risk adjusted basis, such a protection seller can expect to make a payment of $5.2 million under the terms of this contract. Given a second-loss piece of $80 million— (30−10) percent × $400 million—the corresponding protection premium is 647 basis points, or 6.47 percent.

21.2   Model-based Valuation Exercise

As with other multi-name credit derivatives, obtaining a loss distribution function for the underlying portfolio is perhaps the most important part of the valuation exercise. In the previous section we skipped this problem altogether as our goal was simply to build some intuition on the valuation process.

Consider, as an example, an equally weighted reference portfolio with 100 companies and corresponding to a total notional amount of $400 million. The portfolio is homogeneous with each of its constituent companies having a risk-neutral default probability of 10 percent over the life of the one-year portfolio default swaps that we will examine. For simplicity, we continue to assume a zero recovery rate. It turns out that we can value any default swap written on this portfolio by relying on essentially the same model- and simulation-based approach that we discussed in Chapter 19, much as we did in Chapter 20 in the valuation of basket default swaps. In partic- ular, to model the credit risk in this portfolio, we assume that individual company returns and defaults behave as in equations (20.5) through (20.7). To examine the likelihood of different default scenarios associated with this portfolio, one could take the following steps:

- **Step 1**: Assign values to the key model parameters, β and C. For instance, as we noted in Chapter 20, an estimated value for β could be obtained by regressing standardized stock market returns for the companies included in the portfolio on the modeler's choice for the common factor, such as standardized changes in a marketwide stock index, and C can be obtained by inverting equation (20.7);

- **Step 2**: Based on the standard normal distribution, draw a large number of random values for the common factor α and for each of the company-specific factors ϵ_i, $i = 1, \dots, 100$;

- **Step 3**: For each reference entity i, use equation (20.5) to compute its return, R_i, for each value of α and ϵ_i and record whether or not that value of R_i constituted a default by entity i, as specified by equation (20.6);

- **Step 4**: Once individual defaults have been counted and recorded for all reference entities under all values of α and ϵ_i, the probabilities associated with different default outcomes can be computed by taking the ratio of the number of occurrences of that outcome over the total number of random draws in Step 1.[2]

---

[2] Each outcome corresponds to a given number of defaults in the portfolio, as in Table 21.1, and each random draw corresponds to a value for the vector $[\alpha, \epsilon_1, \epsilon_2, \dots, \epsilon_{100}]$.

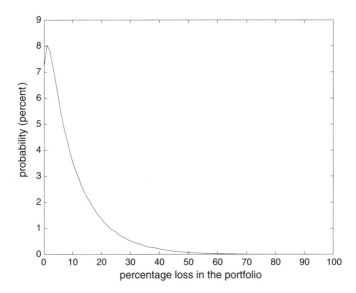

FIGURE 21.1. Loss Distribution Function for a Portfolio with 100 Assets (one-year horizon)

Once the above steps are followed, one has essentially obtained the loss distribution function associated with the portfolio, which is shown in Figure 21.1 for $\beta = .5$. Given the loss distribution function, which effectively corresponds to columns 1 and 2 in Table 21.1, the rest of the valuation exercise proceeds in exactly the same fashion as in the numerical example illustrated in that table.

Take, for instance, the valuation of two one-year portfolio default swaps written on the portfolio underlying the loss distribution function shown in Figure 21.1. The first swap is a first-loss contract covering losses of up to 20 percent of the portfolio, and the second is a second-loss contract covering losses between 20 and 50 percent. We will discuss the valuation results by examining the maximum and expected default-related losses of three investors, one who is long the entire portfolio without having bought any default protection, one who has sold protection via the first-loss contract, and another who has sold protection via the second-loss contract. We shall call each of these the unhedged investor, the first-loss investor, and the second-loss investor, respectively.

Table 21.2 displays key statistics for each investor. Column 2—rows 1 through 3—shows the corresponding maximum losses, which are $400 million for the unhedged investor, $80 million—20 percent of $400 million—for the first-loss investor, and $120 million—$(50 - 20 = 30)$ percent of $400 million—for the second-loss investor. Thus, similar to basket swaps, portfolio swaps give investors an opportunity to lever up their

TABLE 21.2

Valuation of Portfolio Default Swaps[a]

($\beta = .5$; total notional = $400 million; individual recovery rates = 0)

Investor type	Maximum loss ($ millions)	Expected loss	
		($ millions)	(percent[b])
(1)	(2)	(3)	(4)
1. unhedged investor	400	40	10
2. first-loss investor	80	34	43
3. second-loss investor	120	5	4.4

Memo:
  Prob[portfolio loss $\geq$ 20%] = 14.7 percent
  Prob[portfolio loss $\geq$ 50%] = 0.6 percent

[a]Results based on 500,000 simulations of the credit risk model.
[b]Percentage losses for first- and second-loss investors are reported relative to their maximum losses—see column 2.

credit exposure. For instance, while the first-loss investor is exposed to all reference entities in this $400 million portfolio, he or she is liable only for the first $80 million of default-related losses, all while enjoying, as we shall see below, a substantial premium. Of course this "substantial premium" is there for a reason. For instance, as the memo lines in Table 21.2 show, there is a 14.7 percent chance that the first-loss investor will lose the entire first-loss piece, whereas the probabilities of complete losses for the second-loss and unhedged investors are, respectively, 0.6 percent and virtually zero.

To compute the fair value of the premiums owed to the first- and second-loss investors in Table 21.2, we use the loss distribution function associated with the reference portfolio—Figure 21.1—and carry out the same calculations described for Table 21.1. The results are shown in columns 3 and 4. For instance, the expected losses of the first-loss and unhedged investors are relatively close, at $34.4 million and $40 million, respectively. However, relative to their maximum losses, expected percentage losses are much higher for the first-loss investor (about 43 percent) than for the unhedged investor (10 percent).

Thus assuming that no money changed hands at the inception of the first-loss contract and that market forces acted to rule out any arbitrage opportunities, the first-loss investor receives a premium from the protection buyer in that contract that amounts to 43 percent of the first-loss piece, or 4,300 basis points. Likewise, the fair value of the premium for the second-loss portfolio default swap is about 440 basis points as the risk-adjusted expected loss of the second-loss investor is approximately 4.4 percent.[3]

21.3   The Effects of Asset Correlation

As with the default basket, the degree of correlation among the entities included in the reference portfolio is an important determinant of the portfolio swap premium. We illustrate this point in Figure 21.2, which shows the premiums for three one-year portfolio default swaps written on the portfolio described in Section 21.2 for values of β varying from 0 to 1. The first two contracts—labeled first- and second-loss—are the ones examined in Section 21.2. The third one—labeled third-loss—is essentially a contract that would absorb any residual losses after the protection provided by both the first- and second-loss contracts is exhausted. One can think of a protection-selling position in the third contract as equivalent to the residual risk exposure of an investor who owns the entire portfolio, but who has bought protection through the first two contracts.

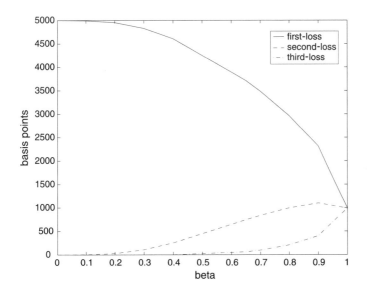

FIGURE 21.2. Portfolio Swap Premiums and Asset Correlation

---

[3] Recall, as noted in Chapter 19, that we are assuming that all parties to the contract discount expected future payments at the same rate and that the premium is paid at the maturity date of the contract.

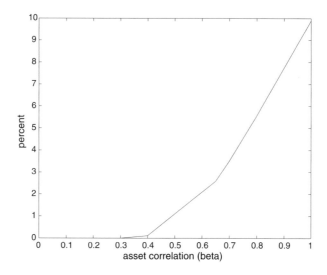

FIGURE 21.3. Probability of Portfolio Losses Equal to or Greater than
50 Percent

Figure 21.2 shows that as the degree of correlation in the portfolio increases, the premium owed to first-loss investors decreases. Although this may seem counterintuitive at first, a closer look at the nature of the contract proves otherwise. As the degree of correlation in the portfolio increases— see Figure 21.3—so does the probability of large losses. This happens because higher correlation increases the chances that several reference entities default together. Thus greater correlation increases the risk that second- and third-loss investors will be called upon to cover default-related losses, i.e., that they will have to pay up for losses beyond those covered by the first-loss investors. Thus, the second- and third-loss investors need to be compensated with larger premiums as more of the total risk in the portfolio is being borne by them as β increases. Indeed, for very high correlation, even the premium owed to second-loss investors starts declining in this example as a substantial portion of the total risk in the portfolio is now also shared with the third-loss investors. (The premium that would be owed to a third-loss investor is shown as the dash-dotted line in Figure 21.2.)

One final note: When $\beta = 1$, the portfolio essentially behaves like a single asset because either all reference entities survive or all default together. In this extreme case, Figure 21.2 shows that all investors earn the same premium, 1,000 basis points, which corresponds to the 10 percent default probability of the individual entities included in the portfolio.[4]

---

[4] As noted in Chapter 10, with nonzero recovery rates, the equality of premiums across different classes of investors when $\beta = 1$ generally does not hold. The positive

21.4   The Large-Portfolio Approximation

In Chapter 19 we discussed the large-portfolio approximation method for computing loss distribution functions for a given portfolio. In particular, see equation (19.33), we found that the following expression approximates the probability that default-related losses in a large homogeneous portfolio will not exceed θ percent over a given time period:

$$\text{Prob}[L \leq \theta] = N(-\frac{C - N^{-1}(\theta)\sqrt{1-\beta^2}}{\beta}) \qquad (21.2)$$

where L is the percentage default-related loss in the portfolio; $N(.)$ is the standard normal cumulative distribution function; $N^{-1}()$ is its inverse; and C and β have their usual definitions.

We can then use (21.2) to compute an approximate value for the probability that the first-loss investor described in Section 21.2 will lose the entire first-loss piece as a result of defaults in the underlying portfolio. That probability is approximately

$$1 - N(-\frac{C - N^{-1}(.2)\sqrt{1-\beta^2}}{\beta})$$

or 13.5 percent, which is close to the 14.7 percent probability reported in Table 21.2. The analogous figures for the second-loss contract are 0.5 percent and 0.6 percent, respectively.

One can also compute approximate expressions for the premiums for the first- and second-loss portfolio swaps described in Section 21.2, but these calculations involve some mathematical manipulations that go beyond the scope of this book. Interested readers will find the following formula in O'Kane and Schlogl (2001)[64] for the premium owed under an arbitrary portfolio swap written on a large homogeneous portfolio:

$$\frac{N_2\left(-N^{-1}(L_{lb}), C, -\sqrt{1-\beta^2}\right) - N_2\left(-N^{-1}(L_{ub}), C, -\sqrt{1-\beta^2}\right)}{L_{ub} - L_{lb}}$$

$$(21.3)$$

where $N_2()$ is the bivariate normal cumulative distribution function, and L_{lb} and L_{ub} are, respectively, the lower and upper bounds of the range of losses covered by the contract. For instance, for the first-loss contract featured in Section 21.2, $L_{lb} = 0$ and $L_{ub} = .2$, whereas, for the second-loss contract, $L_{lb} = .2$ and $L_{ub} = .5$.

---

recovery value of the assets in the reference portfolio provides an additional cushion to higher-order investors, potentially reducing their expected losses.

Using the above formula, we obtain (approximate) premiums of 4,356 and 417 basis points for the first- and second-loss portfolio swaps, respectively, which are indeed close to the results reported in Table 21.2.[5]

21.5 Valuing CDOs: Some Basic Insights

The basic framework laid out in this chapter for the valuation of portfolio default swaps easily translates into the foundation for a simple method for valuing the tranches of CDOs (synthetic or cash flow). Indeed, as we shall see in Chapter 22, some of the methods used in practice in the valuation of CDO structures can be cast as extensions of this simple framework.

For the sake of illustration, let us take a closer look at the synthetic CDO structure. From our discussion in Chapter 14 we know that we can think of a synthetic CDO approximately as a structure made up of one or more portfolio default swaps combined, in the case of a funded synthetic CDO, with an outright position in highly rated assets (the SPV collateral).

It is relatively straightforward to see that equity investors in a CDO structure have a position that is akin to that of first-loss investors in a portfolio default swap (or of second-loss investors if the institution that originated the CDO retained the first-loss piece). Likewise, mezzanine and senior tranche investors are long positions that are analogous to that of second- and third-loss investors in portfolio swaps.

Indeed, Figure 21.2 would be very informative for someone considering a CDO where equity tranche investors absorb the first 20 percent in default-related losses, mezzanine tranche investors absorb losses between 20 and 50 percent, and senior investors absorb any remaining losses. Essentially, one can reinterpret Figure 21.2 as showing the expected default-related losses for each class of investors in this CDO under varying degrees of asset correlation, assuming that the individual one-year default probability of the underlying entities is 10 percent.[6]

21.5.1 Special Considerations for CDO Valuation

Crucial as they are, default correlation and the credit quality of the underlying reference entities are not the only factors determining the valuation of CDO structures. For instance, an important difference between CDOs and

---

[5] Not surprisingly, the large-portfolio approximation works better for larger portfolios. For instance for a 500-asset portfolio, the second-loss premium based on the simulation method is 420 basis points.

[6] A reading of, say, 2,500 basis points in Figure 21.2 can be thought of as a (risk-neutral) expected loss of 25 percent of the notional amount represented by each CDO tranche.

portfolio default swaps is that the former typically incorporate so-called "coverage tests" provisions, but the latter do not. These tests are part of the legal structure of CDOs and are intended to protect investors in more senior tranches against a deterioration in the credit quality of the pool of collateral assets. In particular, a CDO structure may specify that its senior tranches will be provided a certain cushion such that the ratio of the structure's total par value to that of that tranche's will not fall below a certain "overcollateralization" level.

Should defaults occur among the assets in the collateral pool and bring overcollateralization ratios for senior tranches below the prescribed minimum ("trigger") levels, the CDO is said to have failed its overcollateralization tests. As a result, the CDO structure may require the diversion of principal and interest cash flows from lower tranches to pay down enough of the principal of more senior tranches to bring the structure back into compliance with its overcollateralization requirements. In the context of this book, it suffices to say that coverage tests bring an additional level of complexity to the valuation of CDOs, one that was not captured by the portfolio default swap valuation exercise discussed in this chapter.

Some CDO structures call for the diversion of cash flows away from lower tranches even in the absence of default, if, for instance, the credit quality of the underlying assets is deemed to have deteriorated significantly. In contrast, if no defaults have occurred, a deterioration in the credit quality of the reference portfolio has no cash-flow implications for protection sellers in portfolio default swaps.

We mentioned other salient differences between CDOs and portfolio default swaps in Chapter 14. These include the credit quality of the SPV collateral in a synthetic CDO, reinvestment and "manager" risk associated with structures that include ramp-ups, removals, and replenishments, as well as other aspects of the CDO's legal structure. Along with coverage tests, these factors should not be ignored in real-world attempts to value CDO structures.

21.6 Concluding Remarks

The techniques described in this chapter are intended to serve as introductory illustrations of some of the key factors that influence the valuation of multi-name credit derivatives. Before using these or any other methods to value portfolio products in the real world, the reader should consider several key questions:

- Is the model a good description of return and default dynamics of the underlying reference entities?

- Should I allow for more than one common factor to determine the extent of correlation among the reference entities?
- To which extent can I rely solely on market prices, such as CDS premiums, as a proxy for the risk-neutral default probabilities that are fed to the model?

Other issues such as non-normal shocks, uncertain recovery rates, and time-varying correlations (e.g., greater default correlation during economic downturns), which were not addressed by the simple modeling framework described in this chapter, should also be taken into account and serve as a reality check to would-be portfolio credit risk modelers. Still, imperfect as the basic modeling framework described in this chapter may be, it constitutes the basis for understanding more complex models that are used in commercial applications. For instance, as we shall see in Chapter 22, the CreditMetrics model, developed by the RiskMetrics Group, is essentially a more elaborate version of the modeling framework discussed here and in Chapters 19 and 20.[7]

Lastly, as we noted elsewhere in this part of the book, our basic model represents only one of several approaches to assessing the extent of default-related losses in a portfolio of credit-related instruments. For instance, a well-known alternative method for valuing CDOs is the intensity-based model of Duffie and Garleanu (2001)[22].

---

[7] CreditMetrics is a trademark of J.P. Morgan.

22

A Quick Tour of Commercial Models

As the credit markets have grown in both size and sophistication so have the technical skills required to assess the risk-reward characteristics of an ever-expanding array of new products and structures, such as multi-name credit derivatives. Rather than developing in-house the analytical tools and databases required to fully understand and examine these new products, many investors have turned to outside experts for technical assistance. Indeed, several firms have come to be known as leading providers of analytical services regarding portfolio credit risk. In this chapter we briefly discuss some of the better-known models developed and marketed by these firms and compare them to the basic credit risk model discussed in Chapters 19 through 21.

We shall focus on four commercially available modeling approaches to the analysis of portfolio credit risk: Moody's Investors Service's Binomial Expansion Technique (BET), J.P. Morgan/RiskMetrics Group's Credit-Metrics model, Moody's KMV's KMV model, and Credit Suisse Financial Products' CreditRisk+ model.[1] Given the number of approaches just mentioned, however, as well as the length and scope of this introductory book, our discussion of each modeling framework will be brief and, for the most part, non-technical. Basic sources for each approach are cited throughout the chapter. In addition, Crouhy, Galai, and Mark (2000)[17] provide a

---

[1] CreditMetrics is a trademark of J.P. Morgan; KMV is a trademark of Moody's KMV Corp.; CreditRisk+ is a trademark of Credit Suisse Financial Products.

comprehensive comparison involving most of the models summarized in this chapter.

22.1   CreditMetrics

Of the modeling approaches discussed in this chapter, this is the one that is most closely related to the basic model described in Chapter 19 and used in Chapters 20 and 21 for the valuation of basket and portfolio swaps. Indeed, one can think of our basic model, described by equations (19.7) through (19.9), as a simplified version of the CreditMetrics model. The CreditMetrics approach is described in detail by Gupton et al. (1997)[37].

Similar to the basic portfolio credit risk model, the CreditMetrics model is a Merton-style model that specifies defaults as situations where a variable R_i, which is assumed to measure the creditworthiness of a given entity i, falls below some threshold C_i. Another similarity regards the evolution of R_i, which CreditMetrics also assumes to be a function of both common (marketwide) and idiosyncratic random factors, where the former are the main determinants of the extent of default correlation in the portfolio.

An important feature of CreditMetrics that was not captured by the basic model discussed in Chapters 19–21 is that it is also designed to examine the likelihood of "ratings transitions," or the probability, for instance, that an A-rated corporate borrower will be downgraded to, say, a BBB rating over a given time horizon. Thus, whereas the basic model only allowed for a reference entity to be in one of two states—solvency and default—CreditMetrics allows for as many states as the number of credit ratings under consideration. The way ratings transitions are modeled in CreditMetrics is similar to the manner in which we described the passage from solvency into default in the basic model. In particular, continuing with the same example just mentioned, the probability of firm i being downgraded from A to BBB is modeled as the probability that R_i falls below the threshold $C_{i,BBB}$. More generally, one can write

$$\text{Prob[downgrade to J-rating]}=\text{Prob}[R_i \leq C_{i,J}] \qquad (22.1)$$

where, as always, the probability is defined with respect to a given time horizon.

22.2   The KMV Framework

We described the basic features of Moody's KMV's single-default model in Part III in our introduction to structural models of credit risk. Moody's

KMV also offers a related tool for analyzing portfolio credit risk, called Portfolio Manager. The main output of Portfolio Manager is the loss distribution of the portfolio under consideration, from which, as we saw in Chapters 20 and 21, one can value a wide array of multi-name credit derivatives.

Portfolio Manager is similar to CreditMetrics in that it incorporates a model where default correlations are captured through the dependence of individual entities' returns on common factors. In addition, as in the CreditMetrics model, individual returns depend on a firm-specific factor, and defaults and credit migrations are characterized as situations where individual returns fall below certain prescribed thresholds. The basic Moody's KMV framework is described by Crosbie (2002)[16].

Differences between the CreditMetrics and Moody's KMV approaches include the fact that the latter uses an empirical distribution for returns based on proprietary data, as opposed to the normal distribution used in the CreditMetrics framework. Another difference regards the fact that the RiskMetrics Group makes the details of its model specification publicly available, where Moody's KMV does not.

22.3   CreditRisk$^+$

Unlike the full versions of the CreditMetrics and Moody's KMV models, and similar to the basic model used in this book, the CreditRisk$^+$ model allows for firms to be in only one of two states, solvency or default. Thus CreditRisk$^+$ is essentially a model of default risk that is not designed, for instance, to mark portfolios to market when one or more of their components are downgraded.

The incorporation of default correlation into the CreditRisk$^+$ framework is, in some aspects, analogous to the approach adopted by CreditMetrics and Moody's KMV. In particular, individual default probabilities are assumed to be functions of several "risk factors" that are common across different assets in the portfolio.

A key difference between CreditRisk$^+$ and the models discussed in Sections 22.1 and 22.2 regards technical assumptions regarding the random nature of defaults. Rather than relying either on the normal or empirical distributions for modeling the evolution of risk factors, CreditRisk$^+$ assumes the factors to be independently distributed according to the gamma distribution, which, subject to some approximations, allows the model to produce analytical results for unconditional probabilities of various losses in the portfolio. In contrast, the reader may recall that the derivation of the loss distribution function of a given portfolio generally involved either Monte Carlo simulations or, for large portfolios, approximation methods.

Methodologically, CreditRisk$^+$ also differs from CreditMetrics and Moody's KMV in that, while these two latter models are structural models that follow the spirit of the BSM framework discussed in Chapter 17, CreditRisk$^+$ is closer to the reduced-form approach, also discussed in that chapter. In particular, CreditRisk$^+$ is based on actuarial methods that have long been used in the insurance industry to analyze event risk. Similar to intensity-based models, CreditRisk$^+$ does not explicitly link the likelihood of default to the fundamentals of the firm. Instead, defaults occur exogenously according to the probabilities implied by the model.

Credit Suisse Financial Products (1997)[67] describes the CreditRisk$^+$ model in further detail. The model is also summarized by Gordy (2000)[35], who compares and contrasts it to the CreditMetrics approach.

22.4   Moody's Binomial Expansion Technique

In Chapter 19 we showed that, conditioned on the common factor α, individual defaults were uncorrelated in the basic credit risk model, and the (conditional) loss distribution function of the homogeneous portfolio was given by the binomial probability distribution—see equations (19.20) and (19.21). As we saw then, one attractive feature of the conditional loss distribution function implied by the basic model was that its computation involved no Monte Carlo simulations, which can be computer-intensive, and no approximation methods, such as the large-portfolio method. Moody's binomial expansion technique is designed to take advantage of this convenient feature of portfolios with zero default correlation.

For a given credit portfolio with J potentially correlated assets, Moody's BET essentially aims at arriving at an otherwise equivalent homogeneous equally weighted portfolio with D uncorrelated assets, where D is dictated by the "diversity score" of the original portfolio. We say that this idealized portfolio is otherwise equivalent to the actual portfolio we are interested in because it shares many of the fundamental characteristics of the original portfolio. For instance, the individual default probability of each constituent of the idealized portfolio is set to the average default probability of the assets included in the original portfolio.

The diversity score of the original portfolio is a measure conceived by Moody's to capture the degree of industry diversification represented in the portfolio. For instance, a portfolio with a high degree of concentration in a given industry would be one with a low diversity score, resulting in an idealized portfolio with a number of assets, D, that could fall well short of the actual number of assets in the original portfolio. Intuitively, the smaller number of assets in the idealized portfolio controls for the fact that the large number of assets in the original portfolio tends to overstate the portfolio's true degree of diversification when two or more of its constituents have a tendency to default together.

Once the idealized portfolio is constructed, and the main characteristics of the actual portfolio are mapped into it, one can derive its loss distribution function in a way that is entirely analogous to the derivation of the conditional loss distribution function in Chapter 19. In particular, the probability of, say, k defaults in the idealized portfolio can be derived from the binomial distribution as in

$$\text{Prob}\,[k \text{ defaults}] = \frac{D!}{k!(D-k)!}\omega^k(1-\omega)^{D-k} \qquad (22.2)$$

where ω is the probability of default of each reference entity represented in the idealized portfolio.

Armed with equation (22.2), as well as Moody's estimates of the diversity score and of individual default probabilities in the portfolio, it is then relatively straightforward to value, for instance the tranches of a CDO. Indeed, the BET method is an important component of Moody's rating methodology for rating both traditional and synthetic CDOs—see, for instance, Cifuentes and O'Connor (1996)[12] and Yoshizawa (2003)[75]. Other components include qualitative adjustments made to take other features of individual CDOs into account, such as the legal aspects of the structure.

Moody's has found the BET approach to work well for relatively homogeneous portfolios, but less so for portfolios where individual assets' default probabilities are markedly different. For such situations, Moody's has developed a modified approach, dubbed the double binomial expansion method, whereby the portfolio is divided with different portions that are mutually uncorrelated, but where each portion has a different individual default probability—see Cifuentes and Wilcox (1998)[13]. A further variation on the method, called the multiple binomial method, is employed for portfolios with further heterogeneity in individual default probabilities (Yoshizawa, 2003)[75].

22.5   Concluding Remarks

There is obviously much more to the credit risk models discussed in this chapter than has been covered in this brief overview. In addition, there are a number of other well-regarded commercially available models that we did not address here. Our choice of models, as well as the coverage provided for each model discussed in this chapter, was driven by a main guiding principle, which was to provide some insight into how the key concepts and methods described in Chapters 15 through 21 have actually been incorporated into credit risk analytical services that are bought and sold in the marketplace.

23

Modeling Counterparty Credit Risk

In the context of the credit derivatives market, counterparty credit risk refers mainly to the chance that a protection seller will fail to make good on its promise to make previously agreed-upon payments in the event of qualified defaults by reference entities.[1] We have thus far mostly sidestepped the issue of counterparty credit risk when discussing the valuation of credit derivative contracts. We have done so in part because existing arrangements among market participants—such as collateralization agreements and netting—help mitigate such a risk, but also for analytical convenience—factoring counterparty credit risk into the valuation exercise often adds a layer of complexity to the analysis that, for the most part, goes beyond the scope of this book. We say "for the most part" because we can in fact use a variant of the simple model discussed in Chapters 19 through 21 to capture some of the key insights regarding the role of counterparty credit risk in the valuation of credit derivatives.

---

[1] Strictly speaking, the protection seller is also subject to the risk that the buyer will fail to make the agreed-upon protection premium payments. The seller's potential exposure, however, is essentially limited to the marked-to-market value of the contract, which, as we saw in Chapter 16, is a function of the difference between the premium written into the contract and the one prevailing in the market place at the time of default by the protection buyer. Thus the contract could well have negative market value to the seller, which would be the case if the credit quality of the reference entity had deteriorated since the inception of the contract. Under such circumstances, the seller would in principle experience a windfall upon default by the buyer, although, before defaulting, the buyer would likely have a strong incentive to seek to monetize the positive market value of the contract.

Our focus will be on the ubiquitous single-name credit default swap, which we discussed in some detail in Chapter 6. We shall assume that the CDS contracts examined in this chapter are uncollateralized agreements that are not subject to netting and that do not include any other credit enhancement mechanism. Towards the end of the chapter we outline ways to extend the model for the analysis of more complex contracts, such as baskets and portfolio default swaps.

23.1   The Single-Name CDS as a "Two-Asset Portfolio"

One might wonder why include a discussion of counterparty credit risk—especially one that focuses on single-name credit default swaps—in this part of the book, which, after all, deals with portfolio credit risk. The answer lies in the following simple insight: In the presence of counterparty credit risk, and from the perspective of the protection buyer, one can think of a single-name CDS as being akin to a portfolio involving risk exposures to two entities: the one referenced in the CDS and the protection seller. Indeed, the protection buyer has a default-contingent exposure to the protection seller, in that it will have to rely on the seller to cover any losses resulting from a default by the reference entity. Thus, the protection buyer effectively also has some residual exposure to the reference entity because, if the protection seller does not make good on its commitment, the buyer will have to bear any losses associated with a default by the reference entity.

We have to be careful not to take the portfolio analogy too far, however. In contrast to a traditional portfolio setting, the protection buyer only really bears a loss upon default by the reference entity if that entity happens to default at around the same time as the protection seller. (Or if the reference entity defaults after a default by the seller, and the original contract was not replaced.) Still, the basic insight that an uncollateralized single-name CDS shares some of the basic characteristics of a two-asset portfolio has some insightful implications for the analysis of counterparty credit risk. Indeed, as we shall see below, we can examine the effects of counterparty credit risk on the valuation of CDS contracts by relying on a modified version of the portfolio credit risk model that we discussed in Chapters 19 through 21.

23.2   The Basic Model

To admit explicitly the possibility that the protection seller can default on its obligations under the CDS contract, we assume that the seller is a risky entity whose standardized returns $R_{p,t}$ follow the same basic model introduced in Chapter 19:

$$R_{p,t} = \beta_p \alpha_t + \sqrt{1 - \beta_p^2} \epsilon_{p,t} \qquad (23.1)$$

where, as indicated in that chapter, α_t is a common factor (systematic risk) driving the returns on the protection seller; $\epsilon_{p,t}$ represents a risk factor that is specific to the protection seller (idiosyncratic risk); and β_p denotes the degree of correlation between $R_{p,t}$ and the common factor α_t.

We assume that any protection payment owed by the protection seller will be made only on one of the premium payment dates of the CDS. In addition, we define a default by the protection seller as the first instance when its return R_p is equal to or below its default barrier C_p on any of those dates.[2]

Given equation (23.1), and assuming that α and ϵ_p have zero mean and unit variance and are mutually independent and normally distributed, we saw in Chapter 19 that, conditional on all information available at time t, and given survival through that time, the risk-neutral probability that $R_{p,T}$ will be at or below $C_{p,T}$ at some future date T is

$$H_p(t,T) \equiv \text{Prob}_t[R_{p,T} \leq C_{p,T}] = N(C_{p,T}) \qquad (23.2)$$

where $N(.)$ is the standard normal cumulative distribution function. More generally, $H_p(t,T_j)$ is the time-t probability that R_{p,T_j} will be at or below C_{p,T_j} at time T_j.

The evolution of returns associated with the entity referenced in the CDS is modeled in an entirely analogous way. If we let $R_{r,t}$ denote the standardized return on the reference entity, and make the same assumptions made for the protection seller, we have:

$$R_{r,t} = \beta_r \alpha_t + \sqrt{1 - \beta_r^2} \epsilon_{r,t} \qquad (23.3)$$

$$H_r(t,T) \equiv \text{Prob}[R_{r,T} \leq C_{r,T}] = N(C_{r,T}) \qquad (23.4)$$

Equations (23.1) through (23.4) constitute our basic framework for analyzing the effects of counterparty credit risk in credit default swaps. As we will see later in this chapter, these equations capture two important determinants of counterparty credit risk effects: the credit quality of the protection seller (H_p) and the degree of default correlation between the seller

---

[2] In contrast to Chapters 19 through 22, where we limited ourselves to one-year contracts, we are now dealing with multi-period contracts. That is why we are characterizing the time of default as the first premium payment date in which R_p touches the default barrier from above.

and the reference entity, which is mainly determined by their respective values of β.

We should note that, although it may not be clear from the simplified notation used thus far, the basic model is flexible enough to allow for time-varying, even stochastic, probabilities of default. Such features could be incorporated, for instance, by modeling the evolution of the default thresholds accordingly.

23.3   A CDS with No Counterparty Credit Risk

If collateralization and other credit enhancement mechanisms embedded in the contract are such that the protection seller poses no risk to the protection buyer, we can proceed as if $H_p(t, T) = 0$ for all T, and we can thus ignore equations (23.1) and (23.2) when valuing the CDS. In essence, this is what we did in Part III of this book. We shall take the case of no counterparty credit risk as a benchmark against which to compare valuations derived from our counterparty credit risk model, but first we recast some of the main results derived in Part III in terms of the modeling framework described in the previous section.

Let us consider a J-year CDS written on the firm described by equations (23.3) and (23.4). We assume that the CDS has a notional amount of \$1, is entered into at time t, and involves the annual payment of premiums, at dates $T_1, T_2, \ldots, T_J$, i.e.,

$$\delta_j \equiv T_j - T_{j-1} = 1 \text{ year}$$

for all j. For notational convenience we set $T_0 = t$. As we saw in Chapter 16, valuing such a swap involves, first, finding the expected present values (PV) of its protection and premium legs and, second, determining the value of the premium $S_{r,J}$ such that the CDS has zero market value at its inception. We follow the spirit of Merton's (1974)[59] model and assume that a default by the reference entity, if any, only occurs at specific times. In the context of this chapter, those times are the premium payment dates of the CDS.

As we saw in Chapter 16, the expected (risk-adjusted) present value of the premium leg for this CDS can be written as

$$\text{PV[premiums]}_t = \sum_{j=1}^{J} Z(t, T_j) Q_r(t, T_j) S_{r,J} \tag{23.5}$$

where $Q_r(t, T_j)$ is the risk-neutral probability, conditional on all information available at time t and given no default by that time, that the reference entity will survive through time T_j, and $Z(t, T_j)$ is the time-t price of a risk-less zero-coupon bond that matures at time T_j—$Z(t, T_j)$ is the time-t value of a dollar that will be received/paid at time T_j.[3]

The relationship between Q_r and H_r at time T_1 is straightforward:

$$Q_r(t, T_1) = 1 - H_r(t, T_1) = 1 - N(C_{r,T_1}) \qquad (23.6)$$

and, generalizing for $j > 1$,

$$Q_r(t, T_j) = \prod_{i=1}^{j} [1 - N(C_{r,T_i})] \qquad (23.7)$$

where the last equation follows from the fact that R_{r,T_j} is serially uncorrelated, i.e.,[4,5]

$$Q_r(t, T_j) \equiv \mathrm{Prob}_t[R_{r,T_1} > C_{r,T_1} \text{ and } R_{r,T_2} > C_{r,T_2} \text{ and } \dots R_{r,T_j} > C_{r,T_j}]$$

$$= \mathrm{Prob}_t[R_{r,T_1} > C_{r,T_1}] \, \mathrm{Prob}_t[R_{r,T_2} > C_{r,T_2}] \dots \mathrm{Prob}_t[R_{r,T_j} > C_{r,T_j}]$$

$$= \prod_{i=1}^{j} \mathrm{Prob}_t[R_{r,T_i} > C_{r,T_i}]$$

In Chapter 16 we also showed that the expected risk-adjusted present value of the protection leg can be written as

$$\mathrm{PV[protection]}_t = \sum_{j=1}^{J} Z(t, T_j)[Q_r(t, T_{j-1}) - Q_r(t, T_j)](1 - X_r) \qquad (23.8)$$

where X_r is the recovery rate associated with the reference entity ($0 \leq X_r < 1$).

---

[3] Equation (23.5) implicitly assumes that no accrued premium is due to the protection seller upon a default by the reference entity. This simplifying assumption, and a simple approach to relax it, was discussed in Chapter 16.

[4] As we saw in Chapter 19, serial uncorrelation of R_r, which is normally distributed with zero mean and unit variance, means that $R_{r,T}$ and $R_{r,T-s}$ are uncorrelated random variables for all nonzero values of s. Thus, for instance,

$$\mathrm{Prob}_t[R_{r,T} > C \text{ and } R_{r,T-s} > C] = \mathrm{Prob}_t[R_{r,T} > C]\mathrm{Prob}_t[R_{r,T-s} > C]$$

[5] The notation $\prod_{i=1}^{j} G(i)$, for any function $G(i)$ of i, denotes the product operator:

$$\prod_{i=1}^{j} G(i) \equiv G(1)G(2)\dots G(j)$$

Given equations (23.5) and (23.8), the fair value of the CDS premium when there is no counterparty credit risk is

$$S_{r,J|H_p=0} = \frac{\sum_{j=1}^{J} Z(t,T_j)[Q_r(t,T_{j-1}) - Q_r(t,T_j)](1 - X_r)}{\sum_{j=1}^{J} Z(t,T_j)Q_r(t,T_j)} \tag{23.9}$$

and, thus, the model-implied CDS premium in the absence of counterparty credit is

$$S_{r,J|H_p=0} = \frac{\sum_{j=1}^{J} Z(t,T_j) \prod_{i=1}^{j-1}[1 - N(C_{r,T_i})]N(C_{r,T_j})(1 - X_r)}{\sum_{j=1}^{J} Z(t,T_j) \prod_{i=1}^{j}[1 - N(C_{r,T_i})]} \tag{23.10}$$

23.4   A CDS with Counterparty Credit Risk

A first step in understanding how the model presented in Section 23.2 can be used to value a CDS that involves counterparty credit risk is to lay out the possible default outcomes regarding the contract and then to compute the risk-neutral probabilities associated with each outcome, just as we did with baskets and portfolio default swaps in Chapters 20 and 21. As noted earlier, we shall approach this problem from the perspective of the protection buyer in a CDS.

The protection buyer will pay the premium due on the dates T_j specified in the contract, $j = 1, \ldots, J$, for as long as both the protection seller and the reference entity remain solvent on those dates. Let $Q_{rp}(t,T_j)$ denote the probability of such an event at time T_j, conditional on all available information at time t and given survival by both entities through that time. If we also assume that the protection seller is entitled to no accrued premium upon its own default, we can write the expected present value of the premium leg of a CDS that is subject to counterparty credit risk as:

$$\text{PV[premiums]}_t = \sum_{j=1}^{J} Z(t,T_j)Q_{rp}(t,T_j)S_{r,J} \tag{23.11}$$

which is entirely analogous to equation (23.5), except that we have replaced the survival probability of the reference entity with the probability that both the reference entity and the protection seller will survive through different dates in the future. The intuition is quite clear. If either the protection seller or the reference entity defaults at T_j, the protection buyer has no reason to continue to make premium payments. In the former case (seller's default), the default protection provided by the contract becomes worthless; in the latter case (reference entity's default) the contract is triggered and it is the seller that owes a payment to the buyer.

As for the protection leg of the swap, the buyer will receive the protection payment at a given time T_j only if two events occur at that time: the reference entity defaults *and* the protection seller is solvent. Let $H(t, T_j)$ denote the probability that these events take place at T_j, conditional on all information available at time t and on survival by both entities through t. Then, similar to equation (23.8), the expected present value of the protection leg is:

$$\text{PV[protection]}_t = \sum_{j=1}^{J} Z(t, T_j) H(t, T_j)(1 - X_r) \qquad (23.12)$$

where, for simplicity, we assume a zero recovery rate associated with the protection seller.[6]

Given equations (23.11) and (23.12), the fair value of the credit default swap premium in the presence of counterparty credit risk is:

$$S_{r,J|H_p>0} = \frac{\sum_{j=1}^{J} Z(t, T_j) H(t, T_j)(1 - X_r)}{\sum_{j=1}^{J} Z(t, T_j) Q_{rp}(t, T_j)} \qquad (23.13)$$

Equation (23.13) is a model-independent expression for the premium for a CDS that is subject to counterparty credit risk. To obtain expressions for the probabilities $H(t, T_j)$ and $Q_{rp}(t, T_j)$, we need to go back to the credit risk model. We discuss below two methods for doing so. The first is based on deriving explicit solutions for these probabilities in terms of parameters of the model—C_{p,T_j}, C_{r,T_j}, β_p, and β_r. The second is based on Monte Carlo simulation methods and is similar in spirit to the approach emphasized in Chapters 20 and 21.

23.4.1 *Analytical Derivation of Joint Probabilities of Default*

Unlike the case of no counterparty credit risk, where the probabilities included in the formula for the CDS premium depended only on the

---

[6] Extending the framework to allow for a nonzero recovery rate for the protection seller would be relatively straightforward. We would add terms involving $X_p(1 - X_r)$—where $0 \le X_p < 1$ is the recovery rate of the protection seller—and the risk-neutral conditional probabilities, $G(t, T_j)$, associated with a default by both entities at time T_j, as in

$$\text{PV[protection leg]}_t = \sum_{j=1}^{J} Z(t, T_j) H(t, T_j)(1 - X_r) + \sum_{j=1}^{J} Z(t, T_j) G(t, T_j) X_p(1 - X_r)$$

To keep things simpler, however, and because this extension is relatively trivial, we choose to set X_p to zero and leave the nonzero X_p case as an exercise for the reader.

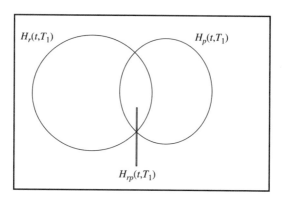

FIGURE 23.1. Diagrammatic Representation of Probabilities of Defaulting at Time T_1

distribution of future returns for the reference entity, we now need to use equations (23.1) through (23.4) to compute joint probabilities of various default and survival scenarios involving the reference entity and the protection seller. As we saw in Chapter 19, the derivation of these joint probabilities can quickly become very messy for a portfolio with several assets, even for the simplest case of a homogeneous portfolio. But computing joint default and survival probabilities for the "two-asset portfolio" implicit in a CDS with counterparty credit risk can be a significantly simpler exercise.

Consider, for instance, the derivation of $Q_{rp}(t,T_1)$ and $H(t,T_1)$. Figure 23.1 shows a diagrammatic representation of the probabilities attached to possible default and survival outcomes involving the reference entity and the protection seller at T_1.[7] In particular, the area labeled $H_r(t,T_1)$ represents the conditional risk-neutral probability that the reference entity will default at time T_1, and the one labeled $H_p(t,T_1)$ is analogously defined for the protection seller. The region of overlap between the two areas, labeled $H_{rp}(t,T_1)$ in the figure, is the probability that both the reference entity and the protection seller will default at time T_1.[8]

Relying on the same arguments laid out in the beginning of Chapter 19, the probability that both the protection seller and the reference entity will survive through time T_1 is

$$Q_{rp}(t,T_1) = 1 - [H_r(t,T_1) + H_p(t,T_1) - H_{rp}(t,T_1)] \qquad (23.14)$$

---

[7] We first discussed the use of such diagrams in Chapter 19.

[8] We continue to assume that these probabilities are conditional on all information available at time t, given survival by both entities through t.

which is simply one minus the probability that at least one of the two entities—the protection seller and the reference entity—will default by time T_1.

Given the definition of default events—equations (23.2) and (23.4)—$H_{rp}(t, T_1)$ can also be characterized as the probability that both R_{p,T_1} and R_{r,T_1} will fall below their respective default thresholds. Because both R_{p,T_1} and R_{p,T_1} are normally distributed and, as we saw in Chapter 19, have a coefficient of correlation equal to $\beta_p\beta_r$, this probability is given by

$$H_{rp}(t, T_1) = N_2(C_{r,T_1}, C_{p,T_1}, \beta_p\beta_r) \tag{23.15}$$

where $N_2()$ is the cumulative distribution function of the bivariate normal distribution.[9]

Thus, in terms of the model parameters, the probability that both the reference entity and the protection seller will not default at time T_1 is:[10]

$$Q_{rp}(t, T_1) = 1 - [N(C_{r,T_1}) + N(C_{p,T_1}) - N_2(C_{r,T_1}, C_{p,T_1}, \beta_p\beta_r)] \tag{23.16}$$

Going back to Figure 23.1, it is relatively straightforward to see that the probability that the reference entity will default at time T_1 and that the protection seller will remain solvent is

$$H(t, T_1) = H_r(t, T_1) - H_{rp}(t, T_1) = N(C_{r,T_1}) - N_2(C_{r,T_1}, C_{p,T_1}, \beta_p\beta_r) \tag{23.17}$$

The derivation of expressions for $Q_{rp}(t, T_j)$ and $H(t, T_j)$ for $j \geq 2$ requires only a bit more work than the computations just described for $Q_{rp}(t, T_1)$ and $H(t, T_1)$. Take, for instance, the computation of $Q_{rp}(t, T_2)$. If we let PS and RE denote the protection seller and reference entity, respectively, and define $R_{T_j} \equiv [R_{r,T_j}, R_{p,T_j}]$ and $C_{T_j} \equiv [C_{r,T_j}, C_{p,T_j}]$ we can write

$$Q_{rp}(t, T_2) \equiv \text{Prob}_t[\text{PS and RE survive through } T_2]$$

$$= \text{Prob}_t[R_{T_1} > C_{T_1} \text{ and } R_{T_2} > C_{T_2}]$$

$$= \text{Prob}_t[R_{T_1} > C_{T_1}] \, \text{Prob}_t[R_{T_2} > C_{T_2}]$$

---

[9] Appendix B provides a brief overview of the bivariate normal distribution.

[10] Those familiar with the bivariate normal distribution have probably noticed that the right-hand side of (23.16) is equivalent to $N_2(-C_{r,T_1}, -C_{p,T_1}, \beta_p\beta_r)$.

where, as in the case of no counterparty credit risk, the last equality follows from the fact that returns are serially uncorrelated.[11]

Thus, given

$$\text{Prob}_t[R_{T_i} > C_{T_i}] \equiv \text{Prob}_t[R_{r,T_i} > C_{r,T_i} \text{ and } R_{p,T_i} > C_{p,T_i}] \qquad (23.18)$$

it is straightforward to see that we can write:

$$Q_{rp}(t, T_2) = \prod_{i=1}^{2} \{1 - [H_r(t, T_i) + H_p(t, T_i) - H_{rp}(t, T_i)]\} \qquad (23.19)$$

As for the derivation of a model-implied expression for $H(t, T_2)$, we once again recall its definition:

$$H(t, T_2) \equiv \text{Prob}_t[\text{RE defaults at } T_2 \text{ and PS survives through } T_2]$$

$$= \text{Prob}_t[(\text{RE def. and PS surv. at } T_2) \text{ and}$$

$$(\text{PS and RE surv. through } T_1)]$$

Serial uncorrelation of returns implies that the two events in parenthesis above are independent. Thus we can write:

$$H(t, T_2) = \text{Prob}_t[\text{RE def. and PS surv. at } T_2]$$

$$\times \text{Prob}_t[\text{PS and RE surv. through } T_1]$$

The expressions for the two probabilities on the right-hand side of the above equation are entirely analogous to the ones derived for T_1. Thus,

$$H(t, T_2) = [H_r(t, T_2) - H_{rp}(t, T_2)]Q_{rp}(t, T_1) \qquad (23.20)$$

Generalizing for T_j, $j \geq 2$, and expressing all probabilities in terms of the parameters of the model, we obtain:

$$Q_{rp}(t, T_j) = \prod_{i=1}^{j} \{1 - [N(C_{r,T_i}) + N(C_{p,T_i}) - N_2(C_{r,T_i}, C_{p,T_i}, \beta_r\beta_p)]\}$$

$$(23.21)$$

$$H(t, T_j) = [N(C_{r,T_j}) - N_2(C_{r,T_j}, C_{p,T_j}, \beta_r\beta_p)]Q_{rp}(t, T_{j-1}) \qquad (23.22)$$

---

[11] R_p and R_r are only contemporaneously correlated. Serial uncorrelation of Z, which is the only source of contemporaneous correlation between R_p and R_r implies that returns on the protection seller and the reference entity are intertemporally uncorrelated.

which we can substitute into equation (23.13) to write an explicit formula for the CDS premium in the presence of counterparty credit risk.

23.4.2 Simulation-based Approach

Rather than using the model to derive explicit formulae for the probabilities in equation (23.13), one may choose to rely on a Monte Carlo simulation approach similar to the one described in Chapter 19 and used in Chapters 20 and 21. In the context of the J-year CDS studied thus far, each simulation of the model involves relying on equations (23.1) through (23.4) to generate J values for the vector $R_{T_j} \equiv [R_{p,T_j}, R_{r,T_j}]$, for $j = 1$ to J. For each generated pair of returns, we record whether any of the two basic default outcomes of interest—survival by both entities and default by the reference entity while the protection seller survives—took place.

Thus, for $j = 1$ to J, we define

- $q(j) \equiv$ total number of simulations where both the reference entity and the protection seller survive through time T_j

- $h(j) \equiv$ total number of simulations where the reference entity defaults at time T_j and the protection seller survives through T_j.[12]

After running a sufficiently large number of simulations, we can compute approximate values of $Q_{rp}(t, T_j)$ as

$$Q_{rp}(t, T_j) \approx \frac{q(i)}{M} \tag{23.23}$$

Likewise, we can approximate $H(t, T_j)$ as

$$H(t, T_j) \approx \frac{h(j)}{M} \tag{23.24}$$

where M is the total number of simulations of the model. Thus, the method involves generating M values of R_r and R_p for each of the J premium payment dates of the CDS.

To improve the accuracy of the results, it is common practice to perform these computations a large number of times and then report the average of the results obtained. For instance, we may run $M = 500{,}000$ simulations of the model 200 times and compute the average of the 200 results obtained.

---

[12] Recall that the time of default is defined as the first time that the asset return reaches or falls below the default barrier on a premium payment date.

23.4.3 An Example

We examine the effects of counterparty credit risk on the valuation of a
five-year CDS written on a reference entity with a 5 percent risk-neutral
probability of default over the next year and a flat credit curve. We assume
that the swap involves no credit enhancement mechanisms such as collateralization and netting, that $\beta_r = \beta_p = \beta$, and that the premium is paid
annually.

Figure 23.2 shows premiums for the CDS just described under various
assumptions regarding the credit quality of the protection seller and for
different values of β. Accordingly, β varies from zero to .99, and $H_p(t, T_j)$
ranges from zero to 4 percent. These results are based on the analytical
results derived in Section 23.4.1 and were confirmed by Monte Carlo simulations.[13] Before we proceed, we should note that this exercise involves
several simplifying assumptions, such as a zero recovery rate for the protection seller and no accrued premiums or interest in the event of default
by the reference entity. In more realistic settings, these factors should not
be ignored.[14]

Each curve in the figure corresponds to a given value of β. For instance,
the solid line shows values of the CDS premium when $\beta = 0$, which corresponds to the case of no default correlation between the protection seller
and the reference entity. The values along the horizontal axis correspond
to risk-neutral default probabilities of potential protection sellers in this
contract.

Consistent with one's intuition, Figure 23.2 shows that, for a given degree
of default correlation between the reference entity and the protection seller,
the fair value of the CDS premium declines as the credit quality of the protection seller deteriorates. Nonetheless, such an effect is barely noticeable
for very low levels of default correlation. This occurs as the protection
and premium legs of the CDS are about equally affected by counterparty
credit risk when the coefficient of default correlation between the protection seller and the reference entity is low. Take the case of a protection
seller that has a risk-neutral default probability of 4 percent, which is only
marginally below the risk-neutral default probability of the reference entity.
With $\beta = .2$—a coefficient of default correlation of about 1 percent—the
fair value of the CDS premium that such a seller would be able to charge
is only about 3 basis points lower than that charged in a contract that
involves no counterparty credit risk.

---

[13] We assume a flat credit curve for the protection seller.

[14] For instance, a nonzero recovery rate associated with the protection seller would lead
to a smaller effect of counterparty credit risk on CDS premiums than the one suggested
by this example.

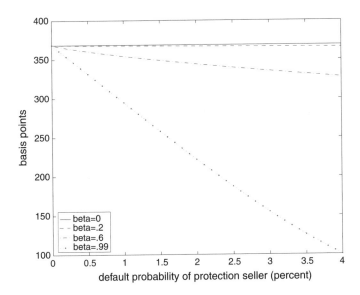

FIGURE 23.2. Effects of Counterparty Credit Risk on Five-year CDS Premiums. (The reference entity is assumed to have a recovery rate
of 30 percent. The riskless yield curve is assumed to be flat at
5 percent.)

Figure 23.2 also illustrates the effect of default correlation on the CDS
premium. As one would expect, higher correlation (higher β) increases the
likelihood that the seller and the reference entity will default together and,
thus, makes the CDS less valuable to the protection buyer, resulting in a
lower premium. For instance, with $\beta = .6$, which amounts to a default correlation of approximately 12 percent, the drop-off in premiums as the credit
quality of the protection seller declines is much steeper than in comparable
cases with lower default correlation. Under this scenario, the same protection seller described in the previous paragraph—one with a risk-neutral
default probability of 4 percent—would have to offer roughly a 40 basis
point concession on the five-year premium relative to the premium charged
in a comparable contract with no counterparty credit risk.

Taken together, the results in Figure 23.2 suggest that, although counterparty credit risk can have a significant effect on the extent of default
protection effectively provided by a CDS, protection buyers can substantially mitigate their exposure to sellers by being mindful of the potential
degree of default correlation between the seller and the reference entity.
That mitigation would be over and above that conferred by relatively common contractual arrangements such as collateralization and netting, and

by the fact that protection sellers tend to have a high credit quality to begin with.

23.5   Other Models and Approaches

In keeping with the introductory nature of this book, we have focused on a very simple approach to analyzing the effects of counterparty credit risk in credit derivatives contracts. Nonetheless, our basic framework captures many of the key elements and insights of other approaches developed in the credit risk literature. For instance, a model that is closely related to the one described in this chapter is the one developed by Hull and White (2001)[42].

Similar to our basic model, the Hull-White specification follows the structural approach to modeling credit risk and assumes that there is a variable $X_j(t)$ that describes the creditworthiness of entity j at time t and that the entity defaults at t if $X_j(t)$ falls below a certain level $K_j(t)$. Hull and White also used their model to examine the valuation of credit default swaps that are subject to counterparty credit risk. Their model allows for defaults to occur at any time, not just at the premium payment dates specified in the CDS, and also allows for accrued premiums and interest rate payments to be factored into the valuation exercise. These features are not difficult to incorporate into the model discussed in Sections 23.1 through 23.4. For instance, accrued premiums can be introduced as noted in Chapter 16.

Many other methods and approaches for modeling the effects of counterparty credit risk exist and have varying degrees of complexity and effectiveness. For instance, a well-known framework rooted on the intensity-based approach was proposed by Jarrow and Yu (2001)[47]. Additional methods are discussed by Arvanitis and Gregory (2001)[2].

One issue that was not explicitly addressed by our basic model is the replacement value of a credit derivative contract in the event of default by the protection seller while the reference entity is still solvent. By replacement cost we mean the cost, to the protection buyer, of replacing a contract where the protection seller has defaulted with another one written on the same reference entity and with the same remaining maturity.

If the credit quality of the reference entity has not changed since the inception of the original contract, then the replacement cost is zero. Thus, for instances of low asset default correlation between the protection seller and the reference entity, the replacement cost should generally be very small. For high (positive) correlation, however, the replacement cost of the contract may be non-trivial, in that the credit quality of the reference entity is more likely to have deteriorated than improved when that of the protection seller has worsened to the point of leading it to default on its obligations. For negative default correlation between the protection seller and the reference entity, the replacement cost could actually turn out to be negative, in which case the protection buyer could experience a windfall upon a default by the seller.

23.6 Counterparty Credit Risk in Multi-name Structures

We have thus far focused on approaches for assessing the effects of counterparty credit risk on the pricing of single-name credit default swaps. It turns out that the basic framework described in Sections 23.1 through 23.4 can be extended for the analysis of more complex structures. For instance, in the case of the first-to-default basket, we can expand the set of possible default outcomes—shown in Table 20.1 for a five-asset example that involves no counterparty credit risk—to allow for scenarios where the protection seller defaults during the life of the basket. By carefully keeping track of all possible outcomes and their respective risk-neutral probabilities implied by the model, one can rely on Monte Carlo simulation methods similar to the one described in Section 23.4.2. A similar logic applies to the valuation of portfolio default swaps, which we discussed in Chapter 21.

23.7 Concluding Thoughts

As we mentioned in the beginning of Part IV, the portfolio credit risk literature has been growing rapidly and is technically demanding. Indeed, we have barely scratched its surface in this introductory book. We do hope, however, that we have managed to provide a broad overview of some of the main issues that are germane to the valuation of multi-name credit derivatives and of counterparty credit risk. More important, we hope we have been able to provide a base from which one can expand one's knowledge of the subject and grow into this important segment of the credit derivatives market.

Part V

A Brief Overview of Documentation and Regulatory Issues

24
Anatomy of a CDS Transaction

This chapter provides an overview of legal and documentation issues involving credit default swaps (CDS), the most prevalent of all credit derivatives.[1] Similar to other over-the-counter derivatives instruments, credit default swaps are typically initiated with a phone call in which the basic terms of the transaction are agreed upon by the two prospective counterparties.[2] That initial oral agreement is then followed up by a confirmation letter, which, together with any supporting documentation referenced in the letter, spells out the rights and obligations of each counterparty, as well as the procedures for fulfilling them.

From a legal standpoint, the confirmation letter and related documents are the core of any CDS transaction and jointly constitute what we shall refer here as a CDS contract. In this chapter, we take a closer look at the main features and provisions of CDS contracts and the role that they have played in the rapid growth of the credit derivatives market. We also look at how developments in the marketplace have helped shape the contracts.

In keeping with the scope of this book, we limit ourselves to providing a broad, and thus necessarily incomplete, overview of documentation

---

[1] Many other credit derivatives instruments are negotiated on the basis of a similar documentation framework.

[2] In recent years, it has become increasingly common for transactions to be initiated "on-line" via various electronic platforms.

issues regarding CDS transactions. Needless to say, this chapter does not constitute legal advice regarding CDS, or any other credit derivatives contracts.

24.1   Standardization of CDS Documentation

As we mentioned in Chapter 2, CDS contracts are largely standardized, with the marketplace mostly relying on documentation sponsored by the International Swaps and Derivatives Association (ISDA), a trade group whose members include major dealers and end-users of over-the-counter derivatives products ranging from interest rate swaps to credit derivatives. We say "largely" because there are some contractual variations across national borders. Indeed, while the ISDA documentation for credit derivatives is preeminent worldwide, it coexists, in a few countries, with alternative, locally drawn, documentation frameworks.

To appreciate the role that the so-called ISDA contracts for CDS have played in the development of the credit derivatives market, it is useful to imagine the counterfactual. Suppose that, to this date, market participants still had to contend with different forms of CDS contracts, both within and across jurisdictions, depending on the counterparty, each with its own stipulations and definitions of key terms of the agreement. To reduce the inherent "legal risk" that would prevail in a world with a multitude of contract types, participants, and their lawyers, would have to devote valuable time and resources to scrutinizing each agreement, often negotiating its terms on a case-by-case basis. Such a situation would hardly be conducive to the impressive growth in liquidity and size that the credit derivatives market has experienced in recent years.

The fact is that, starting in the early days of the credit derivatives market, participants came to realize the need for a common set of contractual provisions and practices, following the example of other successful over-the-counter derivatives markets, most notably that for interest rate swaps. In essence, that is how the ISDA framework has become the most prevalent standard for documenting CDS transactions both at the national and international levels. Thus, our discussion of legal and documentation issues involving CDS transactions is centered entirely on the ISDA legal framework.

Broadly speaking, the ISDA framework for credit default swap contracts revolves around the following main components:

- The **Master Agreement** is a contract between the two prospective counterparties that often preexists the CDS transaction in which they are about to enter. The master agreement governs those aspects of the legal relationship between the two counterparties that are not specific to the CDS transaction at hand. For instance, the agreement may specify that the laws of the state of New York should be the applicable law to any contracts entered into by the two counterparties. The master agreement may also specify that netting provisions should be applicable to any over-the-counter derivatives contract entered by the two counterparties and covered by the master agreement.[3] Procedures relating to default by one of the counterparties in any of the types of contracts covered by the master agreement are generally also dealt with in this document. Highlighting the general nature of the master agreement, it is not uncommon for the same agreement to cover several types of over-the-counter contracts, not just credit derivatives.

- The **Confirmation Letter** is the document that follows up on the initial (generally oral) agreement between two prospective counterparties to enter into a specific CDS. As its name indicates, this document confirms the "economic" terms of the swap such as the identity of the reference entity, the notional amount of the contract, and the protection premium. In the early days of the credit derivatives market, the confirmation letter was a relatively lengthy document that described the terms of the contract in great detail. That so-called long-form of the CDS confirmation letter has effectively been replaced by its short-form, which is basically a template that allows the counterparties to "fill in the blanks" with the appropriate information and "check" the boxes that apply for the transaction at hand. For instance, the parties might have to agree on which types of default events are covered by the contract. The use of the short-form of the confirmation letter became widespread as the degree of standardization of acceptable provisions and definitions became significant enough that those terms and provisions could be listed in a separate document, called the ISDA Credit Derivatives Definitions.

- The **ISDA Credit Derivatives Definitions**, as just noted, is a list that defines key terms referred to in the confirmation letter. Examples include definitions of the credit events allowable in the confirmation letter, as well as additional detail on deliverable obligations and settlement procedures.

- **Supplements** are separate documents issued by ISDA that amend, update, or clarify terms in the Definitions.

- **Credit Support Documentation** involves agreements that call for the collateralization of net exposures between the counterparties in

---

[3] See Chapter 2 for a brief discussion of netting provisions.

order to mitigate counterparty credit risk considerations. Not all CDS contracts include credit support documentation, but contracts that do are becoming increasingly common, especially when a lower-rated counterparty is involved.

The legal framework sponsored by ISDA is primarily intended to promote standardization of legal provisions and market practices, but it does recognize that some of the legal stipulations of the transaction may need to be tailored to the needs of the counterparties. For instance, the master agreement has two parts, the so-called "printed form" and the "schedule." While the former contains key standard provisions of the master agreement, the latter allows any two counterparties to agree to make certain choices specified in the printed form and/or to amend any provisions.

We could go on at length in a discussion of master agreements and other legal issues involving credit derivatives, but that would go beyond the intent of this book. Those interested in learning more about the ISDA documentation framework may want to visit ISDA's website, *www.isda.org*.

24.1.1 Essential Terms of a CDS Transaction

In addition to the names of the two parties in the contract—the buyer and seller of default protection—essential terms that need to be specified front and center in the confirmation letter include, obviously, the identity of the reference entity, the types of obligations of that entity that are covered by the contract, the specific events that will trigger a payment by the protection seller, and the procedures for settling the contract in the event of default by the reference entity. As basic and self-evident as some of these terms may seem, they need to be carefully defined in the text of the agreement. Any ambiguity regarding these key terms can result in significant legal and financial headaches down the road.

24.1.1.1 The Reference Entity

With regard to the reference entity, if all that the contract did were to name it, one might reasonably ask whether a default by a fully owned subsidiary of that entity is enough to trigger payments by protection sellers, or whether following the merger or demerger of the reference entity, the successor entity or entities become the new reference entity in the CDS. These questions, and other related issues, have been addressed in the Definitions and in various Supplements over the years. For instance, a default by a subsidiary generally does not trigger a contract written on the parent company, provided that company itself has not defaulted. Only contracts referencing the subsidiary are triggered. On the second question, the documentation determines that if an entity assumes 75 percent or more of the bonds and loans of the original reference entity, then the assuming entity becomes the new reference entity.[4]

24.1.1.2   Reference and Deliverable Obligations

The reference obligation is a debt instrument issued by the reference entity that is designated in the CDS contract. The characteristics of the reference obligation are important for several reasons. First, it dictates the level of the reference entity's capital structure at which default protection is being bought and sold. Typically, the reference obligation is a senior unsecured debt instrument of the reference entity, although some contracts are written with reference to subordinated debt. Second, in the case of physically settled CDSs, the reference obligation is always a deliverable obligation (see Section 24.2.2), but a deliverable obligation need not be a reference obligation. For instance, most contracts in the United States accept obligations that have the same rank in the reference entity's capital structure as the reference obligation, generally subject to certain restrictions such as the currency in which the instrument is denominated and, in the case of bank loans, the ability to transfer the obligations to someone else.

The confirmation letter generally also specifies the range of obligations in which a default must occur in order for a credit event to take place. Most contracts simply specify the catch-all category "borrowed money," although, as we shall see below, there are some safeguards to prevent the contract from being triggered prematurely, for instance, because of certain events involving small dollar amounts or short delays in repayment.

24.1.1.3   Settlement Method

As we saw in Chapter 6, upon default by the reference entity, a CDS can be either physically or cash settled. The choice of settlement method is specified in the confirmation letter, which, as noted above, also determines the types of debt securities that can be delivered in the case of physically settled contracts.

Cash-settled CDS contracts are more common in Europe than in the United States, where physical settlement is the method of choice. We discuss settlement procedures in greater detail in Section 24.2.

24.1.1.4   Credit Events

One of the most important definitions in a credit default swap contract is that of "default." Which event, or events, must take place for the protection

---

[4] If no single entity assumes 75 percent of the bonds and loans of the original reference entity, then the notional amount of the CDS contract is split pro rata among all entities assuming at least 25 percent of the bonds and loans of the original entity.

payment to be triggered? There are several "credit events" that constitute default in the ISDA documentation framework for credit derivatives and each are detailed in the Credit Derivatives Definitions. The following is a brief description of each event:

- **Bankruptcy** constitutes a situation where the reference entity becomes insolvent or unable to repay its debts. This credit event does not apply to CDS written on sovereign reference entities.

- **Obligation Acceleration** occurs when an obligation has become due and payable earlier than it would have otherwise been.

- **Failure to Pay** means essentially what it says. It occurs when the reference entities fails to make due payments.

- **Repudiation/Moratorium** is deemed to have occurred when the reference entity rejects or challenges the validity of its obligations.

- **Restructuring** is a change in the terms of a debt obligation that is adverse to creditors, such as a lengthening of the maturity of debt. We discuss restructuring in greater detail later in this chapter.

Not all of the above events apply to all contracts. The parties to the contract can agree to exclude certain events. For instance, the market consensus has moved towards excluding obligation acceleration as a credit event in newly entered CDS contracts in the US. In addition, as we shall see in Section 24.3, there is a certain degree of bifurcation in the marketplace, where some contracts allow for restructuring to be included in the list of credit events, whereas others do not.

24.1.2 Other Important Details of a CDS Transaction

Other important terms and provisions included in the confirmation letter and accompanying documentation include:

- The maturity of the contract, also referred to as the "scheduled termination date" of the contract.

- The notional amount of the contract, called the "fixed rate payer calculation amount" in the language of the confirmation letter.

- the CDS premium, which the contract calls the "price" or "fixed rate," normally expressed in terms of basis points per annum.[5]

---

[5] The protection payment and the protection seller are often referred to as the floating-rate payment and floating-rate payer, respectively, borrowing on language commonly used in the interest rate swap market. One interpretation of the use of this terminology

- The day-count conventions that should be applied, for instance, to the calculation of accrued premiums in the event of default by the reference entity while the contract is in force.

- The frequency with which CDS premium payments are made—payments are typically made on a quarterly basis on dates specified in the confirmation letter.

24.1.3   A Few Words of Caution

The standardization of CDS documentation has worked to reduce, but not eliminate, the legal risks associated with CDS transactions. Nonetheless, standardized documents are no guarantee of universal agreement as to the interpretation of those documents. Indeed, the effort to improve on the existing documentation framework is an ongoing one, especially as unanticipated market developments have come to expose deficiencies and limitations of earlier contracts, an issue that we discuss in Section 24.3.

Moreover, given that the CDS market is, as discussed in Chapter 2, still a relatively young marketplace, there is potentially much to be learned regarding how CDS documentation will be interpreted by the parties involved and by the courts. For instance some market observers have expressed concerns about the eventual enforceability of the language in ISDA contracts in national courts, especially in cases involving non-OECD parties.

24.2   When a Credit Event Takes Place...

The contract specifies in detail all the procedures that must be followed in the event of default by the reference entity while the CDS is in place. But before the settlement phase of the contract goes fully into gear, the ISDA documentation provides for some safeguards to ensure that a bona fide credit event has indeed taken place.

24.2.1   Credit Event Notification and Verification

A credit event is not a credit event until it meets certain minimum payment and default requirements under the terms of the CDS contract. For instance, a qualifying failure-to-pay event must take into account any applicable grace periods and must involve a minimum dollar threshold—e.g., a

---

is that, unlike the protection buyer who knows exactly when and how much to pay for as long as the contract is in force and the reference entity is solvent, uncertainty about the recovery rate means the seller does not know in advance the timing or size of the protection payment, if any, that it will have to make to the buyer.

loss of at least $1 million. Repudiation, moratorium, and restructuring events also are subject to minimum dollar thresholds. In addition to meeting the minimum payment and default requirements, a credit event has to be verifiable through at least two sources of public information, such as Bloomberg, Reuters, or similar services. The event notification and verification process is generally formalized via the delivery of the Credit Event Notice and the Notice of Public Information by the party triggering the contract.[6]

These pre-settlement requirements are designed to protect the interests of both sellers and buyers of protection. From the seller's perspective, a premature triggering of the contract involving an otherwise solvent reference entity may mean that the seller will end up making a payment in a situation where no bona fide credit event ever takes place during the life of the CDS. From the buyer's perspective, the seller may end up receiving a small protection payment now while foregoing valuable protection down the road when a bona fide event takes place.

24.2.2 Settling the Contract

Once the occurrence of a credit event is verified, usually via acceptance of the Credit Event Notice and Notice of Publicly Available Information, the contract goes into its settlement phase.

For cash-settled contracts, upon default by the reference entity the protection buyer is entitled to receive from the seller the difference between the par and market values of the reference obligation. The latter tends to be a bond issued by the reference entity as bond prices are typically easier to determine in the marketplace than those of loans. The market value of the reference obligation is commonly determined by a dealer poll typically conducted a few days after the credit event. The contract generally allows the settlement price to be determined on the basis of a similar obligation of the reference entity if the original reference obligation is no longer available, which could be the case if, for instance, it was prepaid by the reference entity.

For physically settled contracts, the protection buyer has the right to decide which of the eligible obligations of the reference entity will be delivered to the seller. Once that decision is made, the buyer delivers a Notice of Intended Physical Settlement to the seller and then commits to delivering the designated obligations. The physical settlement period is capped at 30 business days. If delivery is not successful during that period because,

---

[6] Commonly, the Credit Event Notice and the Notice of Publicly Available Information can be delivered up to 14 days after the maturity date of the contract, provided the event itself took place while the contract was still in place.

say, the buyer was not able to buy the obligations in the marketplace, the contract usually allows for "fallback" settlement procedures, which are described in ISDA's 2003 Credit Derivatives Definitions.

24.3 The Restructuring Debate

One of the most prominent documentation issues in the history of the credit derivatives market has evolved around the definition of restructuring as a credit event. The scope of the issues debated by market participants over the years has ranged from the very definition of restructuring to the question of whether restructuring should be included in the list of allowable credit events in the first place.

In the early days of the marketplace, restructuring was defined only in very broad terms in ISDA's standard CDS documentation. Indeed, the then-prevailing definition, which had been adopted by ISDA back in 1991, characterized restructuring essentially as any change in the terms of the obligations of a reference entity that was "materially less favorable" to its creditors. The Asian crisis of 1997 and the Russian default of 1998 brought to light some of the problems with the subjectivity of the 1991 definition, and, in 1999, market participants adopted a new definition of structuring.[7] That definition basically provided a narrower characterization of which circumstances would trigger the restructuring clause in CDS contracts. In particular, the 1999 ISDA definition characterized restructuring as:

- a reduction in the rate or amount of interest payable;

- a reduction in the amount of principal;

- a postponement of interest or principal payment;

- a change in the seniority of the debt instrument;

- a change in the currency composition of any payment.

In addition, market participants, through ISDA, adopted the condition that, for any of the above to constitute a restructuring event for the purposes of a CDS contract, they must result "directly or indirectly from a deterioration in the creditworthiness or financial condition of the reference entity."

---

[7] Rule (2001)[68] discusses the events that led up to the adoption of the 1999 definition of restructuring, as well as other important cases in the history of the marketplace, such as the Conseco restructuring episode in the United States, summarized below, and the National Power demerger case in the United Kingdom, which helped shape the successor provisions outlined in Section 24.1.1.1 of this book.

24.3.1   A Case in Point: Conseco

Conseco Inc. is an insurance and financial services company based in the United States. The company was facing a deteriorating financial outlook in the late 1990s and eventually lost access to the commercial paper market, a situation that led it to rely on its back-up lines of bank credit to repay maturing debt. In 2000, even though its business condition was showing some signs of improvement, Conseco's lines of credit were fully utilized and about to become due. Conseco's bankers agreed that it would not be able to repay the maturing bank loans and decided to restructure the loans, extending their maturity while charging a higher interest rate and obtaining some collateralization.

The loan restructuring helped Conseco remain solvent in 2000.[8] Moreover, given the higher coupon and degree of collateralization on the restructured debt, the affected lenders were thought to have been at least partially compensated for the maturity extension. Yet, according to the 1999 definition of restructuring a qualifying restructuring event had taken place, and CDS contracts written on Conseco were consequently triggered.

The Conseco case helped expose one shortcoming associated with the 1999 definition of restructuring. Unlike an outright default or bankruptcy, where the market prices of the bonds and loans of the reference entity broadly converge regardless of their maturity, restructurings often affect the prices of bonds and loans of the reference entity differently. For instance, in Conseco's case, the restructured loans were trading at a substantially smaller discount from their face value shortly after the triggering of the corresponding CDS contracts than were longer-dated senior unsecured bonds previously issued by Conseco. Yet, both the long-dated bonds and the loans were deliverable obligations under the terms of the contract!

As a result, some protection buyers in the CDS market that had made loans to Conseco were more than compensated for their restructuring-related losses regarding Conseco. They suffered a relatively small marked-to-market loss in the restructured loans, but that loss was more than offset by gains derived from their CDS positions, where they could deliver the cheaper longer-dated bonds, as opposed to the loans, and receive their full face value from their CDS counterparties.

To sum up, the 1999 definition of restructuring had the effect of giving protection buyers a potentially valuable cheapest-to-deliver option in their CDS positions. While protection sellers honored the letter of the CDS contracts written on Conseco and made good on their commitments under the contracts, many wondered whether the Conseco episode was consistent

---

[8] The company's troubles were not fully resolved by the 2000 restructuring of its bank debt, however. In late 2002, Conseco filed for Chapter 11 bankruptcy protection. It emerged from its Chapter 11 reorganization process in September 2003.

with the spirit of a CDS agreement. Indeed, most market participants point to the Conseco case, as we do in this book, as a major catalyst of the debate that culminated with the adoption of a new set of provisions regarding restructuring in CDS contracts.

24.3.2 Modified Restructuring

The main thrust of the so-called modified restructuring provision of CDS contracts—which was introduced in the standard CDS documentation in an ISDA Restructuring Supplement adopted in 2001 and later incorporated into the 2003 Credit Derivatives Definitions—was to mitigate the cheapest-to-deliver problem that was at the heart of the Conseco case. Thus, without substantially changing the 1999 definition of restructuring as a credit event, the new provisions had mostly the effect of limiting the range of obligations that would become deliverable when a contract is triggered by a restructuring event. The new provisions also disallowed the applicability of the restructuring clause in cases where restructuring is limited to bilateral loans.

The motivation for the first set of main changes associated with modified restructuring—limiting the basket of deliverables in contracts triggered by restructuring—is very straightforward in light of the Conseco case. Indeed, modified restructuring works primarily by capping the maturity of obligations that are eligible to be delivered in the event of restructuring. As for the second main innovation brought about by modified restructuring—the bilateral-loan exclusion—its primary intent was to address potential "moral hazard" problems, whereby a lender may force the restructuring of a loan on which it bought protection and then attempt to gain from "exercising" any remaining cheapest-to-deliver option embedded in a CDS contract.

Remaining provisions of the modified restructuring clause sought to fine tune other issues related to restructuring as a credit event, including the transferability of any deliverable obligations and the treatment of changes in the seniority of an obligation in the reference entity's capital structure.

24.3.3 A Bifurcated Market

Modified restructuring went a long way towards meeting the interests of both buyers and sellers in the CDS market. Many sellers, especially banks who count on the credit derivatives market to obtain regulatory capital relief, wanted the broadest possible default protection and thus preferred to keep restructuring in the list of allowable credit events. Protection sellers, on the other hand, wanted to minimize the cheapest-to-delivery problem, which, as we discuss below, introduces some tough valuation issues. The modified restructuring clause thus emerged as a compromise between these two positions.

Still, the restructuring debate is most likely not over. Indeed, some degree of bifurcation persists in the marketplace, with some contracts being negotiated with restructuring and some without. In addition, there are some variations in the standard contracts used in North American, Europe, and Asia when it comes to restructuring. For instance, in Europe, contracts typically allow for less stringent maturity limitations than in the United States.

24.4   Valuing the Restructuring Clause

A contract that provides protection, for instance, against restructuring, bankruptcy, and failure-to-pay events ought to cost more than one that provides protection only against the latter two. How much extra should a protection buyer have to pay to have restructuring added to the list of credit events? Drawing an analogy with the vast default risk literature, theory would suggest that the value of the restructuring clause should depend on the probability of a restructuring taking place. Unfortunately, however, there are no well-known models of restructuring probabilities so the analogy between modeling default and restructuring risks does not take us very far in terms of valuing the restructuring clause.

One simple approach to gauging the value of the restructuring clause is to compare premiums actually charged in CDS contracts that include restructuring to those that do not. Based on the limited amount of data generated since the modified structuring clause became part of the standard CDS documentation, some market participants have estimated that premiums that correspond to contracts with the modified restructuring clause are about 5 to 10 percent higher than premiums for contracts without restructuring.

24.4.1   Implications for Implied Survival Probabilities

In Chapter 16 we discussed a simple method for inferring risk-neutral probabilities of default from CDS premiums quoted in the marketplace. Suppose now that all that we have are premiums that correspond to contracts that include the modified restructuring clause, but that we are interested in the risk-neutral probabilities of an outright default over various horizons—where by outright default we mean events like bankruptcy and failure to pay. The discussion in the previous section suggests a simple two-step approach to computing those probabilities. First, we reduce the observed premiums by 5 to 10 percent in order to obtain a rough estimate of premiums that would prevail in the absence of the modified restructuring clause. Second, we follow the same method described in Section 16.1.

Table 24.1 shows the results of the two-step approach when applied to AZZ Bank, one of the hypothetical reference entities examined in

TABLE 24.1

CDS-implied Survival Probabilities and Modified Restructuring

| Horizon/ Maturity | CDS premium (basis points) | Survival Probabilities | | Bias |
		Raw quotes (percent)	Adjusted quotes (percent)	(3) −(4)
(1)	(2)	(3)	(4)	(5)
One year	29	99.42	99.48	− 0.06
Two years	39	98.45	98.60	− 0.15
Three years	46	97.26	97.53	− 0.27
Four years	52	95.88	96.29	− 0.40
Five years	57	94.37	94.92	− 0.55

Note. Assumed recovery rate: 50 percent. All probabilities shown are risk-neutral. All other assumptions are as in Table 16.1.

Chapter 16. Column 2 shows the CDS premiums quoted in the market place, which we are now assuming to be for contracts that include the modified restructuring clause. Column 3 shows CDS-implied survival probabilities based on the unadjusted (raw) quotes shown in column 2—these are the same probabilities shown in Table 16.2. Column 4 shows survival probabilities obtained from the two-step approach, where we reduced the premiums shown in column 2 by 10 percent. The results suggest that, at least for highly rated reference entities such as the one examined in this exercise, the survival probabilities based on the adjusted premiums differ very little from those based on the raw market quotes.

The differences between results derived from raw and restructuring-adjusted premiums—shown in the column labeled "bias"—would be bigger for lower-rated entities such as XYZ Corp., the other entity examined in Chapter 16. Still, the maximum absolute value of the bias for XYZ Corp. would amount to only minus 2.75 percentage points. We should also note that it is often the case that CDS contracts written on lower-rated entities tend not to include restructuring in the list of allowable credit events so the "restructuring bias" in derived survival probabilities is often not an issue for these reference entities.

25

A Primer on Bank Regulatory Issues

We mentioned in Section 3.2 that bank regulatory considerations spelled out in the 1988 Basel Bank Capital Accord—also known as the Basel I Accord—played an important role in the early days of the credit derivatives markets. In particular, banks' use of credit derivatives was, at least initially, significantly motivated by the desire to better align the notion of regulatory capital—the share of risk-adjusted assets that bank regulators require to be set aside to support risk-taking activities—with that of economic capital— a prudent bank's own estimate of the needed capital reserve. For instance, in that chapter we examined the case of a hypothetical bank that made a loan to a corporation and subsequently bought protection from an OECD bank in the CDS market in a contract that referenced that corporation. The protection-buying bank would essentially see its capital charge drop from 8 percent of the total exposure associated with the corporate loan to only 1.6 percent of the exposure, provided the bank could demonstrate to its regulators that the terms of the contract—maturity of the CDS vs. that of the loan, definition of credit events, etc.—effectively granted it appropriate protection against default-related losses on the loans.

The interplay between bank regulatory issues and banks' usage of credit default swaps and related instruments has changed considerably since the formative days of the credit derivatives market, however. Not only have banks increased their use of credit derivatives for reasons other than just regulatory capital management, but the regulatory environment itself has also evolved. We discussed, in Chapter 3, banks' other (non-regulatory-driven) uses of credit derivatives—such as applications to risk management and portfolio diversification. We will now take a quick look at the new regulatory environment facing banks and examine its possible implications for the future development of the credit derivatives market.

Similar to the treatment of documentation considerations in Chapter 24, the coverage of regulatory issues provided in this chapter is of a very broad nature and thus does not constitute advice about what is permissible under current international accords or even under the banking laws of any single country.

25.1   The Basel II Capital Accord

In 1999, member countries of the Basel Committee on Banking Supervision formally started working on a new set of guidelines and standards for their national bank regulators and supervisors.[1] That effort culminated with the New Basel Capital Accord—also known as the Basel II Accord. The Accord was finalized at the Basel Committee level in 2004, and the process now is largely in the hands of signatory countries, which have agreed to start implementing the terms of the new accord by the end of 2006. The process towards implementation will likely include further deliberation at the national level, and, possibly, additional fine-tuning in the language of the accord at the international level. As it was the case with Basel I, the Basel II Accord only provides a framework for the regulation of bank capital. Each national authority then has the discretion to adapt the accord's stipulations to its own needs and reality.

A main drive behind the genesis of the Basel II Accord has been the need to strengthen the regulatory framework for large banking organizations, especially those that are active in the international markets, and, in the process, devise capital requirements that are more reflective of these organizations' somewhat unique risk profiles. We say "unique" because, more so than their smaller cousins, large banking organizations have tended to rely on newer instruments and approaches, including credit derivatives, in measuring and managing risk. Many of these instruments either did not exist or were not widely used when Basel I was conceived and thus were not directly mentioned by the framers of that accord. In addition, the new Basel Accord seeks to address some of the limitations of its predecessor,

---

[1] The Basel Committee on Banking Supervision was established in 1974. Its members include representatives of central banks or other supervisory authorities from Belgium, Canada, France, Germany, Italy, Japan, Luxembourg, the Netherlands, Spain, Sweden, Switzerland, the United Kingdom, and the United States. The committee has no supranational supervisory authority and its conclusions have no legal force. Its goals are to formulate and propose standards and guidelines to encourage and facilitate the adoption of best practices regarding bank regulation among member countries (see Federal Reserve Board (2003))[27].

such as, as noted in Chapter 3, the lack of granularity in the way the original accord assigned risk weights to different categories of borrowers.

As we saw in Chapter 2, despite the phenomenal growth of the credit derivatives market, as well as the fact that banks are major users and dealers of credit derivatives, these instruments represent only a small portion of the total notional amount of derivatives at banks. Thus, it is both logical and natural that the scope and motivation for revamping the Basel I Accord goes well beyond issues directly related to the emergence of the credit derivatives market. Given the subject matter of this book, however, we shall highlight those aspects of the new accord that are most relevant for credit derivatives, especially credit default swaps. Towards the end of the chapter we provide a list of basic sources for readers interested in delving deeper into bank regulatory issues involving credit derivatives.

Similar to the 1988 Accord, the provisions of the Basel II Accord call for regulatory capital to be determined according to the credit risk associated with the range of debt instruments held by a bank. But the new accord is much more discriminating than its predecessor with regard to the credit quality of a banks' debtors when it comes to determining the appropriate risk weights that go into the calculation of regulatory capital.[2] The computation of regulatory capital is analogous to that devised under Basel I, in that it involves multiplying the product of the regulatory risk weight and the basic capital requirement of 8 percent by the notional exposure, as discussed in Chapter 3.

The new accord allows the risk weights to be based on either ratings provided by outside credit-rating agencies, such as Standard and Poor's and Moody's—the so-called standardized approach—or on two methods derived from banks' own internal ratings systems—the so-called internal ratings-based approaches—provided, in the case of the latter, those systems have been explicitly approved by the bank regulator. National bank regulators are free to specify which risk weighting approach(es) are applicable to their jurisdiction and under which conditions.

Based on the standardized approach, Table 25.1 shows Basel II risk weights that correspond to sovereign, bank, and corporate (non-bank) borrowers. These weights stand in sharp contrast to the weighting scheme specified in the Basel I Accord—see Table 3.1 in Chapter 3 for a comparison. In particular, whereas the original accord made no distinction among corporate borrowers, and differentiated banks and sovereign borrowers only according to their OECD status, the new accord allows for a closer correspondence between regulatory risk weights and the credit quality of

---

[2] Similar to the discussion of Basel I, in Chapter 3, we limit ourselves here to the regulatory treatment of obligations on banks' banking books. The new accord also addresses requirements associated with obligations held on the trading book (see Basel Committee on Bank Regulation (2003)[1]).

TABLE 25.1

Risk Weights Specified in the Basle II Accord for Selected Obligors[a]

(percent)

| Obligor | Credit Rating | | | | | |
	AAA to AA−	A+ to A−	BBB+ to BBB−	BB+ to B−	Below B−	Unrated
Sovereign	0	20	50	100	150	100
Bank[b]	20	50	50	100	150	50
Corporate	20	50	100	100	150	100

[a] As specified in the April 2003 version of the Consultative Document on the New Basel Capital Accord (Basel Committee on Banking Supervision, 2003[1]). Weights shown are for the so-called standardized approach to weighting banking book exposures.

[b] The Accord also provides for an alternative risk weighting of claims on banks. The alternative weights are based on the credit assessment of the country in which the bank is incorporated (see Basel Committee on Banking Supervision, 2003[1]).

obligors, a provision that helped narrow the gap that existed in the original accord between regulatory and economic capital. For instance, under Basel I, loans to corporations rated either AAA or B would be subject to the same regulatory risk weight of 100 percent, despite the fact that these corporations are nearly at opposite ends of the credit quality spectrum. In contrast, the Basel II Accord assigns risk weights of 20 and 100 percent to these obligors, respectively.

25.2   Basel II Risk Weights and Credit Derivatives

With regard to credit default swaps, the new accord generally allows protection-buying banks to continue to substitute the risk weight of the protection seller for that of the reference entity in instances where the bank is long an obligation of that entity and where the bank can demonstrate that effective protection has been bought. Thus, banks continue to have an incentive to seek regulatory capital relief in the credit derivatives market, but that incentive is arguably not as strong as under the Basel I provisions, given the closer alignment between Basel II risk weights and true economic risk.

One might be tempted to conclude that the closer alignment between regulatory and economic capital might lead banks to become less important users of credit derivatives. Yet, as we saw in Chapter 3, even before the adoption of Basel II, banks' use of such derivatives had been increasingly driven by nonregulatory considerations, such as the need to manage credit risk exposures in response to greater scrutiny by investors. Indeed, given its closer correspondence between regulatory and economic capital, Basel II may well end up reinforcing banks' incentives to use credit derivatives as a risk management tool.

Another implication of the greater granularity of the risk weighting scheme of the Basel II Accord regards the attractiveness of non-banks as potential sellers of protection to banks. Under Basel I, banks would be granted no capital relief, say, for buying protection from an AA-rated corporation in a credit default swap intended to hedge exposure to a BBB-rated corporate reference entity. They would simply be replacing exposure to one 100-percent risk-weighted obligor—the BBB-rated entity— with another—the AA-rated protection seller. Under Basel II, however, this same contract would result, assuming other regulatory conditions are met, in a decrease in the corresponding regulatory risk weight from 100 percent to 20 percent, a development that bodes well for the greater participation of highly-rated nonbank entities as protection sellers in credit derivatives. (A similar argument applies to highly rated non-OECD banks.)

On the whole, Basel II has multiple, and sometimes offsetting, implications for future developments in the credit derivatives market. On one hand, banks' incentives to use of credit derivatives purely as a regulatory capital management tool may wane further. On the other hand, the new accord is clearly intended to reinforce banks' incentives to monitor closely and manage their credit risk exposures, which could be accomplished with greater use of instruments such as credit derivatives. Outside the banking sector, the risk weighting provisions of the new accord may well promote greater participation of other market players, such as highly-rated corporations, as sellers of protection, which may help facilitate the transfer of credit risk from banks to other institutions.

25.3   Suggestions for Further Reading

A complete discussion of the full regulatory treatment of credit derivatives under the Basel II Accord would go well beyond the scope of this book. Indeed, we have omitted the discussion of several topics, such as the treatment of basket swaps and synthetic securitization. In addition, the new accord covers situations where the default protection bought in a credit derivative contract only partially offsets a bank's exposure to the reference entity, such as is the case when the maturity of a loan to the reference entity is longer than that of the corresponding credit default swap. Readers interested in these and other related topics are encouraged to consult the text of the accord itself, which can be downloaded from the Bank for International Settlements' website (*www.bis.org*).

While the focus of this chapter has been on international bank regulatory standards as they relate to credit derivatives, we should once again remind the reader that the Basel II Accord, like its predecessor, only provides a general framework for national bank regulators in signatory countries. The implementation of the accord's provisions varies from country to country according to local concerns and market characteristics. Moreover, credit derivatives have regulatory implications that go beyond the setting of capital requirements, and these too vary across national borders. The following is a partial list of national bank regulator websites, some of which provide further on-line information on issues related to credit derivatives in their respective jurisdictions:

- Australia: Australian Prudential Regulation Authority (*www.apra.gov.au*);

- Canada: Office of the Superintendent of Financial Institutions (*www.osfi-bsif.gc.ca*);

- France: Commission Bancaire (*www.commission-bancaire.org*);

- Germany: Budesanstalt fur Finanzdienstleistungsaufsicht (*www.bafin.de*);

- Ireland: Central Bank of Ireland and Financial Services Authority (*www.centralbank.ie*);

- Italy: Banca D'Italia (*www.bancaditalia.it*);

- Japan: Bank of Japan (*www.boj.or.jp*);

- Sweden: Swedish Financial Supervisory Authority (*www.fi.se*);

- United Kingdom: Financial Services Authority (*www.fsa.gov.uk*);

- United States: Board of Governors of the Federal Reserve System (*www.federalreserve.gov*), Office of the Comptroller of the Currency (*www.occ.treas.gov*), Federal Deposit Insurance Corporation (*www.fdic.gov*), and the Office of Thrift Supervision (*www.ots.treas.gov*).

Appendix A
Basic Concepts from Bond Math

We briefly discuss in this appendix some of the basic bond and term-structure concepts featured in the book. Hull (2003)[41] provides further details on these concepts at the introductory level.

A.1 Zero-coupon Bonds

A zero-coupon bond, as its name suggests, is a bond that makes no coupon payments. Its yield comes from the fact that it is sold at a discount from its face value. For instance, a one-year zero-coupon bond initially sold for 95 cents on the dollar can be said to have an annual yield of 5.26 percent, or $(1 - .95)/.95$. Indeed, it is straightforward to see that, for this one-year bond:

$$1 = .95(1 + 0.0526)$$

i.e., the annual yield is the annual rate at which the price of the bond will have to grow so that it will converge to its face value at the maturity date of the bond. This is also called the yield-to-maturity of this bond.

The yield-to-maturity, Y_n, of a n-year zero-coupon bond is likewise defined as the constant annual rate at which the bond's price will have to grow so that the bond will be valued at par at maturity:

$$\text{face value} = (1 + Y_n)^n \text{ price} \tag{A.1}$$

A.2   Compounding

The zero-coupon yields discussed above assume annual compounding. If we were to compound twice per annum, the yield-to-maturity of the one-year zero-coupon bond considered above would be:

$$Y_1^{(2)} = 2[(1/.95)^{1/2} - 1] = 0.0520$$

or 5.20 percent, where the above equation comes from the fact that $Y_1^{(2)}$ is such that

$$1 = .95 \left(1 + \frac{Y_1^{(2)}}{2}\right)^2$$

For compounding j times per annum, the one-year yield is:

$$Y_1^{(j)} = j[(1/.95)^{1/j} - 1]$$

and, as j tends to infinity, we obtain the following expression for the yield to maturity:

$$Y_1^{(\infty)} = -\log(.95) = 0.05129$$

which is the continuously compounded yield-to-maturity for the one-year bond.

Generalizing for n-year bonds, the yield-to-maturity with compounding j times per year is

$$Y_n^{(j)} = j\left[\left(\frac{\text{face value}}{\text{price}}\right)^{1/(jn)} - 1\right] \tag{A.2}$$

and the continuously compounded yield is:

$$Y_n^{(\infty)} = -\log\left(\frac{\text{price}}{\text{face value}}\right)/n \tag{A.3}$$

The last two equations trivially allow us to write the price of a zero-coupon bond in terms of its yield-to-maturity. With compounding j times per annum:

$$\text{price of } n\text{-year bond} = \frac{\text{face value}}{\left(1 + \dfrac{Y_n^{(j)}}{j}\right)^{jn}} \tag{A.4}$$

and, with continuous compounding:

$$\text{price of } n\text{-year bond} = \left[e^{-nY_n^{(\infty)}} \right] [\text{face value}] \qquad (\text{A.5})$$

A.3   Zero-coupon Bond Prices as Discount Factors

Zero-coupon bond prices can be thought of as discount factors that can be applied to future payments in order to express them in today's dollars. For instance, the present value of $1 to be received in one-year's time is, by definition, simply today's price of a zero-coupon bond with a face value of $1.

If there is no chance that a given future payment will be missed (no default risk) then the receiver of that payment should discount it on the basis of the price of a zero-coupon bond that involves no credit risk. By the same token, future payments that are subject to default risk should be discounted with prices of zero-coupon bonds that are subject to comparable default risk. This is essentially what we do in equation (4.2) in the text, where we discounted the future cash flows of a corporate security using prices of zero-coupon bonds derived from the security issuer's yield curve.

A.4   Coupon-paying Bonds

Consider a n-year bond that pays a fixed annual coupon C at dates $T_1, T_2, \ldots, T_n$. In addition, the bond pays its face value F at its maturity date T_n. The bond has no default risk. Given the discount-factor interpretation of zero-coupon bond prices, we can write:

$$V(t, T_n) = \sum_{h=1}^{n} Z(t, T_h)C + Z(t, T_n)F \qquad (\text{A.6})$$

where $V(t, T_n)$ is the price of the coupon-paying bond, and $Z(t, T_h)$ is the price of a riskless zero-coupon bond that pays $1 at date T_h.

If the coupon-paying bond has some default risk, the discount factors should correspond to the prices of zero-coupon bonds issued by the same entity issuing the coupon-paying bond. Assuming that the bond has no recovery value upon default, we can write:

$$V_0^d + -(t, T_n) = \sum_{h=1}^{n} Z_0^d(t, T_h)C + Z_0^d(t, T_n)F \qquad (\text{A.7})$$

TABLE A.1
Par Yield Curve for a Hypothetical Issuer[a]

Maturity (years)	Yield to Maturity (percent)
1	2.0
2	2.2
3	2.5
4	2.7

[a]Yields shown are compounded annually and coupons are paid once a year.

where $V^d(t, T_n)$ is the price of the defaultable coupon-paying bond, and $Z_0^d(t, T_h)$ is the price of a defaultable zero-coupon bond that promises to pay \$1 at date T_h. Thus, given the zero-coupon curve for a given issuer, we can price other debt instruments of that same issuer, as we do, for instance, in Chapter 11 when valuing principal-protected notes.

A.5   Inferring Zero-coupon Yields from the Coupon Curve

Zero-coupon bonds with long maturities are rarely issued in practice. Instead, actual longer-dated bonds traded in the marketplace are of the coupon-paying variety. Using (A.7), however, we can back out the zero-coupon yields and prices embedded in an issuer's coupon curve. To see how this can be done, we consider a simple numerical example for a hypothetical issuer. Table A.1 summarizes the main inputs. The table shows the "par" yield curve for the issuer, where by par we mean that the prices of the bonds shown are all equal to their face values, or, equivalently, that the yield-to-maturity of each bond is equal to its respective coupon rate. We show four bonds, with maturities ranging from one to four years, each with a face value of \$1 and a zero recovery rate.[1]

The time-t (today's) price of the one-year zero-coupon bond associated with this issuer, which would be used to discount payments to be made in

---

[1]In a more realistic setting, the issuer may not have outstanding bonds along the entire maturity spectrum, and one may need to resort to interpolation and smoothing methods. See, for instance, James and Webber (2000)[44] for a discussion of these methods.

one-year's time, is simply the price of the first bond shown. Thus, given

$$1 = Z_0^d(t, t+1)(1.02)$$

we have

$$Z_0^d(t, t+1) = 1/1.02 = 0.9804$$

To derive the price of the two-year zero-coupon bond, recall that the price of the two-year coupon-paying bond can be written as

$$1 = Z_0^d(t, t+1)0.022 + Z_0^d(t, t+2)(1.022)$$

Thus

$$Z_0^d(t, t+2) = \frac{1 - Z_0^d(t, t+1)0.022}{1.022}$$

where the value of $Z_0^d(t, t+1)$ was derived in the prior step.

For the three-year bond:

$$1 = Z_0^d(t, t+1)0.025 + Z_0^d(t, t+2)0.025 + Z_0^d(t, t+3)(1.025)$$

and thus

$$Z_0^d(t, t+3) = \frac{1 - \sum_{h=1}^{2} Z_0^d(t, t+h)0.025}{1.025}$$

Generalizing, the price of a n-year zero-coupon bond can be written as a function of the prices of shorter-dated zeros and the coupon of a n-year coupon-paying bond sold by the same issuer:

$$Z_0^d(t, t+n) = \frac{1 - \sum_{h=1}^{n-1} Z_0^d(t, t+h)C_n}{1 + C_n} \tag{A.8}$$

where C_n is the coupon payment of the n-year bond.

A.6 Forward Rates

A forward rate $F(t, T_1, T_2)$ is the annual interest rate agreed upon in the marketplace at today's date (time t) for lending and borrowing during a future period $[T_1, T_2]$, but involving no net cash outlay at time t. One can obtain the fair value of $F(t, T_1, T_2)$ entirely in terms of time-t prices of zero-coupon bonds. Consider the following simultaneous transactions at time t:

- sell one zero-coupon bond that matures at time T_1;

- buy $\frac{Z(t,T_1)}{Z(t,T_2)}$ zero-coupon bonds that mature at time T_2.

Assume that the face value of the bonds is \$1. Note that this transaction results in no net cash flow at time t. Subsequent cash flows are as follows:

- Time T_1: Pay \$1 to the buyer of the T_1-bond sold at t;

- Time T_2: Receive $\$\left(\frac{Z(t,T_1)}{Z(t,T_2)}\right)$ from the issuer of the T_2-bonds bought at time t.

Thus we can see that the time-t transaction involves no initial cost and is akin to contracting to lend \$1 at time T_1 in exchange for receiving $\$\left(\frac{Z(t,T_1)}{Z(t,T_2)}\right)$ at time T_2. The implicit interest payment in this forward loan is $\frac{Z(t,T_1)}{Z(t,T_2)} - 1$. As already noted, the annualized interest rate implicit in this forward loan, which we denote below as $F(t,T_1,T_2)$, is defined as the time-t forward rate for the future time period $[T_1,T_2]$. For instance, in Chapter 4, we examine an example where the length of the future period is 6 months, $T_2 - T_1 = .5$ year, which corresponds to the following expression for $F(t,T_1,T_2)$:

$$F(t,T_1,T_2) = \frac{1}{T_2 - T_1}\left(\frac{Z(t,T_1)}{Z(t,T_2)} - 1\right) \tag{A.9}$$

Using equation (A.5), the time-t continuously compounded forward rate for the future period $[T_1,T_2]$ is the rate $f(t,T_1,T_2)$ that solves the following equation:

$$e^{f(t,T_1,T_2)(T_2-T_1)} = \frac{Z(t,T_1)}{Z(t,T_2)}$$

Thus:

$$f(t,T_1,T_2) = \frac{\log(Z(t,T_1)) - \log(Z(t,T_2))}{T_2 - T_1} \tag{A.10}$$

A.7   Forward Interest Rates and Bond Prices

The rate $f(t,T)$ such that

$$f(t,T) \equiv \lim_{\Delta T \to 0} \frac{\log(Z(t,T)) - \log(Z(t,T+\Delta T))}{\Delta T} = -\frac{\partial \log(Z(t,T))}{\partial T} \tag{A.11}$$

is called the instantaneous continuously compounded forward rate. It can be thought of as the time-t interest rate that applies to the future period $[T, T + dt]$, where dt is an infinitesimal time increment.

Integrating both sides of equation (A.11), we obtain:

$$Z(t, T) = e^{-\int_t^T f(t,v)dv} \tag{A.12}$$

Given the definition of the continuously compounded yield to maturity as the rate $R(t, T)$ such that $Z(t, T) = e^{-R(t,T)(T-t)}$:

$$R(t, T) = \frac{\int_t^T f(t, v)dv}{T - t} \tag{A.13}$$

which says that the time-t yield-to-maturity on a zero-coupon bond can be thought of as the average of all time-t instantaneous forward rates that span the remaining life of the bond.

Appendix B
Basic Concepts from Statistics

This appendix provides a brief review of some key statistical concepts used in the text. We have skipped over some technical details and mathematical proofs involving these concepts. Bain and Engelhardt (1987)[5], Hogg and Tanis (1983)[39], and Grimmett and Stirzaker (1998)[36] provide a more complete coverage of the topics discussed herein.

B.1   Cumulative Distribution Function

The cumulative distribution function (c.d.f.) of a random variable X is defined as

$$F(x) = \text{Prob}[X \le x] \tag{B.1}$$

$F(x)$ is also commonly called the distribution function of X. We highlight two of its basic properties below:

- Because $F(x)$ is a probability: $0 \le F(x) \le 1$;

- $F(x)$ is a non-decreasing function of x, i.e., if $x_1 < x_2$ then if $X \le x_1$ we also have $X \le x_2$, and thus:

$$F(x_1) = \text{Prob}[X \le x_1] \le \text{Prob}[X \le x_2] = F(x_2)$$

B.2   Probability Function

A random variable X is said to be discrete if it can only take on one of the discrete values $x_1, x_2, x_3, \ldots$. If X is a discrete random variable:

$$F(x) = \sum_{x_i \leq x} p(x_i) \tag{B.2}$$

where the sum is computed over all x_i such that $x_i \leq x$, and where $p(x)$ is called the probability function of X.

The function $p(x)$ assigns a probability to each one of the possible values of X:

$$p(x) = \text{Prob}[X = x] \qquad x = x_1, x_2, \ldots \tag{B.3}$$

Note that, for $p(x)$ to be a probability function, it must satisfy the following two properties:

$$p(x_i) \geq 0 \qquad \text{for all } x_i$$

$$\sum_{\text{all } x_i} p(x_i) = 1$$

B.3   Probability Density Function

Let X be a continuous random variable, in that it can take *any* value, for instance, in the interval $[x_1, x_n]$. The c.d.f. of X can be written as:

$$F(x) = \int_{-\infty}^{x} f(s)ds \tag{B.4}$$

where $f(x)$ is called the probability density function (p.d.f.) of X.

Similar to the probability function in the discrete case, a p.d.f. must satisfy the following conditions

$$f(x) \geq 0 \qquad \text{for all real } x$$

$$\int_{-\infty}^{\infty} f(x)dx = 1$$

In the light of (B.4), it can be shown that:

$$\text{Prob}[a \leq X \leq b] = F(b) - F(a) = \int_{a}^{b} f(x)dx \tag{B.5}$$

Because $F(x)$ is a continuous function:

$$\text{Prob}[X = a] = 0 \tag{B.6}$$

which is consistent with the basic result from classic calculus that $\int_a^a f(x)dx = 0$. Thus:

$$\text{Prob}[a < X < b] = \text{Prob}[a < X \leq b] = \text{Prob}[a \leq X < b] = \text{Prob}[a \leq X \leq b]$$

We also highlight the following useful relationship:

$$\text{Prob}[x < X \leq x + dx] = F(x + dx) - F(x) \approx f(x)dx \tag{B.7}$$

where the approximation error is negligible for sufficiently small values of dx. Indeed, given (B.4), from classic calculus we know that, for values of x for which $\frac{\partial F(x)}{\partial x}$ exists:

$$\lim_{dx \to 0} \frac{F(x + ds) - F(x)}{dx} = \frac{\partial F(x)}{\partial x} = f(x) \tag{B.8}$$

B.4   Expected Value and Variance

The expected value of a discrete random variable is simply the probability-weighted average of all of its possible values. If the possible values of X are $x_1, x_2, \ldots, x_n$, its expected value, $E[X]$, is given by

$$E[X] = \sum_{i=1}^{n} p(x_i)x_i \tag{B.9}$$

where $p(.)$ is the probability function of X.

The variance of X is likewise defined as

$$V[X] = \sum_{i=1}^{n} p(x_i)(x_i - E[X])^2 \tag{B.10}$$

If X is a continuous random variable we have

$$E[X] = \int_{-\infty}^{\infty} sf(s)ds \tag{B.11}$$

and

$$V[X] = \int_{-\infty}^{\infty} (s - E[X])^2 f(s)ds \tag{B.12}$$

Note. The square root of the variance of X is called the standard deviation of X.

B.5 Bernoulli Trials and the Bernoulli Distribution

Throughout this book, we often deal with situations where a company can be in only one of two possible states at some given future date, default or survival, and where there are probabilities associated with each state. Statistically, one way to characterize such situations is through the concept of Bernoulli trials.

A Bernoulli trial is a random experiment that can result in only one of two possible outcomes—e.g., a given company will either default or survive. A sequence of independent Bernoulli trials is one where the probabilities associated with the two outcomes are the same from trial to trial.

Let X be a random variable associated with a Bernoulli trial. For instance:

$$X = 1 \text{ if the company defaults and } X = 0 \text{ if it survives}$$

If the probability of default is denoted as w, the probability function of X can be written as

$$p(x) = w^x (1 - w)^{1-x} \qquad x = 0, 1 \tag{B.13}$$

and one can say that X has a Bernoulli distribution.

The expected value and variance of X are:

$$E[X] = \sum_{x=0}^{1} x w^x (1 - w)^{1-x} = (1)w + (0)(1 - w) = w$$

$$V[X] = \sum_{x=0}^{1} (x - w)^2 w^x (1 - w)^{1-x} = w(1 - w)$$

B.6 The Binomial Distribution

Consider a sequence of n independent Bernoulli trials. For instance, given n corporate borrowers, each trial may involve either the default or survival of an individual borrower, where defaults among the n borrowers are mutually independent. Let the default probability for each borrower be denoted as w.

Let Y be the random variable that represents the number of defaults among the n borrowers over a given period of time. The probability function of Y is

$$b(y; n, \omega) = \frac{n!}{y!(n-y)!} \omega^y (1-\omega)^{n-y} \tag{B.14}$$

where y denotes the possible values of Y—$y = 0, 1, 2, \ldots, n$—and Y is said to be binomially distributed.

The c.d.f. of the binomial distribution is

$$B(y; n, \omega) \equiv \text{Prob}[Y \leq y] = \sum_{s=0}^{y} b(s; n, \omega) \qquad y = 0, 1, \ldots, n \tag{B.15}$$

which, continuing with our example, is the probability that at most y companies will default over a given time horizon.

In Part IV we use the results just derived to examine expected default-related losses in an equally weighted homogeneous portfolio where defaults among the issuers represented in the portfolio are mutually independent. With default independence the question of how many issuers are likely to default or survive reduces to a sequence of independent Bernoulli trials, in which case the binomial distribution applies. Without default independence—for instance, a default by one company changes the default probabilities of the others—we cannot directly appeal to results based on the binomial distribution.

B.7   The Poisson and Exponential Distributions

Most reduced-form models make use of the Poisson distribution to characterize the "arrival" process of defaults over time for a given borrower.[1] For this borrower, let X be the discrete random variable that corresponds to the number of defaults arriving (occurring) over a given continuous time interval. We assume that defaults occur randomly at the mean rate of λ per year, with $\lambda > 0$.

From a credit risk modeling perspective, in most cases all that we care about is the first occurrence of default. Nonetheless, in some applications—such as when modeling defaults and corporate reorganizations—one may also be interested in the notion of second default, third default, etc.

---

[1] We will measure time in terms of non-negative real numbers, with 0 denoting "the beginning of time" and time t representing the present time. The unit of measurement will be years so that, for instance, $t = 1.25$ means that we are one and a quarter years away from the beginning of time.

If X is Poisson distributed, the following conditions must be satisfied—see, for instance, Hogg and Tanis (1983)[39]:

1. the numbers of defaults occurring in nonoverlapping time intervals are independent;

2. the probability of exactly one default occurring during a short time interval of length s is approximately λs;

3. the probability of more than one default during a sufficiently short time period is essentially zero.

Assuming the above conditions are met, the probability function of X can be shown to be:

$$p(x; 1) \equiv \text{Prob}[x \text{ defaults in a one-year interval}]$$

$$= \frac{\lambda^x e^{-\lambda}}{x!} \qquad \text{for } x = 0, 1, 2, \ldots \qquad (B.16)$$

which, indeed, has the property, stated above, that the expected number of defaults during a time interval of one year is λ:

$$E[X] = \sum_{x=0}^{\infty} x \frac{\lambda^x e^{-\lambda}}{x!} = \lambda \qquad (B.17)$$

The variance of X can also be shown to be λ.

More generally, let us change the reference time interval to be s years—where $s > 0$—so that, for instance, $s = \frac{1}{12}$ indicates a time interval of about a month. If the mean arrival rate of defaults for this borrower in a one-year interval is λ, then the mean arrival of defaults in a s-year interval is λs. As a result, we can write:

$$p(x; s) \equiv \text{Prob}[x \text{ defaults in a } s\text{-year interval}]$$

$$= \frac{(\lambda s)^x e^{-\lambda s}}{x!} \qquad \text{for } x = 0, 1, 2, \ldots \qquad (B.18)$$

provided, of course, conditions 1 through 3 are satisfied.

Thus, using time 0 as our vantage point, the unconditional probability that no default will take place during a time interval of length s years is:

$$p(0; s) \equiv \text{Prob}[0 \text{ defaults in a } s\text{-year interval}]$$

$$= e^{-\lambda s} \qquad (B.19)$$

Similarly, the unconditional probability of exactly one default occurring during a time interval of length s years is

$$p(1; s) = \lambda s \, e^{-\lambda s}$$

which, consistent with condition 2, is approximately λs for small s.

As discussed in Chapter 17, one concept that is of great interest in the pricing of credit derivatives is the expected time of first default by a given reference entity. Let τ denote the time of first default, which can be thought of as a continuous random variable with c.d.f. $\bar{G}(s)$. (Alternatively, τ can also be thought of as the "waiting time" until the first default, as seen from time 0.) Clearly, for $s < 0$, $\bar{G}(s) = 0$, given that a waiting time cannot be negative. For $s \geq 0$ we can write

$$\bar{G}(s) \equiv \text{Prob}[\tau \leq s] = 1 - \text{Prob}[\tau > s]$$

but note that $\text{Prob}[\tau > s]$ is simply the probability, as seen at time 0, that there will be no default by time s. This probability is given by equation (B.19). Thus, we can write:

$$\bar{G}(s) = 1 - e^{-\lambda s} \tag{B.20}$$

which can be thought of as the unconditional probability of a first default by time s.

The unconditional p.d.f. of τ, defined as $\frac{\partial \bar{G}(s)}{\partial s}$, can be written as:

$$\bar{g}(s) = \lambda e^{-\lambda s} \tag{B.21}$$

Readers with some familiarity with statistics will recognize $\bar{g}(s)$ as the p.d.f. of an exponentially distributed random variable with mean $\frac{1}{\lambda}$ and variance $\frac{1}{\lambda^2}$. Thus, the time of first default is exponentially distributed when defaults occur according to a Poisson process.

The conditional probability of first default by time s, given no default through time t, for $s \geq t$, can be written as

$$G_t(s) \equiv \text{Prob}[\tau \leq s | \tau > t]$$

$$= 1 - \text{Prob}[\tau > s | \tau > t]$$

$$= 1 - \frac{\text{Prob}[\tau > s]}{\text{Prob}[\tau > t]}$$

$$= 1 - e^{-\lambda(s-t)} \tag{B.22}$$

where, to arrive at (B.22), we used the Bayes rule and equation (B.19).

320 Appendix B. Basic Concepts from Statistics

The conditional p.d.f. of τ, given no default through time t, is the function $g_t(s)$ such that

$$g_t(s) = e^{-\lambda(s-t)}\lambda \tag{B.23}$$

which is simply $\frac{\partial G_t(s)}{\partial s}$.

Armed with (B.23), we can, for instance, compute the expected time of the first default, conditional on no default through time t:

$$E[\tau|\tau > t] = \int_t^\infty s\, g_t(s)ds \tag{B.24}$$

which can be shown to be equal to $t + \frac{1}{\lambda}$.

B.8 The Normal Distribution

If X is a continuous random variable that is normally distributed with mean μ and variance σ^2, its p.d.f. is

$$f(x;\mu,\sigma) = \frac{1}{\sqrt{2\pi}\sigma}e^{-[(x-\mu)/\sigma]^2/2} \tag{B.25}$$

and the normal c.d.f. is accordingly given by

$$F(x) = \int_{-\infty}^x \frac{1}{\sqrt{2\pi}\sigma}e^{-[(s-\mu)/\sigma]^2/2}ds \tag{B.26}$$

If we define $Y \equiv \frac{X-\mu}{\sigma}$, then it can be shown that Y is normally distributed with a mean of zero and a variance of one. Y is commonly called the standardized value of X, and its density is referred to as the standard normal p.d.f.

$$n(y) = \frac{1}{\sqrt{2\pi}}e^{-y^2/2} \tag{B.27}$$

The standard normal c.d.f. is

$$N(y) = \int_{-\infty}^y \frac{1}{\sqrt{2\pi}}e^{-s^2/2}ds \tag{B.28}$$

which is used extensively in this book, especially in discussion of structural credit risk models in Part III and in the treatment of portfolio credit risk issues in Part IV.

A key result regarding the normal distribution is that

$$F(x; \mu, \sigma) = N\left(\frac{x - \mu}{\sigma}\right) = N(y) \tag{B.29}$$

so one can rely exclusively on $N(.)$ when handling normally distributed variables. This is especially convenient because there is no analytical formula for the normal c.d.f., and one often has to rely on tabulated values. In addition, most statistical and mathematical software have embedded functions to generate values of $N(.)$ for any given y. Alternatively, Hull (2003)[41] provides a simple approximation that is very accurate.

A useful property of the standard normal distribution, and one that we rely upon in Part IV, is that of symmetry. By symmetry we mean that the standard normal p.d.f. is such that for any real number y:

$$n(y) = n(-y) \tag{B.30}$$

which can be shown mathematically, or verified visually if one recalls that $n(.)$ has a bell-shape and is perfectly symmetric around its mean of zero. It can also be shown that, again for any real number y:

$$N(-y) = 1 - N(y) \tag{B.31}$$

a result that we use in the derivation of the loss distribution of a large homogeneous portfolio in Chapter 19.

B.9   The Lognormal Distribution

If X is normally distributed, with mean μ and variance σ^2, then $Y \equiv e^X$ is lognormally distributed. The p.d.f. of Y is

$$f(y) = \frac{1}{\sqrt{2\pi}\sigma y} e^{-(\log(y) - \mu)^2/(2\sigma^2)} \qquad \text{for } y > 0 \tag{B.32}$$

The distribution of Y is called lognormal because, given $Y = e^X$ and the fact that X is normally distributed, $\log(Y)$ is itself normally distributed with mean μ and variance σ^2.

The lognormal c.d.f. can be expressed in terms of the normal c.d.f. In particular, given that $\log(Y)$ is an increasing function of Y, it can be shown that

$$F(y) \equiv \text{Prob}[Y \leq y] = \text{Prob}[\log(Y) \leq \log(y)]$$

but the term on the right-hand side of the above equation can be rewritten as $\text{Prob}[X \leq \log(y)]$, and thus:

$$F(y) = N\left(\frac{\log(y) - \mu}{\sigma}\right) \tag{B.33}$$

The mean and variance of Y are:

$$E[Y] = e^{\mu + \sigma^2/2} \tag{B.34}$$

$$V[Y] = e^{2(\mu + \sigma^2)} - e^{2\mu + \sigma^2} \tag{B.35}$$

We use the lognormal distribution in Chapters 17 and 18 when discussing structural models of credit risk and in the valuation of credit options, respectively. Lognormality of the value of individual firms is also an important assumption in the basic portfolio credit risk model discussed in Part IV.

B.10   Joint Probability Distributions

The joint probability function of the discrete random variables $X_1, X_2, \ldots, X_n$ is defined as the function $f(.)$ such that

$$f(x_1, x_2, \ldots, x_n) = \text{Prob}[X_1 = x_1, X_2 = x_2, \ldots, X_3 = x_3] \tag{B.36}$$

for all possible values $x_1, x_2, \ldots, x_n$ of $X_1, X_2, \ldots, X_n$. In words, $f(x_1, x_2, \ldots, x_n)$ is the probability that $X_1 = x_1$ and $X_2 = x_2, \ldots,$ and $X_n = x_n$.

The joint c.d.f. of these X_is is the function $F(.)$ such that

$$F(x_1, x_2, \ldots, x_n) = \text{Prob}[X_1 \leq x_1, X_2 \leq x_2, \ldots, X_n \leq x_n] \tag{B.37}$$

i.e., $F(x_1, \ldots, x_n)$ is the probability that $X_1 \leq x_1$, and $X_2 \leq x_2, \ldots,$ and $X_n \leq x_n$.

The joint p.d.f. of the continuous random variables $Y_1, Y_2, \ldots, Y_n$ is the function $g(.)$ such that the joint c.d.f. $G(.)$ can be written as

$$G(y_1, y_2, \ldots, y_n) = \int_{-\infty}^{y_n} \ldots \int_{-\infty}^{y_2} \int_{-\infty}^{y_1} g(s_1, s_2, \ldots, s_n) ds_1 ds_2 \ldots ds_n \tag{B.38}$$

for all possible values of $y_1, y_2, \ldots, y_n$.

B.11   Independence

The random variables $Y_1, Y_2, \ldots, Y_n$ are independent if and only if one of the following holds:

$$G(y_1, y_2, \ldots, y_n) = G_1(y_1)G_2(y_2), \ldots, G_n(y_n) \tag{B.39}$$

$$g(y_1, y_2, \ldots, y_n) = g_1(y_1)g_2(y_2), \ldots, g_n(y_n) \tag{B.40}$$

where $G_i(y_i)$ and $g_i(y_i)$ are the c.d.f. and p.d.f., respectively, of Y_i. (This definition applies to both discrete and continuous random variables.)

A closely related concept is that of serial independence. For instance, if R is a random variable that changes its value over time, R is serially independent if R_t, the value of R at time t, is independent of R_s, its value at time s, for s different from t.

Note: For normally distributed variables, events that are uncorrelated are also independent and vice versa. For such variables, the terms uncorrelation and independence can generally be used interchangeably.

B.12   The Bivariate Normal Distribution

If X_1 and X_2 are two normally distributed random variables with means μ_1 and μ_2 and variances σ_1 and σ_2, respectively, and ρ is the correlation coefficient of X_1 and X_2, then the joint distribution of X_1 and X_2 is bivariate normal.

The bivariate normal p.d.f. is

$$n_2(x_1, x_2, \rho) = \frac{1}{2\pi\sigma_1\sigma_2\sqrt{1-\rho^2}}$$

$$\times e^{-\frac{1}{2(1-\rho^2)}\left[\left(\frac{x_1-\mu_1}{\sigma_1}\right)^2 - 2\rho\left(\frac{x_1-\mu_1}{\sigma_1}\right)\left(\frac{x_2-\mu_2}{\sigma_2}\right) + \left(\frac{x_2-\mu_2}{\sigma_2}\right)^2\right]} \tag{B.41}$$

and the bivariate normal c.d.f. has the usual definition

$$N_2(x_1, x_2, \rho) = \int_{-\infty}^{x_2}\int_{-\infty}^{x_1} n_2(s_1, s_2, \rho)ds_1 ds_2 \tag{B.42}$$

Similar to the univariate normal, there is no analytical formula for the bivariate c.d.f. Hull (2003)[41] describes a numerical approximation that is reasonably accurate.

We use the bivariate normal distribution in Chapter 19, in the treatment of default correlation, in Chapter 21, when discussing premiums on portfolio default swaps, and in Chapter 23, in the valuation of credit default swaps that are subject to counterparty credit risk.

Bibliography

[1] BASEL COMMITTEE ON BANKING SUPERVISION. The New Basel Capital Accord, Consultative Document. April 2003.

[2] A. ARVANITIS AND J. GREGORY. *Credit: The Complete Guide to Pricing, Hedging and Risk Management.* Risk Books, 2001.

[3] A. ARVANITIS, J. GREGORY, AND J. LAURENT. Building Models for Credit Spreads. *Journal of Derivatives*, 1:27–43, 1999.

[4] BRITISH BANKERS ASSOCIATION. *Credit Derivatives Report 2000/2002.* British Bankers Association, 2002.

[5] L. BAIN AND M. ENGELHARDT. *Introduction to Probability and Mathematical Statistics.* PSW, 1987.

[6] M. BAXTER AND A. RENNIE. *Financial Calculus: An Introduction to Derivative Pricing.* Cambridge University Press, 2001.

[7] T. BJORK. *Arbitrage Theory in Continuous Time.* Oxford University Press, 1998.

[8] F. BLACK. The Pricing of Commodity Futures Contracts. *Journal of Financial Economics*, 3:167–79, 1976.

[9] F. BLACK AND M. SCHOLES. The Pricing of Options and Corporate Liabilities. *Journal of Political Economy*, 81:637–54, 1973.

[10] R. BLACK AND J. COX. Valuing Corporate Securities: Some Effects of Bond Indenture Provisions. *Journal of Finance*, 31:351–67, 1976.

[11] A. BOMFIM. Credit Derivatives and their Potential to Synthesize Riskless Assets. *Journal of Fixed Income*, December: 6–16, 2002.

[12] A. CIFUENTES AND G. O'CONNOR. The binomial expansion method applied to cbo/clo analysis. Technical report, Moody's Investors Service, December 1996.

[13] A. CIFUENTES AND C. WILCOX. The double binomial method and its applications to a special case of cbo structures. Technical report, Moody's Investors Service, March 1998.

[14] P. COLLIN-DUFRESNE, R. GOLDSTEIN, AND J. MARTIN. The Determinants of Credit Spread Changes. *Journal of Finance*, 56:2177–207, 2001.

[15] J. COX, J. INGERSOLL, AND S. ROSS. A Theory of the Term Structure of Interest Rates. *Econometrica*, 53:385–407, 1985.

[16] P. CROSBIE. Modeling Default Risk. KMV Corporation, 2002.

[17] M. CROUHY, D. GALAI, AND R. MARK. A Comparative Analysis of Current Credit Risk Models. *Journal of Banking and Finance*, 24:59–117, 2000.

[18] S. DAS. *Credit Derivatives and Credit-Linked Notes*. John Wiley & Sons, second edition, 2000.

[19] S. DAS AND P. TUFANO. Pricing Credit Sensitive Debt when Interest Rates, Credit Ratings and Credit Spreads are Stochastic. *Journal of Financial Engineering*, 5:161–98, 1996.

[20] G. DELIANEDIS AND R. GESKE. Credit Risk and Risk Neutral Default Probabilities: Information about Rating Migrations and Defaults. Working Paper 19-98, Anderson Graduate School of Business, University of California, Los Angeles, 1998.

[21] G. DUFFEE. The Relationship between Treasury Yields and Corporate Bond Yield Spreads. *Journal of Finance*, 53:2225–41, 1998.

[22] D. DUFFIE AND N. GARLEANU. Risk and Valuation of Collateralized Debt Obligations. *Financial Analysts Journal*, 57:41–62, 2001.

[23] D. DUFFIE AND D. LANDO. Term Structures of Credit Spreads with Incomplete Accounting Information. *Econometrica*, 69:633–64, 2001.

[24] D. DUFFIE AND K. SINGLETON. Modeling Term Structures of Defaultable Bonds. *Review of Financial Studies*, 12:687–720, 1999.

[25] D. DUFFIE AND K. SINGLETON. *Credit Risk.* Princeton University Press, 2003.

[26] P. EMBRECHTS, A. MCNEIL, AND D. STRAUTMAN. Correlation and Dependency in Risk Management: Properties and Pitfalls. Working Paper, ETH Zurich, 1999.

[27] FEDERAL RESERVE BOARD. Capital Standards for Banks: The Evoluing Basel Accord. *Federal Reserve Bulletin*, September 2003; 395–405.

[28] FITCHRATINGS. Credit derivatives: Risk management or risk? Technical report, FitchRatings, March 2003.

[29] J. FONS. Using Default Rates to Model the Term Structure of Credit Risk. *Financial Analysts Journal*, Sept/Oct: 25–33, 1994.

[30] R. GESKE. The Valuation of Corporate Liabilities as Compound Options. *Journal of Financial and Quantitative Analysis*, 12:541–52, 1977.

[31] R. GESKE AND R. JOHNSON. The Valuation of Corporate Liabilities as Compound Options: A Correction. *Journal of Financial and Quantitative Analysis*, 19:231–2, 1977.

[32] K. GIESECKE. Default and Information. Working paper, Cornell University, 2001.

[33] K. GIESECKE AND L. GOLDBERG. Forecasting Default in the Face of Uncertainty. Working paper, Cornell University, 2004.

[34] L. GOODMAN AND F. FABOZZI. *Collateralized Debt Obligations: Structures and Analysis.* Wiley, 2002.

[35] M. GORDY. A Comparative Anatomy of Credit Risk Models. *Journal of Banking and Finance*, 24:119–49, 2000.

[36] G. GRIMMETT AND D. STIRZAKER. *Probability and Random Processes.* Oxford University Press, 1998.

[37] G. GUPTON, C. FINGER, AND M. BHATIA. CreditMetrics–technical document. Technical report, Morgan Guaranty Trust Co., 1997.

[38] D. HAMILTON AND L. CARTY. Debt recoveries for corporate bankruptcies. Technical report, Moody's Investors Service, June 1999.

[39] R. HOGG AND E. TANIS. *Probability and Statistical Inference.* Macmillan, 1983.

[40] C. HUANG AND R. LITZENBERGER. *Foundations for Financial Economics.* Prentice Hall, 1988.

[41] J. HULL. *Options, Futures, and Other Derivatives.* Prentice Hall, fifth edition, 2003.

[42] J. HULL AND A. WHITE. Valuing Credit Default Swaps II: Modeling Default Correlations. *Journal of Derivatives*, 8:12–22, 2001.

[43] P. J. HUNT AND J. E. KENNEDY. *Financial Derivatives in Theory and Practice.* John Wiley & Sons, 2000.

[44] J. JAMES AND N. WEBBER. *Interest Rate Modelling.* Wiley, 2000.

[45] R. JARROW, D. LANDO, AND S. TURNBULL. A Markov Model for the Term Structure of Credit Risk Spreads. *Review of Financial Studies*, 10:481–523, 1997.

[46] R. JARROW AND S. TURNBULL. Pricing Options on Financial Securities Subject to Default Risk. *Journal of Finance*, 50:53–86, 1995.

[47] R. JARROW AND F. YU. Counterparty Risk and the Pricing of Defaultable Securities. *Journal of Finance*, 56:1765–99, 2001.

[48] E. JONES, S. MASON, AND E. ROSENFELD. Contingent Claims Analysis of Corporate Capital Structures: An Empirical Investigation. *Journal of Finance*, 39:611–25, 1984.

[49] S. KEENAN, D. HAMILTON, AND A. BERTHAULT. Historical default rates of corporate bond issuers, 1920–1999. Technical report, Moody's Investors Service, January 2000.

[50] M. KIJIMA AND K. KOMORIBAYASHI. A Markov Chain Model for Valuing Credit Risk Derivatives. *Journal of Derivatives*, 6:97–108, 1998.

[51] D. LANDO. Cox Processes and Credit-Risky Securities. *Review of Derivatives Research*, 2:99–120, 1998.

[52] D. LANDO AND T. SKODEBERG. Analyzing Rating Transitions and Rating Drift with Continuous Observations. *Journal of Banking and Finance*, 26:423–44, 2002.

[53] H. LELAND. Corporate Debt Value, Bond Covenants, and Optimal Capital Structure. *Journal of Finance*, 49:371–87, 1994.

[54] S. LeRoy and J. Werner. *Principles of Financial Economics.* Cambridge University Press, 2001.

[55] D. Li. On Default Correlation: A Copula Function Approach. *Journal of Fixed Income*, March: 43–54, 2000.

[56] F. Longstaff and E. Schwartz. A Simple Approach to Valuing Risky Fixed and Floating Rate Debt. *Journal of Finance*, 50:789–819, 1995.

[57] D. Lucas. Default Correlation and Credit Analysis. *Journal of Fixed Income*, March: 76–87, 1995.

[58] D. Madan and H. Unal. A Two-factor Hazard Rate Model for Pricing Risky Debt and the Term Structure of Credit Spreads. *Journal of Financial and Quantitative Analysis*, 35:43–65, 2000.

[59] R. Merton. On the Pricing of Corporate Debt: The Risk Structure of Interest Rates. *Journal of Finance*, 29:449–70, 1974.

[60] T. Mikosch. *Elementary Stochastic Calculus with Finance in View.* World Scientific, 1999.

[61] M. Musiela and M. Rutkowski. *Martingale Methods in Financial Modeling.* Springer Verlag, 1998.

[62] S. Neftci. *An Introduction to the Mathematics of Financial Derivatives.* Academic Press, 2002.

[63] D. O'Kane. Credit derivatives explained: Market, products, and regulations. Technical report, Lehman Brothers, March 2001.

[64] D. O'Kane and L. Schlogl. Modeling credit: Theory and practice. Technical report, Lehman Brothers, February 2001.

[65] G. Pan. Equity to Credit Pricing. *Risk*, November: 107–10, 2001.

[66] N. Patel. Credit Derivatives Survey: Flow Business Booms. *Risk Magazine*, February: 20–3, 2003.

[67] Credit Suisse Financial Products. Creditrisk+, a credit risk management framework. Technical report, Credit Suisse Financial Products, 1997.

[68] D. Rule. The Credit Derivatives Market: Its Development and Possible Implications for Financial Stability. *Financial Stability Review (Bank of England)*, June: 117–40, 2001.

[69] O. SARIG AND A. WARGA. Some Empirical Estimates of the Risk Structure of Interest Rates. *Journal of Finance*, XLIV:1351–60, 1989.

[70] P. SCHONBUCHER. Term Structure Modeling of Defaultable Bonds. *Review of Derivatives Research*, 2:161–92, 1998.

[71] P. SCHONBUCHER. A Tree Implementation of a Credit Spread Model for Credit Derivatives. Working paper, University of Bonn, 1999.

[72] D. SHIMKO, N. TEJIMA, AND D. VAN DEVENTER. The Pricing of Risky Debt when Interest Rates are Stochastic. *Journal of Fixed Income*, 3:58–65, 1993.

[73] O. VASICEK. Probability of Loss on Loan Portfolio. KMV Corporation, 1987.

[74] P. WILMOTT, S. HOWISON, AND J. DEWYNNE. *The Mathematics of Financial Derivatives: A Student Introduction*. Cambridge University Press, 1999.

[75] Y. YOSHIZAWA. Moody's approach to rating synthetic CDOs. Technical report, Moody's Investors Service, July 2003.

[76] C. ZHOU. A Jump-Diffusion Approach to Modeling Credit Risk and Valuing Defaultable Securities. Finance and Economics Discussion Series 1997-15, Board of Governors of the Federal Reserve System, 1997.

Index